S0-BFD-315

Rockingham Ware in American Culture, 1830–1930

Rockingham Ware in American Culture, 1830–1930

Reading Historical Artifacts

JANE PERKINS CLANEY

University Press of New England

HANOVER AND LONDON

Published by University Press of New England
One Court Street, Lebanon, NH 03766
www.upne.com
© 2004 by University Press of New England
Printed in the United States of America
5 4 3 2 1

All rights reserved. No part of this book may be reproduced in any
form or by any electronic or mechanical means, including storage
and retrieval systems, without permission in writing from the
publisher, except by a reviewer, who may quote brief passages in a
review. Members of educational institutions and organizations
wishing to photocopy any of the work for classroom use, or authors
and publishers who would like to obtain permission for any of the
material in the work, should contact Permissions, University Press
of New England, One Court Street, Lebanon, NH 03766.

Unless otherwise noted, all photographs are the property of the author.

Library of Congress Cataloging-in-Publication Data

Claney, Jane Perkins.
    Rockingham ware in American culture, 1830–1930 : reading historical artifacts / Jane Perkins
        Claney.—1st ed.
    p.   cm.
    Includes bibliographical references and index.
    ISBN 1–58465–412–0 (pbk. : alk. paper)
        1. Rockingham pottery.   2. Pottery—Social aspects.   3. Pottery, American—19th century.
4. Pottery, American—20th century.   I. Title.
    NK4340.R6C57 2004
    738'.0973'09034—dc22   2004008107

For Jonathan, Jon, and David
  — Thank you

Contents

Plates, Figures, and Tables

Plates, Figures, and Tables

TABLES

Preface: Rockingham Ware in the United States

Edwin AtLee Barber wrote, in 1893, the most comprehensive history of the American ceramics industry ever compiled.[1] He also assembled the great collection of American ceramics at the Pennsylvania Museum and School of Industrial Art in Philadelphia for the purpose of displaying the industry's accomplishments. I researched the collection at the museum—long since renamed the Philadelphia Museum of Art—for reinstallation in the American wing, and so, absorbing Barber's descriptions of the potteries and information gleaned from the old potters, I learned to think about the ceramics as products of American industry rather than as objets d'art. It was a small step from there to beginning to think about them as consumer products, and from there to their uses and meanings in the past.

This predilection bore strange fruit in the form of a ceramics collectors' book I wrote in 1980 for the Buten Museum of Wedgwood in conjunction with their exhibition of eighteenth-century Wedgwood at the Second Bank of Philadelphia. Since the book was a collectors' guide, I would employ an art historical approach, it was assumed, using the considerable resources of the museum library for situating each piece in the Wedgwood oeuvre and identifying its design sources. I felt compelled to stray beyond this format, however, to say something about the buying public for Wedgwood's products and to explain how some of the objects were used. A reviewer in San Francisco rewarded my effort by remarking that the book was filled with societal insights. Thus encouraged, I pursued my interest in the "why's" of ceramic usage and, with the help of historical archaeology, have taken this study of Rockingham ware from the first Rockingham ware made and the first pottery that made it, through to the very individuals who incorporated the teapots and pitchers and spittoons made of Rockingham ware into their daily lives.

Rockingham ware was central to the American ceramics industry— its mainstay, in fact, for much of the nineteenth century. For this inexpensive, mass-produced, brown-glazed, often pictorially embossed earthenware of the mid-nineteenth to early twentieth centuries was, along with its close relative yellow ware, the only Anglo-American ceramic at that time to compete successfully in the American marketplace against British imports. There were economic reasons for this, which are discussed in chapter 3, but I believe fashion played a large part in the initial popularity of Rockingham ware in America. During the decade of the 1840s, when large numbers of English potters were coming to America, many experienced in making Rockingham ware, the rococo-revival style in decorative arts was gaining momentum. "Tortoiseshell ware," produced first in England during the third quarter of the eighteenth century, was a ceramic expression of the eighteenth-century rococo. It had a cream-colored body upon which translucent, colored glazes—often brown—were applied to achieve a mottled effect with the cream-colored ground. In the next century, the newly-increased ranks of Rockingham-ware manufacturers, experienced at working with brown glazes, were quick to jump in with their own "tortoiseshell" glazes and capitalize on the revival in progress.

In chapter 2, I have quoted two comments by Rockingham-ware potters about design intentions and methods related to the rococo, but otherwise my conjecture is undocumented, for such documents are extremely rare. Both immigrant and native-born American potters were familiar and comfortable with Rockingham ware and, consequently, said little about it that survives in the written record. They wrote more about their efforts to produce the more technologically difficult whitewares, porcelain, lusterwares, and other staples of English and continental European ceramics production. Nor have I discovered any first-period documentary information about Rockingham-ware consumption beyond dealer invoices and price lists. These tell us what vessel forms were sold, their prices, and sometimes the names of their designs but nothing about the people who bought the wares and certainly nothing about why they bought them and how they used them. A few scraps about Rockingham-ware usage appeared around the turn of the twentieth century when certain forms in Rockingham ware and the products of particular factories gained a new regard as antiques. But this information is suspect, bathed as it was in the rosy glow of nostalgia.

Originality of design was demonstrably not uppermost in the minds of the Rockingham-ware makers. They copied English sources and they copied each other. Surviving price lists as well as marked Rockingham-ware pieces or those whose makers can be identified through glazing differences, production style, factory histories, or other approaches to connoisseurship reveal that most manufacturers offered the same designs in the same vessel forms often from similar or identical molds. After the first decades, moreover, their offerings narrowed down to relatively few vessel forms made in a variety of designs. The intriguing question to me is why this was so. What needs did these particular

Rockingham-ware vessels satisfy that kept them in production for a hundred years? And to which Americans did they appeal?

Getting to the sources of nineteenth-century America's long-lasting preference for Rockingham ware—even figuring out how to approach the subject—took me from a general understanding of material culture and a nodding acquaintance with historical archaeology to an utter reliance on the methods and theory intrinsic to these fields of learning. This book, then, is not only an attempt to understand Rockingham ware in its historical production and marketing contexts, and to interpret its multiple meanings in the cultural contexts of nineteenth- and early-twentieth-century America, it is also an account of the methodological approaches I used to uncover these meanings—approaches, in short, to reading historical artifacts.

Acknowledgments

Rockingham-ware fragments recovered from archaeological sites by historical archaeologists are the core database for this work, and I am indebted to the many historical archaeologists and laboratory analysts who shared information with me and guided me through their artifact collections: Julie Abell, Louise Akerson, William V. Askins, Sherene Baugher-Perlin, Jeff Carscadden, Deborah Crichton, Jo Ann Cotz, Verna L. Cowin, George Cress, Pamela J. Cressey, Irene G. A. Davis, Charles Fithian, Robert A. Genheimer, Denise Grantz, M. Colleen Hamilton, Preston Hawks, Scott D. Heberling, Silas D. Hurry, Meta Janowitz, Julia A. King, Jed Levin, William Liebeknecht, Kim A. McBride, W. Stephen McBride, Larry McKee, Linda F. Carnes McNaughton, Barbara H. Magid, Floyd R. Mansberger, Trina C. Maples, Ann Smart Martin, Patrick E. Martin, Terrance J. Martin, Jerry J. Moore, Angela Nellor, Virgil E. Noble, Charles E. Orser, Jr., Joseph S. Phillippe, Johnney Pollan, Adrian Praetzellis, Mary Praetzellis, Mike Rodeffer, Karen Rubinson, Jeanette K. Schulz, Nancy S. Seasholes, Andrew Shick, Samuel D. Smith, Suzanne Spencer-Wood, Nancy Stehling, Timothy A. Thompson, Matthew Virta, Steven Warfel, Michael D. Wiant, LouAnn Wurst, Betty Cozens Zeebooker, and Martha Zierden.

Decorative-arts and material-culture scholars and Rockingham-ware collectors who have generously provided me with information, photographs, or access to their collections include Charles and Barbara Adams, Kenneth L. Ames, M. Lelyn Branin, Warren F. Broderick, James S. Brown, Ellen Paul Denker, Robert L. Edwards, Robert Freiman, Alice Cooney Frelinghuysen, Arthur Goldberg, Jay A. and Emma Lewis, Elizabeth and David McGrail, James Mitchell, Ruth Justice Nebus, Arlene Palmer Schwind, Diana and J. Garrison Stradling, and Catherine Zusy.

The following museums, historical societies, archivists, librarians, and curators have kindly provided me with information, access to their collections, permission to photograph objects from their collections, and permission to reproduce documents and photographs: Pamela Henderson, the Antique Collector's Club; Jeffrey Ray, Atwater Kent Museum; Catharina Slauterback, the Boston Athenaeum; Diane Pilgrim, the Brooklyn Museum; the Chester County (Pennsylvania) Library; Richard Malley, the Connecticut Historical Society; Debra

Hughes and Maureen Quimby, the Hagley Museum; Cathleen R. Latendresse, Henry Ford Museum; Dr. R. K. Henrywood; Robert Giannini and Steven Patrick, Independence National Historical Park; Susan H. Myers, the National Museum of American History, Smithsonian Institution; Susan Anderson and Linda Martin-Schaff, the Philadelphia Museum of Art; Nancy Waters, Richmondtown Restoration; the Society for the Preservation of New England Antiquities; Susan Williams, the Strong Museum; Julie C. McKelvey, the Ulster County Historical Society; Gaye Blake-Roberts, the Wedgwood Museum; and Neville Thompson and Dorothy Wiggins, the Winterthur Museum and Library.

Susan Dawson Thomas and Sally Boyd kindly offered suggestions about parts of the work that contributed welcome clarification. Lu Ann DeCunzo's comments and suggestions on earlier versions of part of the manuscript redirected my emphasis from descriptive to interpretive, and her comments at a later stage helped to reshape the book. Robert L. Schuyler's considered reading brought forth suggestions that I deeply appreciate. George L. Miller questioned some of my interpretations along the way; I heeded his comments, and I believe the book is better for it. Karin Calvert has guided and supported this project through every permutation from its beginning as a term paper in a course on American material culture. Some of her ideas are acknowledged in the book, but many, offered in conversations over a fifteen-year period, have simply become part of my thinking. Phyllis D. Deutsch, Mary W. Crittendon, Ann Brash, Elizabeth Rawitsch, and, especially the book's designer, Katherine Kimball at the University Press of New England, have been creative, affirming, supportive, and flexible, and Leslie Cohen's copy editing has contributed accuracy as well as polish.

The support, suggestions, and aid in problem solving that Jonathan, Jon, and David Claney have so graciously given have made the project possible and are only inadequately acknowledged by my dedicating the book to them.

Rockingham Ware in American Culture, 1830–1930

Introduction

The Role of Context in Artifact Interpretation

> *To be at all critically, or as we have been fond of calling it, analytically, minded—over and beyond an inherent love of the general many-colored picture of things—is to be subject to the superstition that objects and places, coherently grouped, disposed for human use and addressed to it, must have a sense of their own, a mystic meaning proper to themselves to give out: to give out, that is, to the participant at once so interested and so detached as to be moved to a report of the matter.*
>
> —HENRY JAMES, *The American Scene*

The American novelist Wright Morris used this passage to introduce *The Home Place*, a fictionalized account in a real setting of both the *mentalité* and material life of a farm family in Nebraska during the first half of the twentieth century. A central theme in the work is that objects acquire meaning through daily usage: "Where the heel drags, the carpet is gone, worn into the floor. The pattern doesn't come with the house, nor the blueprints with the rug. The figure in the carpet is what you have when the people have lived there." Organizing his work around the corollary that objects "give out" their meanings, Morris alternated each page of text with a full-page photograph—of the items on a bureau top, a rut in the road, the corner of a porch, a shaving mug. The photographs, uncaptioned and unexplained, were meant to interact poetically with the text, which itself employed object imagery as much as narrative or dialogue to convey meaning. While the condition of an old Axminster rug stood for the fullness of long lives spent in one place, an elderly woman's accommodation to her aging body is encapsulated in her placing a lightweight basket of corn cobs for fuel next to the kitchen stove as she was no longer able to lift the heavy lid of the cob bin.[1]

Henry James enunciated and Wright Morris made use of the core truth of what we now call "material culture": objects in context can convey cultural meaning. Morris understood the immediacy of their impact—perhaps the quality that the historical archaeologist James Deetz was responding to when he referred to "the emotional content of the [archaeological] material."[2] Morris also understood that unhampered by the explicitness of words, objects may carry more nuanced, if less specific, information about the people who made or used them. Social scientists study the interaction of people and artifacts for the same reason. In *The Meaning of Things: Domestic Symbols and the Self,* Mihaly Csikszentmihalyi and Eugene Rochberg-Halton conducted an interview study asking members of households to describe which objects in the house were "special" to them and why, the premise of their study being that

the study of the objects of the household represent, at least potentially, the endogenous being of the owner. Although one has little control over the things encountered outside the home, household objects are chosen and could be freely discarded if they produced too much conflict within the self. Thus household objects constitute an ecology of signs that reflects as well as *shapes* the pattern of the owner's self. It might be noted in this context that the term 'ecology' literally means households.[3]

By differentiating between "household objects," which are by definition "coherently grouped," to use Henry James's phrase, and "things encountered outside the home," Csikszentmihalyi and Rochberg-Halton are declaring the crucial role of context in understanding the meanings artifacts held for those who owned or interacted with them.

Relating artifacts to a cultural context is integral to my understanding of the term "material culture," although many scholars use the term simply as a synonym for artifacts. In a short essay written about twenty-five years ago, James Deetz reported on a "cursory review of traditional definitions and concepts," in which he found that "material culture and artifacts are vaguely synonymous." He had gathered definitions such as "'the products of man's technology,'" or "'all those things made by man,'" but enlarged the concept to include anything that man shaped, altered, or modified. Topiary work, animal domestication, parades, body tattooing, and a song were "just as much material culture as our beloved shell edged pearlware."[4] Retaining much the same definition in his revised (1996) version of *In Small Things Forgotten: An Archaeology of Early American Life,* Deetz greatly expanded the definition of material culture by expanding the definition of artifacts, but the terms were still synonymous. The historian Bernard L. Herman uses the phrase "material culture" interestingly to mean a particular function of artifacts. He defines material culture as "the discourse of objects," where "the element of discourse focuses on the expressive or textual aspects of artifacts." However, by defining material culture solely as the communicative property of artifacts, Herman excludes their consideration in contexts such as production or marketing. For example, George L. Miller's "Classification and Economic Scaling of Nineteenth Century Ceramics" provides pricing information about English ceramics, which augments the ability of scholars to interpret the "expressive or textual aspects" of these particular ceramics as they were used in nineteenth-century homes.[5] I consider Miller's work a material culture study, but by Herman's definition it would not be because its focus is not directly on artifact meaning. I prefer a more inclusive definition of material culture than Herman's and suggest "the relationship of artifacts to a cultural context."

In brief outline, by "context" is understood the physical location of artifacts in space and time, the people to whom the artifacts were meaningful, and the social and cultural universes in which they existed. The contexts examined in material culture studies can be as broad as the society that produced or used the artifacts or as narrow as the very spot on earth and moment in time that saw them used, then lost, abandoned, or discarded, subsequently to be buried by the accumulations and activities of succeeding generations. Such ultimately specific contexts are the province especially of archaeology and historical archaeology, the latter being the discipline that seeks to understand past cultures by combining systematic excavation of discarded or abandoned material with documentary investigation of the lives and culture of those who used the sites and artifacts—a combination that produces insights not attainable through exploration of either body of data alone. Size of context, however, is not the main issue that distinguishes the historical-archaeological approach from other methods of material culture study. Nor is whether the material under study is located underground or above ground. Rather, emphasis on contextualized interpretation is key.

I would argue that what most differentiates historical archaeology from other material culture studies is the primacy of questions about who used the objects, in what settings, why these particular objects, and how they were used to negotiate such life circumstances as environment, family, age, gender, race, class, and social, economic, and political life.[6] For example, the concept of context does not play a part in the interpretive approach of Jules David Prown, a distinguished theorist in material culture studies. Prown works directly from artifact to mind, finding that "artifacts express culture metaphorically," that they "materialize belief." He writes: "The underlying premise [of the study of material culture] is that human-made objects reflect, consciously or unconsciously, directly or indirectly, the beliefs of the individuals who commissioned, fabricated, purchased, or used them, and, by extension, the beliefs of the larger society to which these individuals belonged."[7]

This widely used approach, sometimes referred to as Prownian analysis, posits a structural relationship between a culturally expressive artifact and the culture of which it was a part. This is a relationship in stasis: the beliefs and outlook intrinsic to the culture shape the artifact and are, in turn, reflected by it. By contrast, the contextual approach sees an active relationship between the artifact and the culture. It explores the ways in which artifacts are used to express as well as construct, maintain, and reinforce cultural and social meaning and to both implement and adjust to culture change.

Paradoxically, if one can narrow down the users of objects from the larger society to the very individuals or class of individuals to whom they were meaningful, the range of objects that can be read for cultural meaning is immensely broadened. This is because many objects are too generic in style to reflect cultural beliefs in their design, as Prown implies when discussing "how objects can be gauged for potential cultural expressiveness prior to subjecting them to analysis."[8] But with their context known, objects such as these can be understood not as reflectors of belief through their design but as agents in the expression of belief through their usage. For example, the large, brown, generically shaped mixing bowls discussed in chapter 7 of this book appear unpromising for deep cultural analysis out of context. But because their archaeological distribution reveals a distinct pattern of usage—the bowls were used mostly on farms, rarely on urban sites—and with economic or availability issues ruled out, only cultural factors could have accounted for this pattern of distribution. Aspects of rural and urban culture operative during the time the bowls were used suggest that farm families used them to demonstrate their knowledge of and compliance with urban middle-class dining practices.

Not all artifacts can be associated with specific cultural contexts. For artifacts that survive above ground there must be a traceable provenance, or they must appear in records—household inventories, probate documents, and so on—or in pictorial images or such oral accounts as stories or songs. Archaeological recovery establishes a specific context, but not all kinds of artifacts are likely to be found archaeologically. Many objects disintegrate if buried in the soil for any length of time, and valuable objects tend to be protected against loss, breakage, or discard. Prior to the throw-away culture of today, metal objects, for example, were infrequently discarded because of their durability and, in earlier times, their value. If broken beyond repair, their metal could be melted down and reused. If metal objects do end up in the ground, they also decompose to varying degrees. Thus such artifacts as the globular pewter teapot that Jules Prown famously interpreted as a metaphor for the maternal breast, while eminently suited for interpretation out of context, would in all likelihood not have turned up in the archaeological record. Moreover, lesser objects that may have been discarded with little consequence would not always have been enumerated separately in household records even if they had not been discarded. James Deetz's book title *In Small Things Forgotten* is a quote from a seventeenth-century household appraisal in which minor items were given a lump valuation.[9] These are the material data given context and interpretive value through the work of historical archaeologists.

If an artifact class had been invented to suit all material culture scholars, it would have been ceramics. For those who seek to find the mind of the maker or user in the object itself, ceramics can have unlimited forms, shapes, designs, and decoration with which to reflect ideas. For archaeologists, ceramics have fragility. Frequently broken and discarded—once broken, ceramics were virtually unrecycleable—ceramics together with glass are the most common artifact types on archaeological sites, particularly on domestic sites and especially on those after the 1830s, the beginning date of the material addressed in this book. Earthenware by then was an inexpensive commodity, and households often had numerous tableware forms since such table pieces for individual use as plates, cups, and mugs had become common. Moreover, once buried in the earth, ceramic objects can remain intact indefinitely except for occasional discoloration where there is crazing of the glaze or spalling. Thus ceramic artifacts, numerous and relatively unchanged from their original state except for being, usually, in fragmentary condition, constitute a rich body of data for archaeological analysis and interpretation.

Compared with other goods, ceramics typically represented only a tiny fraction of household expenditures. They amounted to less than one percent of general merchants' sales, according to studies of eighteenth- and nineteenth-century account books, so they were probably seldom considered among the most important categories of objects in a householder's inventory of possessions.[10] But as ceramics constituted the majority of vessels for the service and consumption of food by the 1830s, and because, as Anne Yentsch observes, "food, an everyday substance, is a remarkably revealing cultural domain that ranks in importance with other major cultural foci," these plates, cups, teapots, and bowls became vessels of cultural meaning as well as sustenance.[11]

Supporting this argument is the frequency with which eating and drinking vessels are mentioned or illustrated in literature and art, for artifacts in these media are chosen for their ability to embody and communicate meaning. The sitters' gentility or lack of gentility as well as

FIG. 1. *Anna Humphreys.* Oil painting attributed to Richard Brunton, ca. 1800. (Courtesy of the Connecticut Historical Society, Hartford, Conn.)

economic status are the meanings the eating and drinking vessels in both the following illustrations signify. The proper service of tea, with its numerous vessels and utensils of specialized function and its requirement of leisure time, was one of the defining rituals of the genteel life. Accordingly, Mrs. Reuben Humphreys, a jailer's wife in East Granby, Connecticut, chose to be shown at her tea table in a portrait painted about 1800 by Richard Brunton, a prisoner in her husband's jail (figure 1).[12] The careful display of her tea set made up of matched pieces of floral-decorated painted creamware signaled both the sitter's desire to appear refined and her ability to set a tea table that was reasonably fashionable. As recently as ten or eleven years before Mrs. Humphreys sat for her portrait, Josiah Wedgwood's creamware, introduced by the trade name "Queensware" during the 1760s, retained sufficient cachet for clients to order it for use in conjunction with porcelain, as the wording

FIG. 2. *Old Pat, the Independent Beggar.* Oil painting by Samuel Lovett Waldo, 1819. (Courtesy of the Boston Athenæum.)

of a Queensware order placed with Wedgwood confirms. Mrs. Eliza Mainwaring ordered, in 1789, "a Desert set to match each other . . . designed to be used after China, therefore I'd wish to have it elegant." [13]

In the second portrait, a redware porringer and a bone apparently gnawed clean were the props of *Old Pat, the Independent Beggar,* painted in 1819 by Samuel Lovett Waldo (figure 2). By the early nineteenth century, when inexpensive fine earthenware, mostly from England, was widely available in the United States, red earthenware dining vessels, made from locally obtained clays in numerous small potteries throughout the country, would have been the ceramics of choice to symbolize low economic status. Similarly, in terms of vessel forms, the porringer was at the opposite end of the status scale from tea ware, for it was used for inexpensive foods such as soups, porridges, or stews made from small pieces of meat. The bone was the remains of an expensive cut, but, consumed without utensils, it shares visual prominence with the worn-out coat to signal not only Old Pat's poverty but his lack of refinement as well.[14]

Further evidence for the embodiment of meaning in ceramic eating and drinking vessels is the finding by Csikszentmihalyi and Rochberg-Halton that these vessels comprised the tenth most frequently mentioned category of meaningful objects out of a list of forty-one categories in their interview study. The meanings given most frequently ("ties to a person or a place"; "shared origins or a common issue") were personal meanings that individuals attached to individual objects rather than meanings shared by a social group or culture, but it is unlikely that specific pieces from the category "eating and drinking utensils" would have held personal iconic value for numerous individuals if the category in general were not culturally meaningful.[15]

Ceramics, usually food related and from residential archaeological sites, have contributed to our understanding of issues ranging from economic status to religious ideology. Miller's "Classification and Economic Scaling of Nineteenth Century Ceramics" and a subsequent revision provide access to the pricing structures of the ceramics that comprised the bulk of the American market during the nineteenth century—English creamware, transfer-printed earthenware, and plain whiteware—enabling historical archaeologists to study comparative household expenditures on ceramics and, by extension, economic status and its intersections with such factors as class, ethnicity, geographic location, and the like.[16] Body and glaze types, vessel forms, shapes, and decoration have aided historical archaeologists in probing such issues as ethnicity and the syncretism of ethnic cultures; ethnicity, class, and gender in urban life; class-related behavior involving smoking, drinking, and temperance; boardinghouse dining behavior; and religious expression in the home.[17] Another area of investigation has been the study of food-related ceramics as material manifestations of the ideals of gentility and refined living, as they spread and gained cultural power in various places, among different ethnic groups, classes, and occupational groups.[18]

Contributing to each of the interpretive studies cited in the preceding paragraph are a variety of material culture studies that provide information about the artifacts used as data. As an example, Anne Yentsch's "Minimum Vessel Lists as Evidence of Change in Folk and Courtly Traditions of Food Use" relies in part on a typology for seventeenth- and eighteenth-century vessels set forth by Mary C. Beaudry and others in "A Vessel Typology for Early Chesapeake Ceramics: The Potomac Typological System." These authors, in turn, gathered some of their data from a three-hundred-year-old material culture study that illustrated and described the uses of objects employed as symbols in English heraldry.[19] Most researchers working with ceramics as data rely on catalogues, collectors' guides, and the like that describe the objects. For example, works cited in the studies of ceramics and gentility mentioned above include *Arts of the Pennsylvania Germans,* by Scott T. Swank; *White Ironstone: A Collector's Guide,* by Jean Wetherbee; *English Cream-Coloured Earthenware,* by Donald C. Towner; and *Tea Drinking in Eighteenth Century America: Its Etiquette and Equipage* by Rodris Roth. Probably no one for nearly half a century has tackled tea without the help of Roth's monograph.

For the period covered in this book, the mid-nineteenth to early twentieth century, white earthenwares and porcelains, decorated and undecorated, are the types of ceramics researchers employ most frequently in cultural interpretation, for the majority of table- and tea wares were made of these materials. In the preceding discussion of topics explored through ceramics, all the ceramics analyzed, with the exception of those used for seventeenth- and eighteenth-century studies and in the piece on "Class Conflict and the Rhetoric of Temperance," were white-bodied earthenware or porcelain. Yet vessels, even food-group vessels, of other types of ceramic wares were probably present on most if not all the archaeological sites used for these studies. In my search for Rockingham ware in nineteenth- and early-twentieth-century ceramics assemblages, I happened to examine four sites that were used in three of the studies, and Rockingham ware was present on all of them but not specifically mentioned.[20] It may have been subsumed in Martha Zierden's category "some less common ceramics" (p. 80), and Diana DiZerega Wall's "other vessels" ("Sacred Dinners and Secular Teas," p. 75), but typically the less common ceramic types are not mentioned in interpretive studies. The argument I am presenting here is that other types of ceramic ware that were widely distributed, if less numerous, can become equally valuable interpretive tools once their cultural meanings are understood.

Rockingham ware in the United States richly exemplifies this thesis. As I pointed out in the preface, while much of the American manufacture of ceramics introduced from Europe during the eighteenth and nineteenth centuries struggled or failed against competition from imported wares, the manufacture of Rockingham and yellow ware survived for a century. Moreover, the research of historical archaeologists informs us that a wide cross section of Americans used Rockingham ware. They have found it all over the United States in the remains of houses, restaurants, taverns, offices, and a great variety of public places.

As the historical archaeologists Daniel G. Roberts and Betty J. Cosans noted in a 1980 archaeological site report: "At least some pottery of this type [Rockingham ware] is usually recovered from mid-Nineteenth-Century proveniences."[21] My research has shown that, unlike the variety of forms made in whitewares, which included ceramics for virtually all uses, Rockingham-ware production was limited to a relatively few forms after its first decade or so. Archaeological excavations, surviving Rockingham manufacturers' price lists, and Rockingham ware found in antiques venues provide evidence that cooking vessels, teapots, pitchers, and spittoons predominated.

I would argue that this long-lasting vessel-form specialization, even without any other information, implies that there was either a functional or a culturally meaningful link between the brown, often mottled glaze and the vessel forms. The functional relationship between the spittoon form and the Rockingham glaze is obvious since spittoons were meant to receive tobacco juice, and I will discuss in chapter 5 the larger implications of this felicitous union of form and glaze both for the Rockingham-ware industry and for the refinement of America. Dark teapots also have practicality in that they tend to hide stains caused by tea seeping through imperfectly watertight glazes or ceramic bodies. My research suggests, however, that cultural meaning was the far more compelling explanation for the popularity of Rockingham-ware teapots, pitchers, and even one form of cooking vessel, the large bowl. The key to unlocking this information was Rockingham-ware distribution as revealed by archaeological sites. Although Rockingham ware per se was used at all social class levels and in all types of communities on the urban to rural continuum, choice of vessel forms and decoration differed markedly along the lines of these social factors. In the absence of an economic cause, only cultural dynamics can explain these patterns. Bringing together the patterns of usage with cultural and societal information about the time, place, and people provides evidence that these Rockingham-ware vessels and designs aided in the enactment of cultural roles at the intersections of gender, class identity, and urban or rural life.

Unlike white earthenwares and porcelain, which have been the subject of many books, I know of only one book devoted exclusively to Rockingham ware. Mary Brewer's *Collector's Guide to Rockingham the Enduring Ware: Identification and Values,* published in 1996, contains some useful description but is rife with historical inaccuracies.[22] Histories of American ceramics include Rockingham ware as do books about British ceramics, although to a lesser extent despite the fact that Rockingham ware originated in England. (The reason for the lack of emphasis on Rockingham ware in English ceramics literature will be explained in chapter 3.) The most comprehensive general history of American ceramics is still Edwin AtLee Barber's *Pottery and Porcelain of the United States,* published first in 1893, with second and third editions in 1901 and 1909. The third edition was reprinted in a combined edition with Barber's *Marks of American Potters* (1904) in 1976. Arranged chronologically—by geographic region within time periods, and by manufacturer within region—the work mentions Rockingham ware throughout, but the subject is inadequately indexed. Llewellynn Jewitt's *Ceramic Art of Great Britain,* first published in 1877 and revised in 1883, was the model for Barber's work. Jewitt discussed the first Rockingham ware but did not index any subsequent references, so that one must search through the text to find out who manufactured it. A more comprehensive source of information about the origin of Rockingham ware is *Rockingham Pottery and Porcelain, 1745–1842,* a history of the Rockingham Pottery at Swinton, Yorkshire, by Alwyn and Angela Cox. Later British Rockingham ware is mentioned briefly in Hugh Wakefield, *Victorian Pottery.*

In addition to Barber's book, American ceramics histories and collectors' guides that include information about Rockingham ware are John Spargo, *Early American Pottery and China;* John Ramsay, *American Potters and Pottery;* Arthur W. Clement, *Our Pioneer Potters;* Marvin D. Schwartz, *Collectors' Guide to Antique American Ceramics;* Ellen and Bert Denker, *The Warner Collector's Guide to North American Pottery and Porcelain;* and William C. Ketchum, Jr., *The Knopf Collectors' Guides to American Antiques: Pottery and Porcelain.*

A number of publications that discuss potters and potteries in various regions of North America include information about Rockingham ware: Lura Woodside Watkins, *Early New England Potters and Their Wares;* M. Lelyn Branin, *The Early Potters and Potteries of Maine* and *The Early Makers of Handcrafted Earthenware and Stoneware in Central and Southern New Jersey;* William C. Ketchum, Jr., *Potters and Potteries of New York State;* Warren F. Broderick, "The Potters of Mechanicville and Their Unusual Wares"; John F. Remensnyder, "The Potters of Poughkeepsie"; Ellen Paul Denker, "Ceramics at the Crossroads: American Pottery at New York's Gateway, 1750–1900"; Newark Museum *The Pottery and Porcelain of New Jersey, 1688–1900;* Susan H. Myers, *Handcraft to Industry: Philadelphia Ceramics in the First Half of the Nineteenth Century;* Arthur W. James, *The Potters and Potteries of Chester County, Pennsylvania;* William C. Gates, Jr., and Dana E. Ormerod, "The East

Liverpool, Ohio, Pottery District: Identification of Manufacturers and Marks"; and Elizabeth Collard, *Nineteenth-Century Pottery and Porcelain in Canada.*

A number of Rockingham-ware vessels are illustrated and described in the Sotheby Parke Bernet Catalogue, *The Jacqueline D. Hodgson Collection of Important American Ceramics.* Specific Rockingham-ware potters and potteries are discussed in David J. Goldberg, "Charles Coxon: Nineteenth-Century Potter, Modeler-Designer, and Manufacturer"; Susan H. Myers, "Edwin Bennett: An English Potter in Baltimore"; Richard Carter Barret, *Bennington Pottery and Porcelain* and *How to Identify Bennington Pottery;* and Richard A. Bourne, *Bennington Pottery: The Robert B. and Marie P. Condon Collection.*[23] A specific Rockingham-ware vessel is discussed in J. F. Gates Clarke, "Rebekah at the Well Teapots"; and J. G. Stradling, "Puzzling Aspects of the Most Popular Piece of American Pottery Ever Made."

Two books about yellow ware, John Gallo, *Nineteenth and Twentieth Century Yellow Ware* and Joan Leibowitz, *Yellow Ware: The Transitional Ceramic,* discuss Rockingham ware, although they identify it as brown-glazed yellow ware. Since only some Rockingham ware is made from yellow-ware clay, and since different vessel forms were made in Rockingham ware and yellow ware with only partial overlapping, this classification is misleading. But these books illustrate Rockingham-ware vessels and provide manufacturing information about potters who made both Rockingham and yellow ware.

All these sources give physical descriptions of Rockingham ware, and most provide some information about manufacturing methods, factory identification, and factory histories. There is little about marketing and nothing about usage, either the functional uses of Rockingham ware or its role in the construction and expression of cultural meaning. In this work I will explore these meanings after discussing Rockingham ware in its production and marketing contexts.

This book is divided into seven chapters followed by a brief conclusion. The first chapter, "Reading Historical Artifacts," discusses research methodology: formulating research questions; identifying and locating source material; and analyzing artifacts, archaeologically recovered artifact fragments, and period texts and images. Chapter 2, "Defining Rockingham Ware," presents the history of Rockingham-ware production in detail, not only because this has not been done before, but because—unlike such pottery as yellow ware, redware, whiteware, or stoneware, whose names reflect or are intended to promote physical characteristics and which have had a certain amount of homogeneity over time—the only thing that the first ceramic called "Rockingham ware" had in common with a number of variations that shared the name over the next hundred or so years was a brown glaze. "Rockingham ware" was a marketing term. I trace it from its early-nineteenth-century beginnings in the smooth, often gilded, refined English tea ware favored by such elites as the Prince of Wales and the eponymous Marchioness of Rockingham through the next hundred and more years as it lent its cachet to the more coarsely made and decorated spittoons, pitchers, teapots, and cooking ware made, for the most part, in the United States. Chapter 3, "The Americanization of Rockingham Ware," argues that the Rockingham-ware industry literally moved from England to the United States and describes how American iconography was sometimes grafted onto English designs or adapted from them, and sometimes newly conceived in the new environment. Chapter 4, "The Niche Market for Rockingham Ware," examines potters' price lists to show that Rockingham-ware potters introduced their product in a wide variety of vessel forms but specialized in fewer forms as time went on, thus explaining why Rockingham ware was found in only small quantities at any given archaeological site and yet was culturally meaningful to a broad spectrum of nineteenth- and early-twentieth-century Americans.

The last three chapters, "Rockingham Ware and Gender Identity," "Rockingham Ware and Class," and "Rockingham Ware in Rural America," demonstrate that the factors of gender, class, and residence in rural or urban communities all affected the choice of vessel forms in Rockingham ware. They discuss how Rockingham-ware vessels were used to negotiate social change and to express and reinforce cultural meanings according to their owners' location on the intersecting grids of these social factors. My data indicate that working-class women, for example, favored Rockingham-ware teapots, which rarely appeared in middle-class archaeological sites; and middle-class men living in cities formed the market for Rockingham-ware pitchers decorated with hunt scenes. These seldom appeared on lower-class sites and not at all on farm sites. I explain these findings and others—such as the intriguing preference among country dwellers for Rockingham-ware bowls, while city dwellers did not seem to bother with them, and while the exact same models were available in cheaper yellow-ware. Rockingham-ware spittoons were used across class lines and all along the urban to rural continuum. To my surprise, it seems spittoons were not gender specific, although I have seen them in period illustrations only in association with men. But Isabella Lucy Bird, an Englishwoman traveling in the

United States in the 1850s, reported (with some disgust) that spittoons were regular equipment in the hotel parlors and even luxurious steamship saloons reserved for women.

Following the discussion of research methods in chapter 1, this work, then, examines Rockingham ware from two perspectives: Chapters 2–4 discuss the artifacts as objects in their historical production and marketing contexts; it looks at them as products of culture and culture change. Chapters 5–7 consider them as agents of cultural expression and culture change. Employing the artifacts as texts, I demonstrate in this final section how the key to their interpretation lies in identifying and understanding the contexts in which they were once used.

❧ I ❧

Reading Historical Artifacts

This book, which describes the nineteenth- and early-twentieth-century ceramic Rockingham ware, locates it in ceramics and design history, then explores its usage and cultural meaning, is a type of work that has been described as a "material system study." Material system studies, as Lu Ann De Cunzo defines them, "begin with an item of material culture (or a class of items) and move outward to the constellation of associated objects, people, places, processes, performances, and ideas. . . . They teach us about material culture's multiple meanings and active roles." Writing from the perspective of an historical archaeologist, De Cunzo continues: "When we encounter the items again in the context of our sites, the material system we now comprehend enriches and extends our interpretation of the people and their culture."[1]

De Cunzo's definition virtually outlines the methods I followed in researching this project, although, since I started out with knowledge of Rockingham ware as "an item of material culture," I began at "people," the middle of the outline, and then worked forward and backward. I moved back to a detailed description of Rockingham ware and its position in industrial and marketing history only after ascertaining the ceramic's culture-bearing potential. The best way to begin this, I reasoned, was to identify Rockingham-ware users, the people to whom it was meaningful. My research question, then, was, What was the market for Rockingham ware? Who were the people or types of people who bought it? Did their class affiliation or the communities in which they lived have any connection to Rockingham-ware usage? Did gender?

I was familiar with historical archaeology at the time I started this project, although its relevance to my research had not occurred to me. I was a material culture specialist, so, following my usual procedure, I turned first to period textual sources for information about Rockingham-ware usage. But in my search through the usual sources of information about domestic artifact usage (letters, diaries, memoirs,

bills, household inventories, or other consumer-generated documents)
I found no reference to Rockingham ware—at least by the name
"Rockingham ware." Correctly matching historical terms with the artifacts they identified is a common problem in research. In Rockingham
ware, especially, potters making the very same brown-glazed ware used
a variety of names for it over time and in different places, as I explain in
chapter 2. The closest I came to finding confirmation of Rockingham-
ware usage in personal papers was in the papers of a Wiscasset, Maine,
sea captain that included an 1858 invoice for household ceramics, glass,
and britannia ware from a Boston retailer. At the end of the lengthy ceramics list, following white, transfer-printed, yellow, and mocha wares
were "two brown stone spittoons."[2] Given that Rockingham ware was
made in both earthenware and stoneware and that invoices invariably
listed Rockingham ware at the end, the "brown stone spittoons" were
probably Rockingham ware. Nor have I found mention of Rockingham
ware in period fiction, advice, or travel literature. I have seen what appears to be Rockingham ware in only one pictorial image, the black-
and-white photograph in figure 3. The shiny dark-colored pitcher resting on two light-colored plates at the near end of the middle shelf (from
the viewer's perspective) appears to be a molded Rockingham-ware
pitcher with its handle pointing toward the viewer.

One reason for the dearth of textual information about Rockingham
ware is the period of history in which it was a popular item of consumption, the mid- to late nineteenth century. Ironically, many sources
of information about domestic artifacts of the distant past are less useful for more recent artifacts. Household inventories provide an example. As the quantity and variety of industrially produced household
goods, including ceramics, increased during the nineteenth century,
ownership of all but the most expensive varieties became common, thus
unremarkable and less frequently recorded. In inventories and other
household records, descriptive itemization of small items became less
common. Where one hundred years earlier, ownership of "milk pans,
butter pots, and earthen plates" would sometimes be recorded in probate inventories, by the mid-nineteenth century, such goods, including
Rockingham-ware vessels, would, if recorded at all, have been recorded
as a "lot of crockery."[3] It is true that a greater quantity of such supply-
oriented material as price lists and advertising survive from this period,
but these sources address only the availability of artifacts, not their ownership and usage.

A probable reason for this paucity of period material relating to
Rockingham-ware usage was that Rockingham ware was a relatively inexpensive ceramic. Prescriptive literature dealt mostly with white earthenwares and porcelain. Both more costly than Rockingham ware, these

FIG. 3. Housemaid in the kitchen of Fowler house, Danvers, Mass., Photograph, ca. 1901. (Courtesy of the Society for the Preservation of New England Antiquities.)

wares were also used symbolically in art, as was redware. But Rockingham ware, while inexpensive, was not sufficiently inexpensive to signal poverty as does, for example, the redware porringer in the painting *Old Pat, the Independent Beggar.* Rockingham ware, then—cheap, ordinary, ubiquitous—is a textbook example of the phenomenon Edgar Martin observed in *The Standard of Living in 1860:* "What is commonplace at one time is likely to be the most difficult thing to find out about at a later time." [4]

Finding that textual sources were not going to provide enough information to answer my research question about Rockingham-ware usership, I briefly harbored the idea that Rockingham-ware presentation pieces might hold the key if I could gather information about the recipients. The presentation pieces were molded pitchers, mugs, or teapots personalized with separately molded whiteware letters applied to the vessels before glazing and firing. I had found, recorded, and where possible photographed thirty-nine of these by searching through museums, sales and museum catalogues, private collections, and antiques shows such as the giant, weeklong outdoor extravaganzas at Brimfield, Massachusetts, but I soon learned that they would not be very useful in helping me identify the general market for Rockingham ware because, ironically, information about the recipients was too easy to find. By examining federal and state census schedules, city directories, local histories, biographies, property deeds, and probate data all dealing with locations near the producing potteries, I was able to identify twenty-seven of the thirty-nine recipients. They all either lived near the potteries or were otherwise associated with them. Some were hotel keepers or restaurant owners who advertised in the directories of cities where the potteries were located and were thus potential customers for the potteries. If I was able to find twenty-seven out of the thirty-nine recipients so closely associated with the potteries, I could not reasonably assume that presentation-piece making was a widespread commercial enterprise. These data, therefore, did not help in answering my research question, but they became essential evidence for answering questions I did not yet know I would be asking. The discussions about gender and class in chapters 5 and 6 rely in part on the presentation-piece data. Still, I had not yet found a method for identifying Rockingham-ware users.

Scholars are a generous lot, I have found. A fellow graduate student whose name I don't know, whose face I hardly remember, asked me in an anthropology seminar on research projects, "Have you thought about using archaeology?" There it was. Not just archaeology, but historical archaeology would provide me with the data essential to the pursuit of my project, for historical archaeologists have linked a vast number of artifacts, including ceramics—including Rockingham ware—with their historical owners and their owners' cultural universe. By synthesizing the information from these archaeological sites, I could determine if broad patterns of usage existed. For the study of Rockingham ware as a material system, I could find out if people in particular social circumstances used Rockingham ware. Such an approach is a variation from the material systems studies Lu Ann De Cunzo discusses as contributions to archaeological site interpretation. For here the archaeological sites themselves, with all their contextual information, become the primary data sets for understanding the material system. Where direct evidence about usage is lacking in historical documents, as in the case of Rockingham ware, the data synthesized from archaeological contexts are the most productive component of the "constellation of associated objects, people, places, processes, performances, and ideas." Without them, a coherent interpretation of the meanings of Rockingham ware in its historical culture would not be possible.

Archaeologically excavated ceramics assemblages and their contextual data constitute the core database of this study of Rockingham-ware consumption. A summary of the research strategy for acquiring and interpreting the data follows. First I had to determine whether a sufficient number of nineteenth- and early-twentieth-century Americans used Rockingham ware to suggest that it had significant cultural meaning and whether there were sufficient archaeological data available to assess the meaning. I put together a list of mid-nineteenth- to early-twentieth-century archaeological sites from work summarized in such publications as the Society for Historical Archaeology *Newsletter* and newsletters from regional associations such as the Council for Northeastern Historical Archaeology. I then read site reports or contacted project directors to find out whether Rockingham ware had been among the excavated artifacts. This phase assured me that there were plenty of data. There were a sufficient number of sites with Rockingham ware to be meaningful, and although historical archaeologists do not usually incorporate Rockingham ware and other wares of the less common ceramics into their site analyses, they do catalog and store the artifacts. The contextual data associated with sites with Rockingham ware would enable me to identify social characteristics of Rockingham-ware owners. They would not, however, provide the data to distinguish between those who owned Rockingham ware and those who did not. Only analyzing all ceramics inventories from the appropriate time period would accomplish that. Such a project would be interesting and will be practical once all archaeologically excavated artifact inventories are included in a computerized database.

After compiling a list of sites that included Rockingham ware among the excavated artifacts, I visited artifact repositories to examine, photograph, and record details about Rockingham-ware fragments and to study site reports. Where necessary, I examined census records, city directories, property deeds, probate information, estate inventories, obituaries, local histories, and other documents to acquire additional site-specific information. I included a few sites in the analysis where I was unable to examine the artifacts but for which site reports included sufficiently detailed information about the Rockingham ware found on the site.

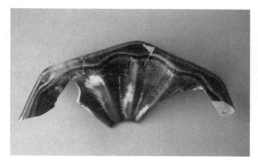

FIG. 4. Spittoon fragment, 1860–1880. Buff earthenware with translucent mottled brown glaze. Excavated from the John Quincy Adams Public School, Philadelphia, site. (Courtesy of the City of Philadelphia and John Milner Associates, Inc.)

Here it is important to mention that the more examples of the objects under study one has seen whole, the more examples he or she is likely to recognize in fragmentary form. This is where visits to museums, antiques shows, and other collections, especially with camera in hand, pay off. For example, the Rockingham-ware fragment illustrated in figure 4 shows grooves or fluting slanting downward and narrowing to an aperture. Even if the only part of this fragment recovered was the fluting, narrowing to a finished, glazed edge, the configuration is recognizable as a spittoon. Likewise the fragment illustrated in figure 5, in combination with documentary

FIG. 5. Teapot fragment, Edwin Bennett, Baltimore, 1856–1860. Buff earthenware with translucent mottled brown and clear glaze. Excavated from an Alexandria, Va., site. (Alexandria Archaeology.)

records relating to the site where it was excavated, indicates that between 1849 and 1860 a teapot matching the sugar bowl shown in figure 19 (p. 49) was discarded at 114 South St. Asaph Street in Alexandria,
Virginia. Rockingham-ware sugar bowls were made in the same molds
as the teapots, but were truncated at the top after molding and given
two handles instead of one large handle and spout. "Handlers" applied the handles and spouts after the vessel bodies had been removed
from the molds. The only difference in the treatment of the vessel bodies was that perforations were punched through the body of the teapot
where the spout would be attached.

The site sample for this study includes 131 consumer sites with a total of 768 Rockingham-ware vessels. Because 477 of these vessels were
spittoons from a single site, the state capitol building in Frankfort,
Kentucky, I removed that extreme from the analysis in order not to
skew the statistics and included only one spittoon to represent the site,
putting the number of Rockingham-ware vessels at 292 for the study.
In addition to consumer sites, I examined one store site with sixteen
Rockingham-ware vessels and a pottery/residence site with four vessels,
but these are not included in the analysis because they were sites of sales
and production rather than consumer activity.

Table 1 shows the distribution of consumer sites by region and type
of community. Ninety-four of the consumer sites were either wholly
residential or primarily residential with some commercial activity also
occurring on the site. In Nathanial H. Roberts's house at 12 North Warren Street, Trenton, New Jersey, for example, a jewelry store occupied
the first floor during the 1840s to 1887 period, and living quarters occupied the upper floors. Eleven of the other consumer sites were hotels or
boardinghouses, seven were restaurants or taverns, and eleven were for
public or semi-public use. These included government buildings, military posts, business offices, a school, an abbey, and a clubhouse. The
historic use of eight sites is unknown, but they did not appear to be potteries or retail sites. Table 2, p. 72, outlines this distribution.

At the beginning of the project, I viewed Rockingham ware as an entity and, because it was an inexpensive ceramic, theorized that most of
it would appear on sites whose occupants had been of low economic status. This did not turn out to be the case. There were slightly more
Rockingham-ware vessels on sites identified with low economic status,
but the difference was not statistically significant. However, from a database that described (1) the form and decoration of each Rockingham-
ware vessel, (2) the location of the site from which it was recovered and
whether the location was rural, urban, or in a village, (3) the date of deposition, and, where known, (4) the historic use of the site, the class of

TABLE I
Distribution of Consumer Sites by Region and Community Type

Region	Urban	Village*	Rural	Frontier army post	Total
Northeast	6	6	3	0	15
Middle Atlantic	40	3	8	0	51
Southeast	23	1	3	0	27
Midwest	10	4	8	0	22
Gulf States	0	0	1	1	2
Southwest	0	1	0	1	2
West Coast	12	0	0	0	12
Total	91	15	23	2	131

SOURCE: Documentary data from archaeological investigations.
*The "village" designation includes one mining and four industrial village sites.

the site occupants as determined by occupational level, and whether or not there were servants in the household—there emerged a markedly significant correlation between the distribution of particular Rockingham-ware vessel forms and the factors of urban or rural residence and class. (The database is reproduced in text form in the appendix.) This finding shifted my thinking from an a priori approach to a strategy, called "grounded theory," that argues for letting the data themselves generate theory.[5] I allowed the evidence from the distribution of Rockingham-ware vessels to change my research question from "Who used Rockingham ware?" to "Why were only certain vessel forms popular in Rockingham ware and why did preference for particular vessel forms differ from class to class and from city to farm?"

Answers to these questions are grounded in the larger cultural context, the "processes, performances, and ideas" of the material system. Before getting there, however, I would like to enlarge a bit on what is to be learned directly from the archaeologically excavated objects and what more is to be learned from associating them with their immediate physical context: the place where they were found, the other objects found with them, and the people who occupied the site at the time the objects were deposited in the earth.

For example, a section from a large brown earthenware bowl is archaeologically excavated from the ground. We know the bowl was large because enough of its rim remains to extrapolate circumference from the curve. From the bit of base remaining, we can see crisscross scratches on the foot ring that indicate the bowl was moved around on hard surfaces—used rather than left in one place. The inside of the base fragment shows worn glaze and scratches, meaning that a hard implement was scraped along the inside, probably repeatedly, to judge from the degree of wear. Although we acknowledge the possibility of any eccentric use at any time, the bowl was probably used to prepare or serve food. The presence of farm implements or floral and faunal remains typical of farm use in the same spatial and temporal context in which the bowl fragment was found suggest that the site had been a farm at the time of deposition. Without further information about the context in which the bowl was found, we can deduce only that a large brown bowl was used for food on a farm that existed at some point in history. Dating the time of deposition, or at least establishing the earliest possible time it could have occurred, the terminus post quem (TPQ), may be possible if something is known or can be learned about the ceramic ware of which the bowl was made or through other, datable artifacts that share the context. (The bowl was Rockingham ware, and manufacturers' price lists suggest a TPQ of the late 1840s or early 1850s, for the bowl form began to appear on price lists about that time.) Textual sources such as real-estate deeds and census schedules might pinpoint ownership and/or occupation of the farm at the time of deposition and provide information about its size, productivity, number of buildings, and the number and names of servants and farmhands if present. Information in local histories, newspapers, and probate documents, as well as any artifacts at the site contemporary with the bowl may help to supply social and cultural identities for the site occupants. Even if there are no textual sources, the recovery of such items as teacups, tobacco pipes, suspender buckles, hat pins, dolls' heads, nursing bottles, and whiskey bottles may provide information about family structure and practices.

Since vessel distribution in this study demonstrated that both class-related issues and differences between rural and urban life affected consumer choice of Rockingham-ware vessel forms, and, as my research began to disclose, so did gender, I initially searched in these areas for cultural explanations of my findings, beginning with such broad secondary scholarly works as Stuart M. Blumin, *The Emergence of the Middle Class: Social Experience in the American City, 1760–1900;* James R. Shortridge, *The Middle West: Its Meaning in American Culture;* Sarah Burns, *Pastoral Inventions: Rural Life in Nineteenth-Century American Art and Culture;* and Carroll Smith-Rosenberg, *Disorderly Conduct: Visions of Gender in Victorian America.* In addition to providing background and further readings in the annotations, such works as these can help the researcher to formulate specifically focused subject searches.

Aside from works directly related or even tangential to the subjects under investigation, almost any text or image created during the period under investigation may be fertile source material because, with the research question simmering in one's consciousness, anything that vaguely relates to it will pop off the page. Thus I zeroed in on a description in Mark Twain's *Life on the Mississippi* of a train trip the author took in 1882 from New York to Saint Louis. On the afternoon of the second day, he recorded: "By and by we entered the tobacco-chewing region. Fifty years ago the tobacco-chewing region covered the Union. It is greatly restricted now." For culturally seating the extraordinary accumulation of 477 Rockingham-ware spittoons at the Kentucky state capitol site mentioned above, no regional history or treatise on tobacco usage could possibly speak with greater clarity than this passage. The artifacts at the Kentucky state capitol and Twain's text are mutually enhancing, for not only does the text explain the artifacts, the artifacts both substantiate the text and contribute to its depth and texture. We know more about tobacco chewing at that time and place from both seeing the remarkable supply of spittoons and reading Twain's comment than we would know from either source alone. In addition, satisfyingly, a comment in a mid-twentieth-century book on economics corroborates Twain's sense of historical timing. The author noted that tobacco chewing was "even more prevalent before the [Civil] war than in later times."[6]

The importance of analyzing both artifacts and documents interactively, however, goes beyond strengthening the impact of both sources. In such an approach, as James Deetz argues, "each body of data is used to inform the other in such a way as to arrive at conclusions that neither data set could provide alone."[7] For example, there is no discussion in any literature that I have discovered that would confirm the archaeological evidence mentioned in the introduction that farm households favored large Rockingham-ware bowls and urban households did not. Nor is there anything that would directly explain the reason. However, hints and clues from various and disparate documentary sources converging with the evidence of the artifacts have furnished a plausible explanation: the use of the bowls on farms expressed their owners' cognizance of and conformity to socially prescribed behavior, while accommodating at the same time and with the same artifact to the practical needs of daily life on the farm. Evidence includes the historical use of the few nonfarm sites from which large Rockingham-ware bowls were also recovered; the economic status of farm families that occupied sites where not only Rockingham- but also yellow-ware bowls were recovered; information about dining practices, both urban and rural; and the controlling role of the concept of respectability. The most telling physical evidence, confirmed by Rockingham-ware potters' price lists, was the absence in Rockingham-ware bowls of a shape modification that was available in yellow-ware bowls. Such textual information — found in the cracks, so to speak, between the lines, and by taking note of what is not there — is a characteristic source of data for the meaning of commonplace things. Chapter 7 describes this evidence in detail and in doing so lays out what I see as a particularly compelling aspect of material culture studies: these types of evidence and the answers they provide, which rarely appear in cut-and-dried explanatory form and usually require sleuthing out, are often the only sources of insight into what was utterly ordinary in the everyday life of the past.

Ironically, indirect evidence—such as Mark Twain's observations on tobacco chewing and a shape difference between yellow-ware and Rockingham-ware bowls—may be a more direct path to interpretation than the seemingly more straightforward route through primary material closely linked to the research question. For example, the primary literature that discussed dining practices during the mid to late nineteenth century was more likely to discuss what they ought to have been than what they generally were. Although there is some evidence that these sort of texts may have worked, exerting some effect on subsequent behavior (see chapter 7, page 120), they and other sorts of prescriptive literature—magazine articles about home furnishings, for instance—should be treated conservatively as statements of the ideal rather than the norm until proven otherwise through cross-checking of other sources. This is not to say that such period literature does not contain eminently valuable information for interpretation: it records the existence in time and place of the objects that it describes or illustrates, and there is no better resource from which to uncover the assumptions and values that inhered in the cultural context under study. But it is a good idea to read period sources skeptically, being alert to built-in biases, both cultural and personal, and to constraints under which the authors may have been working. I have demonstrated the need for this in my discussion in chapter 2 of information from Edwin AtLee Barber's *The Pottery and Porcelain of the United States.*

Illustrations, paintings, drawings, photographs—any period images can be at least as useful as documents for interpreting objects in historical context. If the image is a photograph, it, at the very least, documents that the objects were there. But then the question becomes, "Why were they in the photograph?" Were they intentionally included, or did they just happen to be in view when the camera lens was focused on something else? That is to say, is the photographer or sitter displaying the objects to convey meaning, or is the photograph allowing a fortuitous glimpse into the material culture of the past? The photograph in figure 3 was taken around 1901 in the Fowler House, Danvers, Massachusetts, and shows a person identified as a housemaid, standing in her kitchen beside her stove and work table. (The proprietary terms seem appropriate here because the mantel over the cooking stove, furnished with pictures and decorative objects or mementos as if over a fireplace, suggests that this room is the sitter's domain, her space.) We do not know whether the photographer's intention was to photograph the kitchen, the presence of the cook merely completing the picture, or whether he or she was taking a picture of the cook in her setting. Whichever was the case, all the objects in the photograph help to define the setting, but it is extremely unlikely that they were introduced into the composition for that purpose. We may reasonably assume that the objects we see in the picture were the objects regularly in that kitchen at that time.

If artifacts appear in works of art that are not photographs, we can assume that the artist chose to include them for a purpose. They could have been chosen for any purpose from purely decorative to narrative, but implicit in their choice was the artist's expectation that the audience for the picture would understand their meaning. Sometimes their meanings are equally accessible to us today. One need only know that redware was cheap in the early nineteenth century to understand that in the painting *Old Pat, the Independent Beggar,* discussed in the introduction, Old Pat's eating from a redware porringer underscored his poverty. But often changes in culture since an image was made, even successive small changes, obscure the message originally intended. Here again, just as with texts, multiple lines of indirect evidence from diverse sources—from the images, from textual sources, and from the objects we are trying to interpret—can come together to forge an explanation. They can triangulate, so to speak, to provide sudden clarity.

In researching nineteenth-century images, I came across a number of depictions of men drinking directly from pitchers rather than from mugs, tankards, or other drinking vessels. The reason for this or the meaning signaled, if there was one, was not apparent to me. I found the images in genre paintings, in a magazine illustration, and on several pieces of pottery. Since the pouring lips of pitchers were a modification of the cylindrically necked, bulbous vessels used for centuries for both storing and drinking liquids, drinking from these lipped vessels would not seem remarkable except that in the titles, text references, or associations to literature or popular culture connected to each of the images, there was some implication of excess, either of thirst or alcohol intake. Coming together with the obsolete term "pitcher-man," which I found in a ramble through the *Oxford English Dictionary,* these images provided background to explain a gender-specific usage of Rockingham-ware pitchers, which I discuss in chapter 5. The *OED*'s etymological feature, documenting when words first entered the language and how their meanings changed over time, has been a fruitful research source for me.

Objects from the past whose meanings are completely inexplicable today are the bonanzas of material culture research. As the anthropologist Robert Darnton notes in *The Great Cat Massacre:* "When we run

FIGS. 6A. AND 6B. Pitcher. Attributed to Vodrey & Brother Pottery, East Liverpool, Ohio, 1858–1876. Buff earthenware with translucent mottled brown glaze. H. 8⅞″. In another example of the pitcher on which the molding is better defined, the shape to the right of the skull in fig. 6a can be recognized as a rib cage. (Private collection.)

into something that seems unthinkable to us, we may have hit upon a valid point of entry into an alien mentality." [8] An apparently popular relief-decorated Rockingham-ware pitcher that depicts birds of prey or possibly vultures screeching over a carcass seems to me to qualify as unthinkable. (Figures 6a and 6b; see also plate 1.) To twenty-first-century sensibilities, the sight of skeletal parts picked clean to the bone would not seem a likely stimulus to appetite at the table or good cheer at the tavern, but the pitcher (and an ale jug of the same design) were in mass production in the mid to late nineteenth century. Evidently the design was such a hit in Rockingham ware that one manufacturer even tried it in a heavy-bodied, semi-vitreous porcelain that was somewhat experimental at the time. Since the design does not arouse a sympathetic response in us, we must ask what there was about the culture in which it was produced and, presumably, appreciated that differed from present-

day American culture so much that its members might associate the
scene with pleasurable ingestion. In chapter 5, I discuss how images of
hunting and game animals relate to urbanization and a concomitant
nostalgia for country life; to men's role in the business and professional
world, increasingly separate from the domestic sphere; and to masculinity itself, as it was associated with hunting and predation. The
scene embossed on this pitcher explicitly portrays the predation and violence that, as Kenneth L. Ames explains, were elements of nineteenth-
century Romanticism in which hunting and the Victorian concept of
masculinity were enmeshed, yet birds picking over carrion would seem
unrelated to the romantic or sporting or even food-procuring aspects of
hunting.[9] It is true that the boar and stag on opposite sides of the
pitcher are posed like the fleeing animals in conventional boar-
hunt/stag-hunt pitchers, but the ravaging birds and, on the opposite

side, the peaceful deer—oblivious to danger—do not evoke images of the hunt to present-day viewers. But understood as couched in the conceptual configurations that shaped much of Victorian expression, the embossed images cohere as depictions of hunting that would have been immediately recognizable to their contemporary audience.

An expressive convention that particularly characterized nineteenth-century arts was the casting in narrative form of not only the novel and drama, but the visual arts as well. Paintings that make visual reference to past or future events relative to the primary event the painting was meant to be illustrating—the return home of a wounded soldier, or the family gathered around a young man about to leave home—are familiar examples, as are serial images, such as George Cruikshank's *The Bottle,* produced in 1847, which details in ten separate etchings the fateful consequences of drink to two generations of a family. The popular nineteenth-century art forms panorama and diorama, which often presented the illusion of sequential events or different phases of one event, can be included as narrative forms of visual art.[10] This design format and concept carried over to the decoration of functional objects, as seen in the English stoneware pitcher illustrated in figures 7a and 7b. The narrative involves an event occurring that only the figures closest in space to the event are yet aware of, but which will soon affect all of them. A hound is attacking a herd of deer. The two stags nearest to the hound are running from it, the stag to the right of those is moving away, but not running, and the deer farthest from the hound are standing still or lying down—clearly unaware of danger.

A second conceptual and expressive mode deeply imbued in nineteenth-century culture was the communication of ideas through the use of binary oppositions. The humor and impact of Lewis Carroll's fantasy *Through the Looking Glass and What Alice Found There* turn on such antithetical visions as the opposition of culpability and innocence—colored, respectively, black and white—expressed in the opening lines: "One thing was certain, that the white kitten had had nothing to do with it—it was the black kitten's fault entirely."[11] Nineteenth-century authors frequently employed the narrative contrivance of "the double" to dramatize conflicting impulses, as in Robert Louis Stevenson's *The Strange Case of Dr. Jekyll and Mr. Hyde,* for example. The double was dependent upon the concept of polarities for its effect.

Given the pervasiveness of the narrative convention, the "deer side" of the Rockingham-ware pitcher, illustrated in figure 6b, would have been read by contemporaries as a deer hunt in progress, but with fewer scenes shown than in the deer-hunt panorama illustrated in the stoneware pitcher (figures 7a and 7b). The stag in full flight is at the top of the image, the group as yet unaware is at the bottom. The fleeing

FIGS. 7A. AND 7B. Pitcher.
Stephen Hughes & Co., Co-
bridge, England, 1840–1855.
Green stoneware. H. $7\frac{3}{4}''$.
(From *Relief-Moulded Jugs,
1820–1900,* R. K. Henrywood.
Antique Collectors' Club as
publishers in England. Photograph, Dick Henrywood.)

boar on the opposite side of the pitcher was also a stock hunt-scene figure, and it was invariably on the opposite side of the pitcher from the stag. The reason for this and for the seemingly jarring inclusion of birds of prey with carrion is explained by the culture-wide habit of thinking in antitheses.

Since early recorded history, the red deer has stood for piety and the wild boar has personified evil, according to a history of hunting by Gunnar Brusewitz entitled, simply, *Hunting*. The author quotes a medieval source characterizing the boar as "the wicked man who refuses to repent and, instead, remains forever in his state of black and midnight sin." Brusewitz also writes that birds of prey were hated in the eighteenth and nineteenth centuries because they were thought to ruin the hunting and that hunters trapped them mercilessly in the name of game preservation. He describes the method: "When the eagle settled down on the carrion and began to peck at the meat, the trapper hauled in both the bird and the carcass and quickly grabbed the eagle's legs and pulled his catch into the hide." [12] Thus the despised animals were grouped together on the "evil" side of the pitcher, the boar about to be hounded down, perhaps, and the vultures about to be trapped so that they could no longer compete with the human hunters. It is too much to assume that the potters who grouped the images on these ceramics were consciously commenting on the duality of good and evil. But the folklore that initially dictated the groupings lingered long and fit with the mode of visualizing in polarities that pervaded Victorian culture.

Interpretation of these Rockingham-ware hunt pitchers, with their richly textual imagery that relates in shorthand one of the meaningful themes of their day, and interpretation of the large Rockingham-ware bowls mentioned above, which are minimally informative until knowledge of the contexts in which they were used and understanding of the cultural milieux in which those contexts were imbedded make an explanation possible, represent two different approaches to reading historical artifacts. The first works from the culture directly to the object, exploring what is known about the culture that might explain the otherwise baffling images that have survived from their time to puzzle us in ours. The second approach seeks an explanation by working from the object to its immediate contexts, the "associated objects, people, places," then outward to the "processes, performances, and ideas" of the larger culture. I have pursued both approaches, usually a combination of both, in the artifact interpretations that make up the second half of this book. In the first half, I provide a descriptive and historical matrix for recognizing and understanding Rockingham ware in ceramics and decorative arts history.

✵ 2 ✵

Defining Rockingham Ware

The earliest ware called "Rockingham" was made in England and acquired its name around the turn of the nineteenth century. It was glazed brown over a white body, had a smooth surface, and was restrained in concept. By fifty years later, the United States was producing much of the Rockingham ware that was made. It was still brown-glazed, but made of a variety of earthen- or stoneware bodies that were yellow or buff colored but rarely white. It was usually relief decorated, often with exuberant designs. The only attributes the early and later wares had in common were a brown glaze and the name "Rockingham." Chosen at first for its elite social associations, the name was retained through all the transformations the ware was to undergo, for, unlike the names "yellow ware," "edged ware," "printed ware," "redware," or "salt-glazed ware," which describe physical qualities of the wares, the name "Rockingham ware" was used for its marketing value.

Edwin AtLee Barber, the preeminent late-nineteenth-century historian of American ceramics, defined Rockingham ware as "simply yellow ware covered with a dark brown glaze and often mottled by spattering the glaze before it is fired." Karl Langenbeck, a ceramics chemist and Barber's contemporary, wrote: " 'Rockingham ware' differs from 'yellow ware' only in that it is covered with a brown manganiferous glaze, applied either by spattering the piece, previously dipped in the clear glaze, with the same, thus producing a mottled effect by the melting of the glazes into each other, or by directly dipping the biscuit piece into the 'Rockingham' glaze alone, whereby the fired piece obtains a uniform red-brown finish." He noted that yellow-ware clays, from which firebrick was also made, were "the common 'buff' or 'blue' clays widely distributed in coal seams."[1] Barber and Langenbeck did not discuss shaping or decorating methods, but in the United States Rockingham ware was sometimes wheel thrown but more often press molded, often with relief decoration. Press molding involved lining a mold, usually in two or more parts, with malleable clay and then binding the mold parts together and smoothing and pressing the inside of the piece with a sponge. After the piece was sufficiently dry, a workman removed the mold and smoothed the piece again before firing. Occasionally (but rarely, because of the cost), potters employed a method of hand-applying molded decoration that had been formed in small molds called "sprig molds."

In describing Rockingham-ware glaze colors, Barber and Langenbeck may have been looking to an ideal in their minds' eye, for both surviving and archaeologically excavated nineteenth-century examples reveal a wider range of shades than the "dark brown" or "red-brown" that they mentioned. Glazes ranged from amber through rust to dark chocolate and could be solid colored or variations of streaked or mottled glazes. As Barber and Langenbeck said, the majority of Rockingham ware *was* made of the same earthenware body as yellow ware, a buff-bodied, yellow- or clear-glazed ceramic. Indeed, many potters from the 1840s until the early twentieth century specialized in producing both yellow and Rockingham ware. But stoneware potters produced a substantial minority of the Rockingham ware made. Although some writers on American ceramics consider only what they term "Rockingham-glazed yellow ware" to be "true" Rockingham ware, analysis of documents related to the artifacts in their contemporary contexts reveals that the stoneware versions were marketed as "Rockingham ware" and, presumably, so perceived by the historic consumers who are the subjects of this study.

It should also be mentioned that some wares recognizable as Rockingham by even the narrowest definition appear on historical documents under other names. A notable example is the mottled cream-colored-and-brown Rockingham ware made by the United States Pottery Company of Bennington, Vermont—the ware that has characterized Rockingham to ceramics historians and collectors since the beginning of the twentieth century. It was called "mottled" on the pottery's invoices of the 1850s. Nor did the term "Rockingham" appear on the pottery's bill heads, which included patent flint enamel, parian, agate, yellow, "and other wares."[2]

The first known use of the term "Rockingham" was in an 1807 invoice for Rockingham teapots from the Swinton Pottery, Yorkshire, to Wentworth House, the estate of the marquis of Rockingham, upon whose property the Swinton Pottery was located. (The pottery was renamed

FIG. 8. Cream pitcher, teapot, covered sugar bowl. Swinton Pottery/Rockingham Works, Swinton, Yorkshire, England, 1770–1842. White earthenware with translucent brown glaze and gilt decoration, H. 7½″ (teapot). Mark: ROCKINGHAM (Courtesy, The Winterthur Library: Printed Book and Periodical Collection.)

the Rockingham Works in 1826, the marquis having lent financial support and taken an active part in the business.)[3] Except for a brown glaze, the Rockingham ware to which the 1807 invoice referred was totally different from the later ware that Barber and Langenbeck described. It was white bodied with a smooth, shiny brown glaze, often decorated with polychrome enamel, gilded bands, chinoiserie, or floral patterns. (Figures 8 and 9; see also plate 2.) Fashioned into teapots, cream pitchers, covered sugars, and lidless pots filled from the bottom called "Cadogans," the ware was sufficiently different from the other colored-glazed earthenwares of the day to excite the wholehearted admiration of the nineteenth-century English ceramics historian Llewellynn Jewitt:

This ware, which is of a fine reddish-brown, or chocolate colour, is one of the smoothest and most beautiful ever produced. The body is of fine hard and compact white earthenware, and the brown glaze, by which the peculiar shaded and streaky effect of this class of goods was produced, is as fine as it is possible to conceive, and required to be "dipped" and passed through the firing process no fewer than three times before it arrived at perfection.[4]

Novel, of high quality, and probably expensive because of its three firings, the Swinton Rockingham ware attracted an elite clientele. In production by about 1770, it may have acquired the name "Rockingham"

FIG. 9. "Cadogan" pot. Rockingham Works, Swinton, Yorkshire, England, 1826–1842.
White earthenware with translucent brown glaze, gilt, and applied relief decoration. (Re-
produced in Alwyn Cox, "The Analysis of Rockingham and Rockingham-Type Brown-
Glazed Earthenwares," *English Ceramic Circle Transactions,* 15, part 1, 1993.) (Courtesy, The
Winterthur Library: Printed Book and Periodical Collection.)

through the enthusiastic patronage of the marchioness of Rockingham,
who ordered eighteen teapots in one invoice alone in October 1780.
The order was for "purple tea potts," which an 1816 invoice
to Wentworth House for "8 Rockingham or Purple Tea Pots" reveals,
and archaeological excavations at the pottery site confirm, referred
to manganese-glazed ware. The manganese glaze usually produced a
purplish brown color when sponged or streaked onto the pieces. The
Prince of Wales, later George IV, was also a customer, having ordered
teapots in 1807 after admiring them on a visit to Wentworth House.[5]

It is clear that royal patronage brought on imitators as early as the 1820s,
for in an 1827 newspaper advertisement, the Brameld brothers, owners
of the Rockingham Works, promoted themselves as "original Inventors,
and sole Manufacturers of the *genuine* Royal Rockingham Teapots etc.
to be had here, at the Manufactory and at Mortlock's, London." (Emphasis added.) Some of the imitators, including Wedgwood, Spode, and
other, unidentified potters actually marked their product "Rockingham."[6] Whether or not these other potteries appropriated the name
"Rockingham" before insolvency caused the Rockingham Works to
close in 1842 is not known; but if not before, at least by very soon after,

Wedgwood's product, examples of which were marked both "WEDG-WOOD/ETRURIA" and "ROCKINGHAM," had become the industry standard. Reporting, probably before the end of 1843, on the work he had accomplished during the past year, an emigrant English potter in Utica, New York, wrote back to Staffordshire about his "excellent and beautiful common earthenware, the best in the United States, and as fine a glaze as ever you saw, even on that of the great Wedgwood Rockingham!" (The potter was making brown-glazed redware.) Wedgwood continued to produce the "Rockingham" line well into the twentieth century.[7]

The "Rockingham" made by Spode and Wedgwood was white-bodied, smooth-surfaced tea ware of the type the Rockingham Works produced. Among other potters who continued to make that type were two former workmen at the Rockingham pottery, Isaac Baguley and his son, Alfred, who reopened part of the works in June 1843, decorating ware produced by other potteries and specializing in "brown-glazed wares of Rockingham type."[8]

At the same time other potters stretched the term "Rockingham" to include ware that had nothing in common with the original except a brown glaze. Examples marked "Rockingham" appear in D. G. Rice, *Illustrated Guide to Rockingham Pottery and Porcelain,* and are attributed to the Rockingham Works, but Alwyn and Angela Cox argue that some were made at other potteries. For example, a group bearing a "Rockingham" mark, which Alwyn Cox identified through chemical analysis as not having been made at Swinton, includes a jug with relief decoration of men smoking and drinking; a teapot shaped to resemble a log and decorated in relief with leaves, knotholes, and branches; a Toby jug; and a pitcher with handle in the shape of a hound and decorated with scenes in relief of a boar hunt and stag hunt. All of these were earthier in subject matter and more rustically decorated than the pretty gilt chinoiserie of the Rockingham Works's tea ware. The Podmore, Walker & Company pottery of Tunstall, Staffordshire, placed its own factory mark, "STONEWARE/P W & CO," on its brown-glazed, hound-handled stag- and boar-hunt pitcher, with no additional "Rockingham" mark, but the vessel was identified as "Rockingham" in their invoice to Adam Southern, a Philadelphia crockery-ware dealer. The invoice, dated February 16, 1842—four months before the Rockingham Works was advertised to let and ten months before the remaining stock was offered for sale—listed "10 d[ozen] Rockingham Jugs [size] 4 dog Handle" and "1½ d[ozen] d[itt]o Spittoons 7 In[ch]s."[9]

Thus the term "Rockingham" became generic for a wide variety of wares, all of which drew disdain from Llewellynn Jewitt: "Since that time [the closing of the Rockingham Works] 'Rockingham ware'—in every instance falling far short of the original in beauty and in excellence—has been made by almost every manufacturer in the kingdom." [10]

Relief-decorated Rockingham ware, such as Podmore & Walker's and the group described and illustrated by Alwyn Cox, derived its name from the Rockingham Works ware introduced in the late eighteenth century, but owed more to an older decorative tradition and a newer technological innovation. Hunting subjects appeared on English-made pottery dating back to the Roman occupation, and these and other rustic subjects were rendered in applied relief on thick, salt-glazed stoneware that was either all-over brown or dark brown at the top and light brown at the bottom. Several pottery-making districts in England had made them since the late seventeenth or early eighteenth century. [11] Potters used small molds called "sprig molds" to form the relief decoration, which they then attached, or "sprigged on," to the already formed vessel with liquid clay called "slip." A more economical method than applying decoration to each vessel separately was to form the decoration in the same mold that shaped the vessel. This process, in which molds were made from a relief-decorated master model, had been practical in England since the introduction of plaster of paris molds about 1745. These absorbed water quickly, allowing for fast drying, hence rapid production, and they could be used repeatedly. Relief-decorated molded earthenware; thin, white-bodied, salt-glazed stoneware; and porcelain vessels were made this way. But large-scale production of molded ware with elaborate, finely detailed decoration had to await the development of a dense, finely grained, nonporous stoneware body that could reproduce extremely detailed modeling. [12] Wares produced in this fine stoneware—and eventually also in less expensive, yellow-ware clay—were decorated with the rustic subjects familiar from the coarser, sprig-decorated brown salt-glazed stoneware pitchers and mugs as well as with an expanded range of subjects fashionable in the early nineteenth century. Finished in brown glaze and marketed under the name popularized by the Rockingham Works, they became the new nineteenth-century Rockingham ware.

R. K. Henrywood, writing in *Relief-Moulded Jugs, 1820–1900,* noted that the fine, closely grained stoneware that "was to become the *de facto* standard" for nineteenth-century relief-decorated ware appeared about 1820, and the first to manufacture press-molded relief wares in that body was the firm of Jacob Phillips and John Denton Bagster of the Church Works, Hanley, Staffordshire. Working from 1818 to about 1823, Phillips & Bagster made a hunt pitcher decorated with boar- and stag-hunt scenes that can be identified not through a mark on the bottom of the vessel, but through their firm name incised on the collar of the dog that forms the handle and on the boar hounds' collars. Operations continued at the Church Works through the dissolution of the partnership, through Joseph Mayer's proprietorship after Bagster's death in 1828, and when William Ridgway took over in 1831. The Minton factory of Stoke was also producing these fine stoneware relief-molded vessels by 1831 and Machin & Potts of Burslem by 1834. Moreover, although Henrywood states that "considerable research has failed to identify any other potters involved in producing relief-moulded jugs before 1835," David and James Henderson of Jersey City, New Jersey, were probably making fine, dense stoneware vessels with relief decoration molded in the body as early as 1829 or 1830. Three pieces of evidence lead to this conclusion: an extract from a New York newspaper, a marked D. & J. Henderson pitcher, and a dated price list.

The extract is from the New York *Commercial Advertiser*. Reviewing an industrial fair held by the New York American Institute in October 1929, the reporter notes: "The stone-ware of Henderson, which we hope will be successfully introduced, has several times been mentioned by us in terms of approbation. The pitchers of this material, at the fair, are from classical models, and very elegant." The article doesn't mention whether the decoration was molded in the body or sprigged on, but a surviving example fitting both the *Advertiser*'s description and specifications from an 1830 price list indicates that at least some of Henderson's pitchers were molded in the body by the time the price list was published. Decorated in the classical idiom with gadrooning, stylized leafage, and dancing figures within circlets of trailing vines, the pitcher is marked on the bottom "D. & J. HENDERSON JERSEY CITY" within a circle. The letter "C" is also impressed. Although the mark "D. & J. Henderson" was undoubtedly used until 1833, when D. & J. Henderson incorporated as the American Pottery Manufacturing Company, the pitcher was probably the one marked "C" in the 1830 price list of "Fine Flint Ware, Embossed and Plain, Manufactured by D. & J. Henderson, Jersey City, N. J." In this list, pitchers are specified by letter marks and numbers. The term "flint ware" referred to the composition of the Hendersons' clay body, which, according to an advertisement in the 1849–1850 Jersey City directory, included English ground flint for greater hardness and vitreousness.[13]

The fact that Phillips & Bagster in England and D. & J. Henderson in the United States were innovative in their production of one-step relief-decorated molded wares is underscored by a discussion of molding, specifically sprig molding, published in 1832. The author, Dionysius Lardner, noted that "small ornaments, such as figures, animals, foliage,

FIG. 10. Ewer. Orcutt & Thompson, Poughkeepsie, N.Y., 1830–1831. Buff earthenware with translucent brown glaze. H 11″. (Courtesy of the Ulster County Historical Society, Marbletown, N.Y.; photo, Robert Edwards.)

FIG. 11. Detail, opposite side of fig. 10. (Courtesy of the Ulster County Historical Society, Marbletown, N.Y.; photo, Robert Edwards.)

and the like," were made in plaster or copper molds and then "affixed to the vessel by means of slip. . . . *It is in this manner that drinking jugs are so commonly ornamented with figures in relief.*" (Emphasis added.) [14]

Soon after the New York *Commercial Advertiser* praised D. & J. Henderson's line of classically inspired pitchers, another partnership (1830–1831), that of Eleazer Orcutt and Charles W. Thompson of Poughkeepsie, New York, brought out a large, thinly potted, elegantly shaped ewer, or wash pitcher, with crisp, clear relief decoration consisting of classical palmettes, stars, and stylized flowers against a stippled background. On each side is centered the

American eagle, wings outstretched. On one side is the legend "ORCUTT & THOMPSON/POKEEPSIE"; on the other side, proudly emblazoned, are the words "AMERICAN/MANUFACTURE." (Figures 10 and 11; see also plate 3.) Orcutt & Thompson's pottery was a both "Stone and Earthen Ware Manufactory," according to a newspaper notice published after the dissolution of their partnership; they had introduced the pitcher in red earthenware as well. Orcutt, the practical potter of the partnership, had been both a redware and a stoneware potter in Troy, New York, during the previous decade, and there, during his business partnership with Horace Humiston from 1828 to 1830, his aspiration to produce ware that was out of the ordinary manifested itself in an oversized stoneware water cooler decorated with an applied figure of a muse playing a lyre.[15]

D. & J. Henderson's pre-1833 wares were typically buff colored with a clear smear glaze—a smear glaze being the result of glaze material vaporizing in the saggers during firing and leaving a thin layer on the ware. (Saggers were containers in which pieces were placed for protection during firing.) Or sometimes the early wares were buff colored on the bottom half and dipped in brown glaze on the top, which was the conventional way of glazing the "drinking jugs" that Lardner discussed. The company won "first premium for specimens of superior stone, flint and cane colored earthenware, a great variety," in the American Institute's 1830 exhibition.[16] "Cane colored" was the name at the time for yellow or buff-colored ware, and it is reasonable to assume that the partially dipped wares would have been subsumed under that category. Figure 12 (which dates to 1829 according to the inscription, "UNCLE TOBY/ 1829," on the small pitcher Toby is holding) illustrates an example of the partially dipped ware.

Orcutt & Thompson, however, continuing along Eleazer Orcutt's innovative course, glazed their ewer not with a clear smear glaze or in the traditional half brown, half buff, but with a rich, shiny brown glaze that covered the entire body of the piece. It is the earliest precisely datable American example of what would later become known as "Rockingham ware." In *The Pottery and Porcelain of the United States,* Barber illustrated a "mottled Toby jug" marked "D. & J. HENDERSON, JERSEY CITY" that is completely covered with a dark glaze. (The photograph is black and white, but if the glaze were any color but brown, Barber would have said so.)[17] The piece, which is from the same model as the Toby jug illustrated in figure 12, was probably made before 1833 because Henderson used the American Pottery Company mark after that, but it cannot be dated any more precisely than that. It is unlikely, however, that Henderson's Toby jugs with an all-over brown glaze were

FIG. 12. Toby jug. D. & J. Henderson, Jersey City, N.J., 1829. Buff
stoneware with translucent clear and brown glaze, H. 9¾″. Mark: D&J/
HENDERSON/JERSEY/CITY. (Jay A. Lewis collection; photo, Jay A. Lewis.)

made in any great quantity before the autumn of 1830, for that was the
year the American Institute mentioned only "cane colored."

The practice of glazing embossed wares with a brown glaze continued through the 1830s. Many all-over brown-glazed pieces bear the
mark of the American Pottery Company (D. & J. Henderson's company name after 1833), although none of these can be positively dated to
the 1830s because the mark was used into the 1840s. (See figures 13 and
14; see also plate 4.) Brown-glazed relief-molded wares of another pottery, however, the Salamander Works of New York City, can be positively dated to the 1830s. An inscription, "KIDD'S TROY HOUSE," applied
over the glaze to the shoulder of a marked Salamander pitcher, which is
glazed on the exterior with a translucent brown glaze over buff body,
makes this dating possible. From about 1834 to 1838, Archibald Kidd

was keeper of the Troy House, a riverside hotel in Troy, New York. Troy was the head of steamboat navigation on the Hudson River, and, appropriately, Kidd's pitcher bore a relief decoration of a side-wheeler steamboat. A price list from the Salamander Works dated April 1837 lists "Steam Boat" among ten pitcher designs.[18]

A search through American import documents, records of industrial exhibitions, and the few American potters' records that survive has failed to turn up an instance of potters calling their brown-glazed relief-decorated wares "Rockingham" before the 1840s, when the earliest known reference, the invoice for "Rockingham Jugs" from the English potters Podmore & Walker, appeared in 1842. The Salamander Works was making brown-glazed wares when their price list came out in 1837, but the list was headed "Flint and Fire Proof Ware," emphasizing body quality rather than color. The word "Rockingham" was absent also from the D. & J. Henderson list of "Fine Flint Ware," published in 1830, and from American Pottery Company advertisements during the 1830s. An 1833 advertisement for the latter company itemized "C.C., dipt, painted, and edged Earthenware" among its products and "also, an assortment of Stone Pitchers, variously ornamented: Spittoons, Tea Tubs, etc." The term "dipt," also included in their 1835 advertisement, meant ware dipped in colored glazes or slips (liquid clays) and could have technically included the pottery's brown-glazed pitchers, spittoons, and other forms. ("C.C." meant cream-colored, "painted" usually referred to under-glaze colors applied with a brush, and "edged" meant wares with a band of green or blue glaze over a molded rim.)

We do not know what the American Pottery Company called their brown-glazed wares, but one of their glazes was described in a memoir written in 1901. James Carr, who had emigrated from England and started to work at the pottery in 1844, recalled: "Large pitchers and spittoons . . . were dipped in Albany clay, found in Albany, N.Y., which fused and became a dark-brown colored glaze much like Rockingham glaze." The American Pottery Company Toby jug illustrated in figure 15 may be an example of the type of glaze Carr was describing. It should be pointed out that "Rockingham glaze" to Carr, writing at the turn of the century, would have denoted the same sort of glazes that Barber and Langenbeck described: translucent lead glaze with added colorant rather than slip, which was opaque. However, for many, Rockingham

FIG. 13. Toby jug. American Pottery Company, Jersey City, N.J., 1833–1850. Buff stoneware with translucent brown glaze, H. 5¾″. Mark: AMERICAN/POTTERY/CO/JERSEY CITY NJ. (Jay A. Lewis collection; photo, Jay A. Lewis.)

FIG. 14. Spittoon. American Pottery Company, Jersey City, N.J., 1833–1850. Buff
stoneware with translucent brown glaze. Mark: AMERICAN/POTTERY CO/JERSEY CITY NJ.
(Courtesy of W. M. Schwind, Jr. Antiques.)

ware was a more widely inclusive term than Carr, Barber, or Langenbeck might have allowed. Numerous potters, especially stoneware potters working in New England and New York during the last half of the
nineteenth century, used an opaque glaze on stoneware vessels and marketed the result as "Rockingham ware." [19]

It would be wrong to assume from the absence of other records that
Podmore & Walker were necessarily the first to borrow the prestige of
the Rockingham name for embossed wares decorated with rustic subjects, for few records survive from the many nineteenth-century potteries that existed. Almost certainly many English potteries jumped on the
Rockingham bandwagon and started exporting wares to the United
States under that name around the time the Rockingham Works closed.
Corroborating evidence comes from the Franklin Institute exhibition
notes of 1845, which state that the Rockingham-ware trade was extensive and suggest by their wording that it was a fairly new phenomenon.
Commenting on pottery submitted by Bennett & Brothers of Birmingham (Pittsburgh), Pennsylvania, the judges wrote: "In this invoice
there is a good variety of ware, and all very creditable. The jugs, mugs,
and spittoons are decidedly better than the English Rockingham ware,
which is used extensively in this country, and furnished at prices which
must successfully compete with the foreign article." [20] Presumably, if the
judges felt they had to say "which is used extensively in this country," it

FIG. 15. Toby jug. American Pottery Company, Jersey City, N.J., 1833–1850. Buff stoneware with opaque brown glaze, H. 10⅝". Mark: AMERICAN/POTTERY CO/JERSEY CITY NJ. (Jay A. Lewis collection; photo, Jay A. Lewis.)

was not a universally known fact. They did not call the Bennett submission "Rockingham ware."

The following year, however, Bennett & Brothers used the term in their own advertising: "PENNSYLVANIA POTTERY/BENNETT & BROTHERS/MANUFACTURERS OF/FANCY ROCKINGHAM WARE/IRON STONE CANE WARE, &c. &c./Warerooms—No. 65 Wood Street, Pittsburg." "Fancy Rockingham Ware" was in the largest type and had a line to itself. Still the Franklin Institute committee did not call the Bennett wares "Rockingham," emphasizing instead that they were press molded: "The Bennett Bros, Birmingham, Prest samples show a great improvement over the excellent ware exhibited by them last year. The large water jar is equal to the best ever produced from the English potteries." The "large water jar" was still in the collections of the Franklin Institute when Barber wrote the first edition of

The Pottery and Porcelain of the United States in 1893. He described the piece as an "eight-sided glazed 'tortoise-shell' pitcher, with Druid's head beneath the lip." [21] "Tortoise-shell" meant mottled Rockingham ware.

The Franklin Institute judges' comments suggest that they may have still considered the name "Rockingham," as well as the English ware it described, to be foreign. The theory gains support from the fact that, although the Bennett brothers were English immigrants and used to the name, the American-born potter Christopher Webber Fenton, of Bennington, Vermont, was clearly hesitant about accepting the term whole-heartedly—although the fact that he used it at all indicates that he knew it had sales appeal. In his price lists of 1847 and 1848, Fenton listed "Dark Lustre or Rockingham Ware." A note at the bottom of each list makes it clear that "Dark Lustre" and "Rockingham" were two different names for the same thing, not two different types of ware: "Articles not expressed in the list will be made to order either in Yellow, Dark, White Earthen or China." Fenton's grandniece remembered: "A bit of tradition which is interesting is that Mr. Fenton called Rockingham *dark finish* and *dark lustre,* and my mother called it by these names as much as *Rockingham.*" [22] (The term "luster" had been applied before to American-made wares that were not true lusterwares. In lusterwares, metallic oxides were applied and refired over an already glazed piece.) [23] By 1847, even as Fenton was hedging, the Franklin Institute seems to have become comfortable with the concept of American-made Rockingham ware, listing "Rockingham ware by Harker & Taylor, East Liverpool, Ohio." [24] Although not all Rockingham-ware potters adopted the name "Rockingham"—others used "mottled," "fancy pressed," "chocolate colored," or "brown"—the name "Rockingham" predominated.

In his American ceramics history *The Pottery and Porcelain of the United States,* Barber said that the Bennett brothers, who had operated a pottery in East Liverpool, Ohio, before moving to Pittsburgh in 1844, made the first Rockingham ware in the United States in East Liverpool late in 1841. This was after the pottery's founder, James Bennett, had summoned his three younger brothers from England to aid in the enterprise he had begun in 1839. Barber amended the "first Rockingham-ware" date to 1839 in his chronology of important events in American ceramics history, although, according to James Bennett family history, Bennett's first kiln was not even built until 1840. [25]

Well, when is Rockingham ware, Rockingham ware? While I agree that the Bennetts may have been the first potters in the United States to *call* the ware "Rockingham," a decade earlier Orcutt & Thompson had made the press-molded, relief-decorated ware with translucent brown glaze that would later be called "Rockingham," and the Salamander

Works, the American Pottery Company, and possibly others had made it before 1841—or 1839, for that matter. Barber did not know, evidently, of the existence of Orcutt & Thompson or the Salamander Works when he wrote the first edition of *Pottery and Porcelain* in 1893. By 1904, when he wrote *Marks of American Potters,* he had become aware of Salamander, but not that it had been operating in the 1830s, for he wrote that the pottery "was established in New York City about the year 1848." [26] He must have overlooked D. & J. Henderson's early brown-glazed wares, such as the "mottled Toby jug"—his words—that he pictured in his book, or he just did not make a connection between them and the term "Rockingham."

To understand why Barber credited the first American Rockingham-ware production to the Bennetts in 1839 or 1841 despite the existence of earlier 1830s Rockingham-ware look-alikes, one must understand how Barber acquired the data for his publications. Writing in the 1890s, when there were few museum or private collections of American ceramics, he had at his disposal only a few pieces of historical pottery and bits of information that had descended in the families of potters or were stored in such repositories as historical societies or societies for the promotion of industry—the Franklin Institute is one example. Most of Barber's historical information seems to have come from old retired workers at the potteries or from potters still in business with whom he corresponded in seeking information about their potteries and any other potteries they might have known about. Given the scope of Barber's undertaking, there was little he could have done to verify the accuracy of the replies short of having a reader in every pottery center locating and combing through old newspapers and local records. He seems to have transferred the potters' accounts nearly verbatim into print, perhaps attempting to control for biases or hidden agendas by changing some of the absolute statements into relative ones. The information in *The Pottery and Porcelain of the United States* about Woodward, Blakely, & Company, which operated in East Liverpool, Ohio, between 1852 and 1858, came from William Vodrey, whose father, Jabez Vodrey, had been the experienced potter of the firm. Barber's write-up is a virtual quote from the letter Vodrey wrote to him, except that he downgraded two phrases, changing "they had the largest pottery in East Liverpool" to "they had one of the largest potteries in East Liverpool," and "Rockingham and Yelloware that has not been excelled before or since their time" to "yellow and Rockingham ware of the finest quality." In this instance, Barber modified a statement that was true: Woodward, Blakely, & Company did operate the largest pottery in East Liverpool in the 1850s. [27]

Edwin Bennett had left Pittsburgh in 1846 to start a new pottery in Baltimore, and Barber was in touch with him there while he was doing his research for *Pottery and Porcelain* in the early 1890s. In a letter written to the Edwin Bennett Pottery Company four years after Edwin Bennett's death in 1908, Barber noted that Bennett had sent him several examples of "early wares produced at the Baltimore factory . . . when I was preparing my first book on American Pottery."[28] Probably Bennett believed and told Barber that his family's pottery was the first to make Rockingham ware in the United States. The James Bennett pottery had been the first pottery in East Liverpool, and soon thereafter East Liverpool became the most concentrated yellow- and Rockingham-ware–producing center in the country. Moreover, the Bennett brothers' pottery in Pittsburgh announced their "Fancy Rockingham Ware" with a prideful flourish, to judge from the large bold type in their advertisement. If James, who worked as a newly arrived immigrant at the American Pottery Company during the mid-1830s, had remembered the mottled brown-glazed ware from his sojourn there, it wasn't called "Rockingham" then; and in any case James had been dead for thirty years by the time Edwin had his conversation with Barber.[29] It seems unlikely that Barber, with Bennett's early Rockingham-ware samples in hand, would have thought to question the matter.

Nevertheless, by Barber's and Langenbeck's definitions of Rockingham glaze, and in their likeness to the wares sold and purchased throughout the nineteenth and early twentieth centuries as Rockingham ware, the wares with translucent brown glazes made in the 1830s by Orcutt & Thompson, D. & J. Henderson, and Salamander were, in substance, Rockingham ware and would be recognized as such after the name was adopted in the United States.

When Barber described the glaze of the Bennett & Brothers's 1846 exhibition entry as "tortoise shell," he may have touched on the primary reason for the rapid growth in popularity of Rockingham ware in mid-nineteenth-century America. For, as mentioned in the preface, the introduction of this type of mottled glaze coincided with the rococo revival that was in ascendancy in the decorative arts of that time. A ceramic manifestation of the eighteenth-century English rococo style was tortoiseshell ware, which was cream-colored ware with colored glazes—brown predominating—applied to the body and then covered with a clear lead glaze before firing. The process, popular during the third quarter of the eighteenth century, was developed by Thomas Whieldon and adopted by other potters, including those of the Swinton Pottery, where Rockingham ware was first made.[30] In the simplest tortoiseshell ware, manganese oxide, the colorant in the brown glaze, was spattered onto the body resulting in a spotted look that was copied a hundred or so years later in American Rockingham ware, as illustrated in the Toby jug shown in figure 16 (see also plate 5). The eight-inch plate illustrated in figure 17, on which the brown colorant is fused in spots in the clear lead glaze, looks very like the eighteenth-century plates it was modeled after except that the yellow-ware body is darker than creamware and results in a thicker, heavier plate.

Many potters, a few beginning in the 1840s, more in the 1850s and 1860s, produced mottled or tortoiseshell Rockingham ware. In addition to spattering, they might pour or drip the brown glaze onto the piece, allowing more or less of the buff body to show through. Figure 6, for example, illustrates a piece mostly covered by the brown glaze, and figure 18 shows an earthenware pitcher on which the brown glaze has been dripped sparingly to show much of the yellow-ware body. According to Henry Brunt, manager of the Edwin Bennett Pottery Company in the early part of the twentieth century, Edwin Bennett had devised another method of achieving a mottled effect in the 1850s:

With reference to Mr. Bennetts designs, I find that from about 1846 to 1858 one of his cheif [*sic*] forms was the Octagon. This arose no doubt from his desire to show some variation in his glaze, it being a brown (or rockingham) glaze it would run away from the high points during burning, and settle in the cavities. This would give a great variation in the depth of tone, and bring out all the high lights. This effect was further increased in the latter part of the 50s, by splashing (or spattling) the goods with a soft semi-transparent lead glaze which united with the brown (or rockingham) glaze, giving a mottled appearance which was one of the characteristics of his ware.[31]

Figure 19 shows the glaze effect Brunt described on a marked Bennett vessel and on two attributed to him. (See also plate 6.) The molded hunt pitcher is marked on the base "E & W BENNETT/CANTON AVENUE/BALTIMORE, MD." (The "W" in the firm name at this time stands for Edwin's brother William, who was a partner in the Baltimore pottery from about 1848 to 1856.) None of Edwin Bennett's Rockingham ware made in Baltimore prior to or following his partnership with William is known to have been marked. The molded sugar bowl is identified through provenance provided by Barber: In 1914, the Bennett Pottery Company (the company name after 1990) lent a group of its early pieces to the Pennsylvania Museum, which included a teapot made from the same mold as this sugar bowl.[32] The sugar bowl pictured is defective; the handle that should have been on the left side

FIG. 16. Toby jug. Possibly South Amboy, N.J., 1858–1870. Buff earthenware with translucent mottled clear and brown glaze, H. 8½″. (Private collection; photo, Rick Echelmeyer.)

FIG. 17. Plate. Probably American, 1850–1860. Buff earthenware with translucent
mottled brown and clear glazes, Dia. 8½″. (Private collection; photo, Rick Echelmeyer.)

was never applied. Xs were incised to guide the handler but were glazed
over along with the rest of the bowl, which was evidently then sold as a
second. The thrown mug is attributed to Edwin Bennett on the basis of
the glaze. The mug was found in the South, which was Bennett's territory, judging from numerous nineteenth-century archaeological finds,
and it was lathe turned to finish the base and create the decoration
at the rim. In a letter written to his family in England, one of Edwin
Bennett's fellow potters identified him as an experienced thrower and
turner.[33]

The mottled glaze was markedly different in appearance from the
uniform brown glazes mostly in use before that time—the American
Pottery Company glazes shown in figures 13 and 14, for example. These
glaze effects were achieved by dipping the pieces in the brown glaze—
the process used at Swinton that Llewellynn Jewitt described—rather
than dripping or spattering the glaze on.

In a variant of eighteenth-century tortoiseshell ware, splashes of green
and/or blue, yellow, and grey augmented the brown glaze. Rockingham-

FIG. 18. Pitcher. United States Pottery Company, Bennington, Vt., 1849–1858. Buff earthenware with translucent clear and mottled brown glaze, H. 9″. (Private collection.)

ware potters copied the polychrome ware by applying green and blue (or occasionally yellow) translucent glazes in spots or splashes over or beside the brown, calling the result "variegated" or "enameled" ware. In a price list of 1853 or 1854, the Swan Hill Pottery, of South Amboy, New Jersey, offered "Enameled Rockingham Ware," an example of which, splashed with translucent areas of green and blue glaze, is illustrated in figure 20 (see also plate 7). The pitcher, called a "grape ice pitcher," came both covered and uncovered. The mark on the base of the pitcher, which reads "SWAN HILL/POTTERY/SOUTH AMBOY," is shown in figure 21. East Liverpool price lists, such as the 1864/1865 offering of the Vodrey & Brother Pottery, used the term "variegated." The inkwell guarded by a dog with green patches on his or her

FIG. 19. Pitcher. E. & W. Bennett, Baltimore, Md., ca. 1855. Sugar bowl and mug. Attributed to the Edwin Bennett Pottery, 1856–1860. Buff earthenware with translucent mottled brown and clear glaze, H. 8½″ (pitcher), 4½″ (sugar bowl), 3″ (mug). (Private collection; photo, Rick Echelmeyer.)

FIG. 20. Covered pitcher. Swan Hill Pottery, South Amboy, N.J., 1853–1854. Buff earthenware with translucent mottled brown, blue, and green glaze, H. 12″. (Elizabeth and David McGrail collection.)

FIG. 21. Detail of fig. 20. Mark on the base: An embossed swan above the words SWAN HILL/POTTERY/SOUTH AMBOY. (Elizabeth and David McGrail collection.)

coat (illustrated in figure 22), is attributed to the Vodrey & Brother Pottery. (See also plate 8.)[34] Naturalistic ornament figured prominently in the rococo style and its nineteenth-century revival. Accordingly, a New Jersey pottery, Taylor & Speeler of Trenton, put out a pitcher made to look like the trunk of an oak tree (figure 23). The piece is sparsely dotted with spots of blue glaze, as are the game pitcher and spittoon shown in figure 24 (see also plate 9). Both are attributed to Taylor & Speeler based on their glaze colors and method of application. (The pitcher, shown in frontal view, is discussed in chapter 5; see figure 43.) The blue spots of glaze on the oak-tree pitcher and the green patches of glaze on the dog highlight an aspect of polychrome Rockingham-ware manufacture: it did not matter whether the colorful glazes related realistically to the subject matter. They were applied equally to abstract designs, such as the bottom half of the spittoon illustrated, and to dogs on inkwells; they were simply colorful.

Revived rococo had begun to appear by the 1830s in Europe. In 1836, buyers of French porcelains could choose between neoclassical shapes, in fashion since the late eighteenth century, or the curvilinear shapes of the new aesthetic taste. In July of that year, Henry

FIG. 22. Inkwell. Attributed to Vodrey & Brother Pottery, East Liverpool, Ohio, 1858–1876. Buff earthenware with translucent mottled brown, and green glaze, L. 6¼″. (Private collection; photo, Rick Echelmeyer.)

Middleton wrote from Paris to his mother in South Carolina asking "with regard to the *vases*" would she prefer "the *classical shape* . . . or the Lewis the 14th or 'rococo' form now in Vogue?" Gaining momentum in the United States during the 1840s, the rococo-revival style evidently inspired Edward Tunnicliffe, working in 1848 in Zanesville, Ohio, to design new molds for his Rockingham ware. His wife, Sarah, wrote home to England: "You would say that we had got Rockingham to perfection. Our last kiln was better than ever. We are just bringing out a kind of scroll ware which is likely to gain great credit."[35] In addition to the naturalistic subjects that abounded in Rockingham ware and for which it was particularly well suited, other elements of eighteenth-century rococo, such as Tunnicliffe's "scroll ware," made their reappearance. C-scrolls amid the floral decoration grace the top of the spittoon shown in figure 24, and the fancy variegated Rockingham-ware dish illustrated in figure 25 (see also plate 10) is a virtual index of rococo vocabulary. Its color is mottled pale yellow and brown with splashes of green. A curvilinear molded frame with shellwork, C-scrolls, and floral decoration surrounds a chinoiserie in the form of an embossed picture of three figures in Chinese dress; the seated figure facing the viewer is eating with chopsticks from a bowl.

The rococo-revival style remained in fashion through the 1850s and into the 1860s. Rockingham-ware modelers' designs — their representations of flowers and vines that trailed naturalistically over pitchers and over vessels with asymmetrically tilted flower-shaped finials, such as the sugar bowl in figure 19 and the teapot in figure 38 (see page 82) — contrasted markedly to the neoclassical designs that predominated in the 1830s and into the 1840s. In the Orcutt & Thompson ewer (figure 10) and the American Pottery Company Toby jug and spittoon (figures 13 and 14), the floral motifs are stylized, and decorative elements are discrete and small in scale. Classical motifs were also important design elements in the early wares: anthemia and other classical devices decorate the Orcutt & Thompson and the American Pottery Company pieces cited.

It should be noted that in England the term "Rockingham ware" often referred, and still refers, to the smooth gilded or enameled brown-glazed ware made first at Swinton rather than to the relief-decorated ware under discussion here.[36] But the Swinton type does not seem to have been popular in

FIG. 23. Pitcher. Taylor & Speeler, Trenton, N.J., 1852–1855. Buff earthenware with translucent mottled brown and blue glaze, H 11¼". Mark: TAYLOR/SPEELER/TRENTON/N.J. (Jay A. Lewis collection; photo, Jay A. Lewis.)

FIG. 24. Pitcher and spittoon. Attributed to Taylor & Speeler, Trenton, N.J., 1852–1855. Buff earthenware with translucent mottled brown and blue glaze, H. 9″ (pitcher), Dia. 8½″ (spittoon). (Private collection; photo, Rick Echelmeyer.)

the United States. Rarely do survivals fitting the description appear in ceramics collections, and there was only one such vessel among the 789 excavated Rockingham-ware vessels that formed the archaeological database for this study. It was a gilded teapot from the site of a late-nineteenth-century Pittsburgh home-furnishings store. There is a post–Civil War newspaper reference to a Rockingham County, Virginia, potter named J. H. Kite making "Rockingham ware . . . moulded into shape and beauty . . . comparable with the first English 'Rockingham ware,'" but it is impossible to know what the ware looked like or even if the writer knew what the first English ware looked like.[37] From archaeological evidence, surviving examples, and American potters' price lists, it appears that Americans preferred Rockingham ware with embossed decoration.

The subjects depicted in Rockingham ware were wide ranging and included hunt scenes; national symbols; religious, classical, or literary themes; heroes; such subjects of topical interest as gypsy encampments or the Salamander Works' steamboat of the 1830s; florals; animals, and abstract designs.

FIG. 25. Dish. Probably American, 1850–1860. Buff earthenware with translucent mottled clear, brown, and green glaze, L. 10⅝″. (Private collection; photo, Rick Echelmeyer.)

As fashions in decorative styles changed throughout the period of Rockingham-ware production, which lasted into the 1930s, potters responded with changes in Rockingham-ware designs and glazes. Concurrent with the rococo revival, the gothic revival flourished—six-, eight-, ten-, or twelve-sided paneled vessels being the simplest Rockingham-ware manifestation. The American Pottery Company made a pitcher with the embossed representation of saints standing in niches; Norton and Fenton's 1847 price list offered "Gothic pattern" pitchers, and "Sexigon pattern" was added in 1848. Between 1847 and 1858, Fenton's pottery (variously called "Lyman, Fenton & Park"; "Lyman, Fenton & Company"; and "the United States Pottery Company") offered tobacco jars decorated with pointed gothic arches that are exceeded in elaboration only by the paned gothic windows depicted on the spittoon illustrated in figure 44 (page 95) and plate 14.[38]

Mottled or streaked glazes predominated into the 1870s when, concurrent with the late-nineteenth-century neoclassical revivals, plain brown glazes again became prevalent. The Edwin Bennett Pottery's most famous article in Rockingham ware, the Rebekah-at-the-Well teapot (pictured in figure 38), which the pottery introduced in the 1850s glazed as described in the letter to Barber quoted above, was reissued in the latter part of the nineteenth century, not mottled but dipped in a plain, dark brown glaze. The J. L. Rue Pottery, Matawan, New Jersey, made the pitcher in the form of a bulldog, illustrated in figure 26 (see also plate 11). Produced during the 1880s, it is entirely covered with a plain, dark brown glaze, although, because the glaze ran off of the raised "hairs" of the molded coat, the effect is of highlighting. A visitor to the pottery, describing the glazing process in an account published in the *Matawan [New Jersey] Journal,* noted that pieces to be glazed were "inverted and dipped in to the glazing solution."[39] In keeping with fashion, Rockingham ware at this time was again appropriately classicized, with egg-and-dart borders, palmettes, and portrait medallions of Roman warriors comprising the decoration of teapots, pitchers, and spittoons.

This is not to suggest that mottled Rockingham glazes entirely disappeared with the revival of neoclassicism. As late as 1913, the Yellow-Rock Pottery Company of Philadelphia was making mottled Rockingham ware, some of it decorated with classical motifs.[40] Figure 27 illustrates a hanging flowerpot with a mottled glaze over embossed classical fluting and egg-and-dart decoration, which is in the large scale typical of late-nineteenth-century neoclassicism. It was probably made during the 1870s when many potters advertised hanging flower vases or baskets. It is likely that potters during the entire period of Rockingham-ware production used both glaze methods from time to time and would have been equipped to do both. When the Swan Hill Pottery, South Amboy, New Jersey, was sold to a new owner in 1875, the equipment that was transferred included "dipping tubs" and "mottling tubs."[41]

A glazing method not yet mentioned was a technique in which the potter sponged the brown glaze

FIG. 26. Pitcher. J. L. Rue Pottery, Matawan, N.J., 1881–1890. Buff earthenware with translucent brown glaze, H. 9″. (Private collection; photo, Rick Echelmeyer.)

FIG. 27. Hanging flowerpot. American, 1870–1880. Buff earthenware with translucent mottled brown glaze, Dia. 9¼″. (Private collection; photo, Rick Echelmeyer.)

onto the yellow or buff-colored body rather than dipping, dripping, spattering, or splashing it. This method of glazing characteristically produced repeated discrete patterns rather than the random effect typical of the other methods. It was not, according to William C. Ketchum, author of *American Country Pottery: Yellowware and Sponge-ware*, produced "in any great quantity until the turn of the [twentieth] century." Some ceramics collectors and dealers today consider this ware a separate entity from yellow or Rockingham ware, calling it "sponge-ware," although there is no indication that the potters who produced it used the term.[42] While the name is useful descriptively, to consider this ware a separate class of pottery reifies a distinction that may not have existed in the minds of the potters or their customers. For the potters, sponging may have been yet another means of achieving a (perhaps novel) mottled effect on their Rockingham ware.

❧ 3 ❧

The Americanization of
Rockingham Ware

The Rockingham-ware industry in the United States followed a
pattern unique in the history of Anglo-American ceramics. By
the 1760s, the colonies were becoming an important market
for the English pottery industry, as Josiah Wedgwood, the preeminent
pottery manufacturer of the late eighteenth century, noted: "The bulk
of our particular manufactures are, you know, exported to foreign markets, for our home consumption is very trifling in comparison to what
is sent abroad; and the principal of these markets are the Continent and
Islands of North America." (The context of Wedgwood's correspondence makes it clear that the reference was to the North American continent rather than Europe, and that the "islands" were the West Indies.)
Only temporarily interrupted by the American Revolution and the War
of 1812, this pattern continued well past the middle of the nineteenth
century with the United States absorbing generally between 40 and 50
percent of English export ceramics.[1] These English wares comprised a
major portion of the ceramic wares Americans used throughout the
nineteenth century. In general, despite the American pottery industry's
century-long attempts to compete against imported wares, the imports
prevailed over the home products—with the exception of Rockingham
and yellow ware. I will explain in this chapter why the manufacture of
these ceramics followed a different course.

With the American market offering seemingly boundless sales potential and outstripping the home market for English ceramics, and
with knowledge having long circulated among English potters that the
requisite raw materials existed in America, thousands of English artisan
potters chose to emigrate to the United States during the nineteenth
century. They became, in the words of the economics historian Frank
Thistlethwaite, the "essential cadre" for an American pottery industry.
In "The Atlantic Migration of the Pottery Industry," Thistlethwaite examines the consequences of this migration, basing his study on the ca-
reers of one hundred British emigrant master and journeyman potters.

He found that some arrived during every decade, but the periods of greatest influx were the years between 1839 and 1850 and between the Civil War and 1873.[2]

The first of these periods of increased immigration saw not only the name "Rockingham ware" entering into American usage but the rapidly expanding American manufacture of Rockingham as well, and there is no doubt that the migration of English potters played a critical role in these events. This is not to suggest that production of the brown-glazed ware that began in the 1830s would not have continued without the wave of English migration or that the name "Rockingham ware" would not have been adopted. Two American-born potters, at least, advertised Rockingham ware in the 1840s: Christopher Webber Fenton, starting in 1847 (although, as mentioned in chapter 2, Fenton preferred the name "dark lustre"), and Abraham Miller, of Philadelphia, in 1849. Given the ephemeral nature of documentary evidence, it is more than likely that during the 1840s other American potters made and advertised Rockingham ware, even though the proof of such has not survived. Still, it was undoubtedly the arrival of large numbers of English potters with experience at making yellow and Rockingham ware that gave impetus to the industry. Thistlethwaite emphasizes the paramount importance of such experience: "Potting was an industry involving a high degree of craft skill and artistry, and a comparatively low degree of investment in plant and machinery. The actual migration of the potters themselves is the central fact of the colonization of the industry on the western shores of the Atlantic. The potters carried it in their packs, so to speak."[3]

Usually the English immigrant potters, whether or not they ultimately struck out on their own, worked first for established potters—generally earlier English immigrants—upon their arrival in the United States. As mentioned in the last chapter, James Bennett, who started the Bennett & Brothers pottery in East Liverpool, Ohio, worked first at the American Pottery Company, Jersey City, New Jersey, in 1834. In 1837 he moved to Troy, Indiana, to work with James Clews, the English manufacturer who was attempting to make whiteware. Abandoning that failed project in about a year, Bennett proceeded up the Ohio River to seek a better situation and location.[4] Learning from a fellow steamboat passenger about the existence of potting clays and adjacent coal veins near the tiny river town of East Liverpool, Bennett stopped there to assess the location. He found the clay and coal suitable and abundant and, upon obtaining local financial backing, began construction of a one-kiln pottery with the help of a mold maker and presser named George Hollingshead and a kilnman named William Thomas.[5] His first kiln load, consisting of yellow ware, was fired in 1840, and by 1841 his ware was advertised in the East Liverpool pages of the Pittsburgh business directory.[6] Employing hyperbole not the least uncommon in advertising of the period, the ad cited the "manufactury (now in successful operation) of porcelain, which is carried on by Mr. Bennett, a regular manufacturer from Staffordshire, England. . . . The 'Liverpool Ware' is for sale in Pittsburgh by Mr. George Breed." Bennett was making yellow ware, not porcelain, and Breed was a wholesaler for Queensware.[7] The term "Queensware" had been Wedgwood's brand name for creamware, which subsequently became generic for creamware in general. By the time Bennett was potting and Breed was selling, it had expanded to include yellow ware. That same year James sent for his brothers Edwin, Daniel, and William, with whom he founded Bennett & Brothers. Sometime after the younger brothers' arrival, at least by the time Bennett & Brothers had started advertising their "fancy Rockingham ware," the pottery had started producing Rockingham ware.

Thus began the pottery manufacturing center that, with its concentration of potteries making Rockingham ware, probably did more than any other pottery district to popularize Rockingham ware in the United States. Ten more potteries constructed and manned by Englishmen were operating in East Liverpool by the end of the decade, and these as well as those that opened in the 1850s and 1860s produced both Rockingham and yellow ware. According to William C. Gates, Jr., and Dana E. Ormerod, "except for the shortlived whiteware production of William Bloor (1861–1862) and various experiments by other potters, East Liverpool manufacturers confined themselves to Rockingham and yellow ware prior to 1872."[8]

In addition to being ideally sited for pottery production because of its native clay and fuel supplies, East Liverpool was well located for distribution of the potters' wares. Although the Cleveland and Pittsburgh railroad line to East Liverpool was not completed until 1856, the growing cities of Pittsburgh, Cincinnati, Louisville, St. Louis, and New Orleans, and numerous river towns along the way were all accessible markets to the East Liverpool potters via the Ohio and Mississippi Rivers. In 1844, a thrower at the Bennett & Brothers pottery described the fortunate situation to his relatives and friends in England: "East Liverpool is full of clay and coal, and contains about 700 inhabitants, lying on the Ohio River, 45 miles from Pittsburgh. It lies well for shipping to Cincinnati, also New Orleans and many other markets. . . . I find there are markets open to receive every cup of ware that is made. . . . It is impossible for you to starve."[9]

Descriptions of the pioneer East Liverpool potteries catalog the variety of distribution methods available to potters who had access to navigable waterways. A steamship would have carried James Bennett's wares upriver to George Breed, the Pittsburgh wholesaler who sold his "Liverpool ware" in 1841. Bennett also sold two crates of yellow-ware mugs to Isaac Knowles, an East Liverpool carpenter and cabinetmaker, who himself started a pottery in the 1850s. Knowles acted as middleman, selling the mugs from a trading boat on the river. Richard Henderson, who opened his Salamander Pottery near the end of the 1840s, built his own trading boat. According to a journalist writing in the 1930s, his practice was to fire a supply of Rockingham ware, then close the pottery while he sold his merchandise down the Ohio and Mississippi, returning to replenish until the stock was sold. Trading boats, or "store boats," could be privately owned, or they could function as traveling general stores, picking up supplies and offering their goods at town and farm landings along the river.

Steamboats carried freight as well as passengers, but they were outnumbered by the many keelboats and flatboats that plied the inland waterways. An anecdote involving George S. Harker, son of Benjamin Harker, the founder of East Liverpool's second pottery, colorfully illustrates the river scene: The senior Harker started out selling potting clay from the land upon which he would subsequently operate his pottery. He sent a boatload to Cincinnati "under the pilotage of W. McClure," with George following in a steamboat to sell the clay when it reached the city. George "found but little demand for such an article, and was afraid the venture would prove unsuccessful, when a large steamer, in making a landing at the levee, accidentally sunk the flat containing the clay. The captain of the steamboat, however, cheerfully and promptly paid the bill of damages presented, and the young business man returned home unexpectedly well satisfied with the adventure." [10]

In addition to shipping, potters also peddled their wares locally, going from house to house by horse and wagon. Evidently the purchase of a peddler's wagon could be a material sign of success. Edward Tunnicliffe (the Zanesville, Ohio, potter whose wife, Sarah, had written home to England in 1848 about their "scroll ware") had come to East Liverpool in 1841 with the three younger Bennett brothers, but had moved before 1848 to Zanesville. In her letter, Sarah also reported that "we are doing better now than we have ever done since we left home. E. paid $100 for a peddling wagon last Monday." But not all the pioneer East Liverpool potters could afford a wagon or shipping, at least at first. James Salt and Frederick Mear, who with two partners had started a pottery in 1842, were a three-person operation, with Mrs. Salt consti-tuting the sales force. She is said to have carried the ware in a basket bal-anced on her head, selling or bartering from door to door.[11]

A railroad line was opened in 1852 to Wellsville, Ohio, three miles downriver from East Liverpool, and in 1856 it reached all the way to East Liverpool, affording access to markets far from the banks of the in-land river system: Chicago to the west, and to the east, New York and the other cities of the East Coast. Not surprisingly, the East Liverpool potters took full advantage of this improved transportation. But even before that time, when the routes would have been via Lake Erie, the Erie Canal, and the Hudson River to New York, or from Wheeling, West Virginia (part of Virginia at that time), to Cumberland, Mary-land, via the National Road, East Liverpool ware was selling on the East Coast. A newspaper in Augusta, Georgia, picked up an 1849 article from the *Pittsburgh Gazette* reporting on the "queensware" production of the (then) eight potteries at East Liverpool, finding it "equally as good, be-sides being a great deal cheaper than the English article manufactured from the same kind of clay." (The phrase "from the same kind of clay" would have alerted the reader that East Liverpool was producing yellow ware or Rockingham and not a white-bodied ware, whitewares being more expensive than yellow or Rockingham wares.) The quote contin-ued: "This branch of our manufactures has sprung up within the past few years, and has already driven the English yellow ware from our mar-ket. It is sold in vast quantities in New York, Philadelphia, and other eastern cities, as well as in Pittsburgh, Cincinnati, Louisville, St. Louis, New Orleans, and the rest of the western towns."[12]

In 1851, two years after the newspaper article appeared, the American Institute of the City of New York held an exhibition of industrial prod-ucts at which it awarded the gold medal for Rockingham ware to Wood-ward, Blakeley & Company, of East Liverpool, noting that their speci-mens combined the "soundness which has always characterized the ware of the Messrs. Bennett" with the "beautiful coloring produced in the Bennington ware" plus "the most exquisite modeling." Although the exhibition took place during the year before railroad service was available even as far as Wellsville, the institute judges more than cor-roborated the *Pittsburgh Gazette*'s report that East Liverpool ware was sweeping the East:

In our immediate neighborhood potting has been carried on to [a] limited ex-tent for a considerable time, but with indifferent and varying success. It has remained for the *Great West* to add another branch to the already cumbersome wreath, by springing into active operation on the banks of the Ohio, a com-munity of nearly two thousand souls, supported entirely from the profits of successfully manufacturing various articles of use and ornament from the *soil* upon which their city is built. The difficulties with which our eastern manufacturers have had to contend, in the procuring of coals and materials, are there entirely overcome by the beneficent hand of nature, and we now witness the strange anomaly of Eastern potters *importing* ware from the *West* at cheaper rates than they can manufacture, notwithstanding the heavy cost of transportation.[13]

To "the beneficent hand of nature," the American Institute judges might have added "lucky timing." For the fire clay deposits at East Liverpool were ideally suited to making the newly popular Rockingham ware; the Bennetts and some of the other potters who first exploited them had come experienced from Derbyshire where fire clay deposits were extensive, and yellow and Rockingham ware were specialties of the district.[14]

Even though about as many potters in the East were making Rockingham ware in 1851 as in East Liverpool, where between eight and eleven potteries were operating, the relative novelty of Rockingham ware, and the monolithic impression the East Liverpool potteries must have made—all concentrated into a small area and all producing only Rockingham and yellow ware—may have led the institute judges to see Eastern pottery manufacture, which was more spread out and diverse, as less dynamic. Except for two potteries making only yellow and Rockingham ware in the East that year (Edwin R. Hanks and Charles Fish's Swan Hill Pottery in South Amboy, New Jersey, and Abraham Cadmus's Congress Pottery, also in South Amboy), most of the others who made Rockingham ware were known for other types of wares— with the possible exception of E. & W. Bennett, which may or may not have introduced its blue- and green-glazed molded wares by that year. For example, the New York potters John B. Caire & Company of Poughkeepsie, William Warner of West Troy, and Otto V. Lewis of Greenwich were better known for their salt-glazed stoneware.[15]

The judges' impression of "indifferent and varying success" may have stemmed even more, I suspect, from their awareness of the potters' ongoing struggle to make a market for whiteware. Attempts at making white earthenware or porcelain had occupied potters in America since the seventeenth century, but before the establishment later in the nineteenth century of a sufficiently protective tariff structure for the more technologically complex ware, almost all attempts were commercial failures or, at best, short-lived successes.[16] In 1851, whiteware production was decades from becoming a commercial success. The American Pottery Company, renamed the Jersey City Pottery in the early 1850s, had by 1849 added "white granite ware" (a white earthenware of lighter shade than creamware) to their cream-colored earthenware products of the 1830s and 1840s, but they had to discontinue both white granite and creamware in 1854. According to the ceramics historian Jennie J. Young, "[T]he pressure of foreign competition was so great that they could not gain a foothold in the regular trade. Their wares were chiefly sold by peddlers and itinerant dealers, who were in the habit of going to the factory with wagons, when they knew that a kiln was to be drawn, and carting off the goods before they were trimmed." Among others in the East making white-bodied wares along with Rockingham and yellow ware were Christopher Webber Fenton in Bennington, Vermont, and Abraham Miller and Ralph Bagnall Beech of Philadelphia, who produced white-bodied wares to a limited extent. Miller was particularly diversified, making also red and black tea wares, an extensive line of ceramic products for industry, and a portable furnace that could be used outdoors for laundering and cooking during hot weather.[17]

At some point Jersey City returned to the production of whiteware—in 1878 Jennie J. Young called it their staple product—but they had never discontinued making Rockingham ware. Young wrote: "The popularity occasionally reached by a single form was, perhaps, never better exemplified than by the brown pitcher above mentioned [a hound-handled pitcher introduced in the late 1830s or early 1840s]." Still in production, it had become "so identified with the factory," that the proprietor, wishing to send a gift to a friend at the Derby China Works in England, "thought he could not do better than send him one of these pitchers of a size larger than ordinary."[18]

The career of Ralph Bagnall Beech, who emigrated from England in 1842, also suggests a pattern of producing Rockingham ware as a mainstay. Before emigrating, Beech had been running his own business and before that had worked at the Wedgwood factory. Between 1842 and 1845, he worked in Philadelphia for Abraham Miller, who had started whiteware production by 1844—perhaps under Beech's tutelage. Opening his own pottery in the Kensington section of the city in 1845, Beech was making "Porcelain Flower and Scent Vases" by 1851, according to the Franklin Institute's report on the Exhibition of American Manufactures. The same year he also introduced "Japanning on Earthenware," a technique of decorating on a white biscuit earthenware body with a colored varnish surface that imitated Japanese lacquer. Some of the pieces were further enhanced with inlaid mother-of-pearl or paint and gilding. Both before and after branching out into white-bodied wares, however, Beech made Rockingham ware, winning a Franklin Institute prize for his earthenware in 1846, and using the dated patent mark from his Japanned ware, "RALPH B. BEECH/PATENTED/JUNE 3,

1851/KENSINGTON, PA," on the Rockingham ware he made thereafter. The Metropolitan Museum of Art's collection of American ceramics includes a Rockingham-ware twelve-sided covered dish with the mark.[19]

Evidence is convincing that the young Rockingham- and yellow-ware industry in the United States was becoming increasingly successful, but can East Liverpool really have "driven the English yellow ware from our market" by 1849, as the *Pittsburgh Gazette* stated? Only four years earlier the Franklin Institute had reported that English Rockingham ware was "used extensively in this country." The United States Geological Survey of 1883 seems to confirm the *Gazette*'s assessment: "Before 1861 the several hundred potteries in the United States were small and local. They made stoneware jugs, pie plates, drain tile, yellow crockery et cetera . . . the cheapest and commonest class of pottery products with which foreign competition was powerless because the expense of transportation bore such a large proportion to their costs."[20]

However, contradicting the Survey's opinion about the success of pre–Civil War foreign competition in these inexpensive wares—which included "yellow crockery," which, in turn, included Rockingham ware—are surviving ceramics dealers' invoices demonstrating that importation of English Rockingham ware was indeed taking place. Invoices dated 1849, 1852, 1859, and 1861 from importers and dealers in New York and Boston all give prices for Rockingham-ware teapots, pitchers, and spittoons in pounds sterling translated into dollars. The scarcity of surviving or archaeologically excavated marked English Rockingham-ware vessels as compared to the number of marked American Rockingham pieces that have turned up could be taken as evidence that imports were few, except that the vast majority of Rockingham ware was not marked at all. During the 1830s, 1840s, and 1850s in particular, some American Rockingham-ware potters did mark their wares, but the marks were impressed and frequently rendered illegible because the thick, dark Rockingham-ware glaze filled them up. Thus many potters did not bother to mark their wares; taking this into account, the negative evidence of the scarcity of English marks cannot be given much weight.

Nor is it possible to differentiate positively unmarked English- and American-made wares. Although scholars of American ceramics generally consider a dark brown, uniform, unmottled Rockingham glaze to be characteristic of English Rockingham ware of the mid to late nineteenth century, especially of the Rockingham made in Derbyshire, it isn't always the case: English potters also made mottled Rockingham ware. A sugar bowl marked by the English firm Elsmore & Forster

FIG. 28. Sugar bowl. Elsmore & Forster, Tunstall, Staffordshire, England, 1859–1871.
White earthenware with translucent mottled clear and brown glaze. (Private collection;
photo, Warren F. Broderick.)

(figure 28), made between 1859 and 1871, is very close in appearance to
some of the products of Christopher Webber Fenton's Bennington pottery, made in the 1850s, and to wares made in the 1860s and later by
other potteries such as the J. E. Jeffords Pottery, Philadelphia. (Jeffords's
foreman, Stephen Theiss, had worked for the United States Pottery
Company.)[21] The body of the Elsmore & Forster piece is white, like
some of the United States Pottery bodies, and looks cream-colored in
the clear-glazed parts as do the Bennington pieces. The cream-colored
appearance was the result of simply not adding the bluing agent customarily added to the glazes of whitewares of the period to make them
appear whiter. A marked example of Rockingham ware from the
Wooden Box Pottery, Derbyshire, is also indistinguishable from
mottled American Rockingham; the English ceramics historian
Llewellyn Jewitt wrote in 1883 that the Wooden Box Pottery "manufactures ironstone, cane, buff, and Rockingham wares of the usual kinds
and qualities."[22]

At the same time that some American dealers were selling imported Rockingham ware, others were selling domestic. A Boston importer in 1853 gave whiteware prices in pounds and dollars, but Rockingham-ware teapot prices on the same invoice were in dollars only. In 1856, a Chicago dealer advertised Ohio stoneware, beer bottles, and Rockingham ware, and in 1873, a Milwaukee dealer advertised Ohio stoneware, Rockingham and yellow ware, flowerpots, and garden vases. A Philadelphia importer and general commission merchant advertised in 1870 both "Foreign and Domestic China, Glass, and Queensware." He listed "Glassware and Queensware, open and in original packages, Kerosene Lamp Goods, Yellow & Rockingham Ware, Gray Stoneware." Most compelling is the evidence of *The Crockery Companion,* a salesmen's book of tables giving English and equivalent American prices for an extensive list of table- and toilet-ware vessel forms. Published in 1881 by a Boston importer and dealer, the handbook gives both currencies for all the whiteware, but only dollars for the Rockingham and yellow ware.[23] This document strongly suggests that although the import market for whiteware was active in 1881, the Rockingham and yellow ware for sale were all American made.

Information from a 1929 doctoral dissertation entitled "Factors in the Development of the American Pottery Industry, 1860–1929" supports this interpretation. The author, Herman John Stratton, notes that "there was considerable importation of this type of ware [Rockingham and yellow ware] after, as well as before, the Civil War. But by the eighties, the importers and manufacturers agree, there was practically no importation of such ware, and the American manufacturers had entire control of the market."[24] The statement was drawn from the annual report of the Tariff Commission for 1882 and, fitting with the evidence of the dealers' documents, is probably accurate. Importation of English Rockingham and yellow ware before the Civil War is documented—demonstrating more hope than truth in the *Pittsburgh Gazette*'s 1849 report that East Liverpool potters had "driven the English yellow ware from our market." Importation probably continued after the Civil War, but by the 1880s, it virtually had ceased.

It is hard to know what part the ad valorem protective tariffs of 20 or 25 percent that the American Rockingham- and yellow-ware industry enjoyed during and for thirty years after the Civil War played in the industry's success, but tariffs of twice to three times that were not enough to enable the American whiteware industry to compete successfully against British imports.[25] Throughout the nineteenth century England remained the chief supplier of the ceramic wares Americans used the most: creamware and whitewares. England also supplied such nineteenth-century decorative wares as refined stoneware, lusterware, and Jasper, Wedgwood's trade name for colored, refined stonewares with white relief decoration. But Rockingham- and yellow-ware production for the American market moved to the United States. Where English potters maintained their hold on American trade in other types of wares, often exporting designs especially for American tastes, the immigrant potters successfully took over that role in Rockingham ware, producing images appropriate to American life and culture for their new countrymen.

Some American-made Rockingham ware directly copied English designs, the immigrant potters having brought the molds with them from England. Or the modelers made new designs, many featuring American symbols, especially versions of the American eagle from the Great Seal of the United States. Figures 29 and 30 show an octagonal spittoon decorated with both the stylized American eagle, bearing shield and arrows, and a naturalistically rendered eagle. The short sides display leafage and scrolled decoration characteristic of rococo-revival design. A third design option was to graft American symbols onto English designs. Figure 31 illustrates a pitcher based on an English stoneware pitcher design of wheat ears, registered in April 1861 by James Dudson of Hanley, Staffordshire. In the English version, the wheat ears grow straight upward; in the American version, they have been pushed aside to accommodate the American eagle. An octagonal Rockingham-ware spittoon

FIG. 29. Spittoon. American, 1850–1870. Buff earthenware with translucent mottled brown glaze, H. 5⅝". (Private collection.)

FIG. 30. Detail of fig. 29. (Private collection.)

FIG. 31. Pitcher. Probably American, 1861–1900. Buff earthenware with translucent mottled brown glaze. (Private collection; photo, Warren F. Broderick.)

probably made in New Jersey exhibits scenes from Robert Burns's poem "Tam O'Shanter" taken directly from an English stoneware pitcher made by William Ridgway in 1835. The American potter transferred the Scottish thistle motif from the neck of the Ridgway pitcher to one of the panels of the spittoon, and on the eighth panel he displayed an American eagle. (See figures 32, 33, and 34.) One inventive modeler— tentatively identified as Charles Coxon, who worked for the Bennetts in Baltimore between 1849 and 1858—Americanized a small pitcher with relief figures of huntsmen taken from Staffordshire figure groups, by placing the huntsmen improbably amidst Indian corn, an American plant and an American symbol.[26] (See figure 35.) Another version, probably made at a different pottery, went further: the bearded English huntsmen were transformed into American Indians, having shed their

FIG. 32. Pitcher (detail). William Ridgway, 1835. Blue-grey stoneware, smear glazed.
(Courtesy of Antique Arts Ltd., Newport, R.I.)

FIG. 33. Spittoon (detail). American, 1849–1870. Buff earthenware with translucent
mottled brown glaze. (Private collection.)

FIG. 34. Spittoon (detail).
American, 1849–1870. Buff
earthenware with translucent
mottled brown glaze. (Private
collection.)

beards, boots, and cloth coats in favor of buckskins and feathers. (See
figure 36.)

Another English immigrant, Josiah Jones, was probably the creator
of the quintessentially American design illustrated in figure 37 (see also
plate 12)—a large, generously curved pitcher decorated with a luxuri-
ance of growing corn that suggests the abundance of America. Jones's
brother-in-law Charles Cartlidge, who started a porcelain factory in
Greenpoint, a section of Brooklyn, New York, in 1848, first produced
the design in porcelain. Molds of the pitcher disseminated to other potteries—Jones himself took them to Kaolin, South Carolina, where he
became manager of the Southern Porcelain Company after the closing
of the Cartlidge works in 1856—and the "corn" pitcher appeared in several media: Rockingham ware and redware, as well as porcelain.[27] The
exuberant Rockingham-ware corn pitcher, popular in its appeal and
aesthetically far distant from the elegantly conceived teapots made at
Swinton in the eighteenth and early nineteenth century, eloquently
symbolized the Americanization of Rockingham ware.

FIG. 35. Pitcher. Attributed to E. & W. or Edwin Bennett Pottery, Charles Coxon, modeler, 1855–1860. Buff earthenware with translucent mottled brown and clear glaze, H. 5¼″. (Private collection; photo, Rick Echelmeyer.)

FIG. 36. Pitcher (detail). American, 1855–1870. Buff earthenware with translucent mottled brown glaze, H. 5″. (Warren F. Broderick collection; photo, Warren F. Broderick.)

FIG. 37. Pitcher. American, design attributed to Josiah Jones, 1848–1870. Buff earthenware with translucent mottled brown glaze, H. 11⅛″. (Jay A. Lewis collection.)

❧ 4 ❧

The Niche Market for
Rockingham Ware

rtifact distribution in the archaeological sites included in this study shows that although its usage was widespread, Rockingham ware generally accounted for at most only 1 or 2 percent of the domestic ceramics assemblages in which it was found. In the total count of ceramics assemblages, those with and those without Rockingham ware, it would have represented less. Whiteware, on the other hand, accounted for at least 75 percent, often more. Analysis of the excavated Rockingham-ware vessel forms as well as diachronic tracking of the vessel forms listed in thirty-seven Rockingham-ware potters' price lists showed me why Rockingham ware was seldom found in large quantities on any one site. The reason was not marginal popularity but consumer acceptance of only a few of the vessel forms that were made. Rockingham was a specialty ware.

In formulating the research plan for this study (see chapter 1), I assumed that when I identified the historic users of Rockingham ware, I would find that Rockingham-ware usage per se divided along interpretable lines. I would find it occurring in certain segments of the population, regions of the country, urban or rural loci, or with certain types of property usage. But that did not prove to be the case. From the mid-nineteenth century into the twentieth, Rockingham ware was used in all types of American settings: in rural locations, villages, towns, and cities; in households representing all classes; and in such public establishments as restaurants, taverns, and hotels. At government facilities from the army fort at Apache Pass, Arizona, to Independence Hall in Philadelphia, a Rockingham-ware spittoon seems to have been de rigueur. Even not counting the extraordinary accumulation of spittoons discarded by the Kentucky state legislators, this vessel form accounted for nearly 40 percent of the Rockingham ware on nondomestic sites (see table 2). Rockingham-ware pitchers with gothic paneling were used at the hotel that Mormon prophet Joseph Smith built to accommodate visitors to his settlement at Nauvoo, Illinois; and the tip of

TABLE 2
Distribution of Rockingham-Ware Vessel Forms by Historical Use of Site

	Type and Number of Sites					
Vessel form	Residence (94)	Hotel/ boarding- house (11)	Restaurant or tavern (7)	Public or semi-public** (11)	Historical use unknown (8)	Total vessels
Teapot	65	15	3	2	1	86
Spittoon	30	9	10	9	6	64
Pitcher	41	4	10	0	4	59
Mixing bowl	32	4	1	0	0	37
Baking vessel*	14	0	1	0	0	15
Serving dish	6	0	0	0	0	6
Mug	3	0	0	2	1	6
Jar	0	1	1	1	0	3
Flower pot	2	0	0	0	0	2
Tobacco jar	2	0	0	0	0	2
Marble	1	1	0	0	0	2
Chamber pot	2	0	0	0	0	2
Box	1	0	0	0	0	1
Bottle	1	0	0	0	0	1
Canning jar	1	0	0	0	0	1
Crock	0	0	1	0	0	1
Figurine	1	0	0	0	0	1
Milk pan	1	0	0	0	0	1
Soap dish	0	0	0	0	1	1
Tumbler	1	0	0	0	0	1
Total vessels	204	34	27	14	13	292

SOURCES: Rockingham-ware fragments and documentary data from archaeological investigations.
*Includes nappies, baking dishes, and pie plates.
**Includes government buildings, military posts, business offices, a school, an abbey, and a clubhouse.

a teapot spout indicates that household objects in the slave quarters of Andrew Jackson's Hermitage included a Rockingham-ware teapot.[1]

However, to say simply that virtually everyone used Rockingham ware, while true, is misleading. It implies a monolithic quality to consumer attitudes that is an oversimplification, for everyone did not use the same vessel forms and decorative motifs. The mere presence of Rockingham ware at an archaeological site provides little information except a terminus post quem—a beginning date for the site or the part of the site associated with the datable artifact. Rockingham ware revealed its cultural meaning at the vessel form and decoration level.

More than eighty different vessel forms in a variety of sizes and embossed decorations were made at some point in the history of Rockingham-ware production. The list of forms, compiled from survivals, archaeological recoveries, and potters' price lists or other documents, includes:

Ale jugs
Architectural ele-
ments
Baking pans*
Banks
Basins
Batter jugs
Bedpans
Birdbaths and cups
Bottles*
Bowls*
Boxes*
Bread boxes
Butter dishes
Butter tubs
Cake plates
Candlesticks
Canning jars*
Chamber pots*
Chicken waterers
Coffeepots
Coffee urns
Coin covers
Cookie jars
Covered dishes
Creamers
Crocks*
Cups
Curtain tiebacks

Desk sets
Dishes*
Doorknobs
Ewers
Figurines*
Flasks
Flowerpots*
Footbaths
Foot warmers
Furniture knobs
Garden seats
Goblets
Hall dogs (large
figurines, usually
spaniels)
Hanging baskets
Icewater pitchers
Inhalators
Inkwells
Jars*
Lamp bases
Milk pans*
Marbles*
Molds
Mugs*
Nameplates
Nappies (round
dishes)*
Paperweights

Pickle dishes
Picture frames
Pie plates*
Pipkins
Pitchers*
Plates
Plug basins (sinks)
Salad dishes
Sauce dishes
Shakers
Shaving mugs
Shovel plates
Slop jars
Snuffboxes
Soap dishes*
Spill holders
Spittoons*
Stove supports
Sugar bowls
Teapots*
Tobacco jars*
Toby jugs
Toothbrush holders
Toys
Tumblers*
Wafer pots
Washboards
Water coolers

* Denotes vessels found on archaeological sites in this study.

Only twenty-two of these forms turned up on the sites included in this study, and at that, most were in miniscule quantities. As table 2 shows, only four or five forms appear to have really caught on: teapots (which accounted for 29 percent of the total), spittoons (22 percent), pitchers (20 percent), mixing bowls (13 percent), and nappies, other baking dishes, and pie plates, which together accounted for 5 percent. (Nappies for baking were flat-bottomed, slant-sided vessels, offered in six or eight different sizes.)

The earliest Rockingham-ware potters' price lists offered only a few of the forms listed above. Fenton's Crockery Works and Lyman, Fenton & Park, Bennington, Vermont (1847 and 1848), listed Rockingham-ware pitchers, spittoons, teapots, coffeepots, creams, and sugars. In 1850, John Goodwin of East Liverpool, Ohio, offered a greater variety that included, in addition to the forms made at Bennington, butter tubs, flowerpots, honey bowls, washbowls and ewers, bedpans, salad dishes, and sauce dishes. The Swan Hill Pottery, South Amboy, New Jersey (1853/1854) made nineteen different Rockingham-ware vessel forms, but by far the most ambitious inventory, judging from extant price lists, was that of the United States Pottery Company, Bennington, which, in 1852, offered sixty-two different forms. In addition to the standard pitchers, teapots, and spittoons, they offered cooking ware and such decorative articles as picture frames, figured pocket flasks, "architectural work made to order," and mantel ornaments, two examples being reclining cows and a poodle carrying a basket in its mouth. A former workman, interviewed in 1902, remembered selling the "novelties" from a wagon, traveling as far as Lowell, Massachusetts; and, in 1911, a magazine writer waxed nostalgic about the figures "in the homes of our New England grandmothers . . . [T]he big, rather friendly-appearing lion, or the deer with head held proudly erect, or the healthy, productive-looking cow, each occupying a conspicuous place in the parlor."[2]

Surviving Rockingham-ware objects and the few price lists that still exist indicate that while the United States Pottery's scope was probably the most ambitious, other potteries were also offering a variety of such forms as "figured" candlesticks, fancy cake plates, Toby flasks, and "Octagon" or "Turk" inkstands during the 1850s. The number and variety of vessel forms and designs offered decreased somewhat during the decade, however. In an undated list published in 1855 or 1856, the Mansion Pottery of East Liverpool, for example, offered twenty-five different forms. Some of the vessels were "turned," which meant wheel thrown and finished on a lathe, and they were offered in as many as seven sizes. The rest were molded and, with the number of different designs in different sizes offered, required a total of one hundred and two master molds. By 1857, the year of a financial panic that drove some potteries out of business, the pottery's prices had been reduced, the number of forms offered was down to nineteen, and the number of different designs reduced so that the pottery needed only sixty-six master molds. From the earlier price list to the one issued in 1857, the number of different spittoon designs dropped from thirteen to six, and pitcher designs from seven to six. Despite the general decrease in the pottery's designs, there was a new pitcher design on the 1857 list—"Kansas." The design was an attempt, I imagine, at topical relevance, for the Kansas Territory, which for several years had been a battleground for pro- and antislavery forces, elected a free-state legislature in that year.

One of the designs retained from the first to the second list was the "game" pitcher, and this, as well as other variations on the hunting theme, was one of the staples of the Rockingham-ware industry. I have seen hunt-related pitchers with such titles as "game," "chase," "stagg," [sic] "Indian game," or "hunting pitchers" listed on most Rockingham-ware price lists that can be dated from the late 1840s to the 1880s, and no sooner did it appear that the designs might be petering out in general Rockingham-ware production than the Vance Faience Company, an art pottery in Wheeling, West Virginia, acquired molds of a boar hunt/stag hunt pitcher designed by the mid-century modeler Daniel Greatbach and started reissuing the design in 1901.[3] A pitcher decorated with hanging game is shown in figure 24 (page 52); other variations on the hunting theme appear in figures 6 and 19 (pages 26, 27, and 49).

Rockingham-ware price lists of the 1860s, including those that appeared during the Civil War years, offered nearly as many forms and designs as the Mansion Pottery's 1857 list. But by the last quarter of the century, the Rockingham-ware industry was retrenching as whiteware production gained ground. In 1879, according to Herman Stratton's study of the American pottery industry from 1860 to 1929, "eleven or twelve of the twenty-three potteries in East Liverpool had changed or were changing from yellow to whiteware," and by 1882, twenty-five of thirty potteries in New Jersey and forty-four of eighty-three kilns in East Liverpool were making whiteware.[4] (East Liverpool and Trenton, New Jersey, were at that time the major pottery-making centers in the country.)

However, it is notable that while forty-four kilns were making whiteware in East Liverpool in 1882, thirty-nine were still making Rockingham and yellow ware. Moreover, in addition to nineteenth-century Rockingham- and yellow-ware potteries that continued their operations into the 1930s, new Rockingham- and yellow-ware plants opened during the twentieth century. Confirming the continuing, if smaller, market for Rockingham ware—Stratton reported that Rockingham- and yellow-ware production decreased from $440,000 to $160,000 during the 1890s—the D. E. McNicol Pottery Company, East Liverpool, opened a pottery for making Rockingham and yellow ware in 1902. Formerly called McNicol, Burton & Company, D. E. McNicol had begun making Rockingham and yellow ware in 1869 and added whiteware to its production during the 1880s. It was continuing to make whiteware in the original pottery in 1902 when it opened the second plant for Rockingham and yellow ware.[5]

Judging from available price lists, the number of Rockingham-ware vessel forms and designs in production during the last fifteen or so years of the nineteenth century and in the beginning of the twentieth were far fewer than those offered in the middle decades. The Rockingham-ware industry had evidently restricted production to and made a respectable market of its most popular vessel forms: the teapots, pitchers, and spittoons that so outnumber all other vessels in this archaeological study of Rockingham ware, plus food-preparation vessels and a few other such forms as soap dishes, chamber pots, mugs, flowerpots, and a Rockingham-ware figural specialty called a "hall dog"—a large, seated spaniel that might have served as a doorstop or decoration.[6]

Rockingham ware had actually occupied a niche market from the beginning of its history in the United States. Comparing vessel-form usage between Rockingham ware and the white, transfer-printed, painted, edged, or dipped Staffordshire wares that predominated in the American market emphasizes the specialty status of Rockingham ware. George L. Miller describes an equally limited acceptance of most Staffordshire vessel forms; out of more than ninety forms produced, fifteen comprised 95 percent of the market.[7] Miller's figures disclose an important difference, however, between the Staffordshire- and Rockingham-ware forms that were popular. Analyzing only the periods when Rockingham ware was also in production, individual food consumption forms—cups, saucers, and dinner plates, which were rare in Rockingham ware—comprised more than 80 percent of imported Staffordshire ware, while teapots and pitchers accounted for only slightly more than 3 and 2 percent, respectively. Spittoons did not figure at all or were subsumed under "other vessels." Even if cups, saucers, and dinner plates are left out of the white ceramics analysis, Rockingham-ware teapots, pitchers, and certainly spittoons still accounted for greater shares of the Rockingham-ware market than the same forms in Staffordshire ware.

The Rockingham-ware plate pictured in figure 17 (page 48) attests to the fact that at least one Rockingham-ware manufacturer tested the market for individual dining or tea forms, but it should have come as no surprise that they failed to catch the public's fancy. Throughout the history of whitewares in Europe and America—porcelain, tin-glazed earthenware, eighteenth-century creamware and salt-glazed stoneware, and all the types of nineteenth-century whiteware—Europeans and Americans have favored them for dining and drinking tea. This explains the ratio of whiteware to Rockingham ware characteristic of domestic ceramics assemblages. There would be many more pieces for individual use than those for corporate use such as the forms in which Rockingham ware was favored: pitchers, teapots, spittoons, and cooking ware.

Rockingham ware demonstrates a pattern of vessel-form usage different not only from whitewares but also from any other variety of ce-

PLATE 1. Pitcher. Attributed to Vodrey & Brother Pottery, East Liverpool, Ohio, 1858–1876. (Private Collection.)

PLATE 2. "Cadogan" pot. Rockingham Works, Swinton, Yorkshire, England, 1826–1842. (Courtesy, The Winterthur Library: Printed Book and Periodical Collection.)

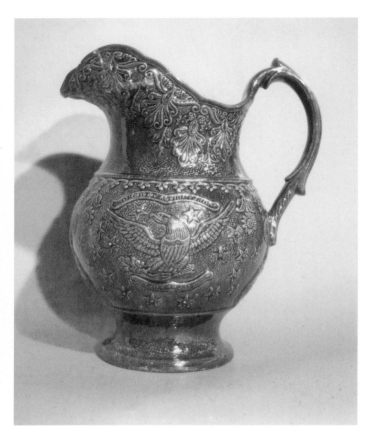

PLATE 3. Ewer. Orcutt &
Thompson, Poughkeepsie,
N.Y., 1830–1831. (Courtesy
of the Ulster County Historical
Society, Marbletown, N.Y.;
photo, Robert Edwards.)

PLATE 4. Toby jug. Ameri-
can Pottery Company, Jersey
City, N.J., 1833–1850. (Jay A.
Lewis collection; photo, Jay A.
Lewis.)

PLATE 5. Toby jug. Possibly South Amboy, N.J., 1858–1870. (Private collection; photo, Rick Echelmeyer.)

PLATE 6. Pitcher. E. & W. Bennett, Baltimore, Md., ca. 1855. Sugar bowl and mug. Attributed to the Edwin Bennett Pottery, 1856–1860. (Private collection; photo, Rick Echelmeyer.)

PLATE 7. Covered pitcher. Swan Hill Pottery, South Amboy, N.J., 1853–1854. (Elizabeth and David McGrail collection.)

PLATE 8. Inkwell. Attributed to Vodrey & Brother Pottery, East Liverpool, Ohio, 1858–1876. (Private collection; photo, Rick Echelmeyer.)

PLATE 9. Pitcher and spittoon. Attributed to Taylor & Speeler, Trenton, N.J., 1852–1855. (Private collection; photo, Rick Echelmeyer.)

PLATE 10. Dish. Probably American, 1850–1860. (Private collection; photo, Rick Echelmeyer.)

PLATE 11. Pitcher. J. L. Rue Pottery, Matawan, N.J., 1881–1890. (Private collection; photo, Rick Echelmeyer.)

PLATE 12. Pitcher. American, design attributed to Josiah Jones, 1848–1870.
(Jay A. Lewis collection.)

PLATE 13. Beer pitcher.
Attributed to the Edwin
Bennett Pottery, 1870–1885.
(Private collection; photo, Rick
Echelmeyer.)

PLATE 14. Spittoon. American, 1845–1870. (Private
collection; photo, Rick
Echelmeyer.)

ramics nineteenth-century Americans used. Whiteware was used across the entire utility spectrum, from food preparation forms used in production areas of the house to tea wares and ornaments for the parlor. Tea and coffee wares were generally the nineteenth-century ceramic vessels most important for validation of social status, and households typically spent more for them than for vessels in other functional groups. A measure of this, historical archaeologists have found, is that ceramics expenditures correlate most directly with the socioeconomic status (determined by other data) of archaeological site residents when only cups and saucers were used in the analysis.[8] Porcelain was used in table- and tea wares, and porcelain chamber sets were not uncommon, but porcelain food preparation forms were. Other ceramic varieties such as yellow ware and a cheap cream-colored ware called "C.C." in the pottery trade were used primarily for food preparation and chamber vessels. Still others such as copper luster and black refined stoneware were used mostly for tea wares. Rockingham ware, however, was not either fancy or utilitarian ware, nor was it a general line, as the white-bodied wares were. In this study, the most frequently found vessel form on residential sites, constituting almost one-third of the entire residential assemblage, was the teapot. Vessels in the functional group of food preparation and storage constituted the second largest category, equaling nearly one-fourth of all vessels from residential sites and including mixing bowls, nappies, baking dishes, pie plates, a bottle, a canning jar, and a milk pan (see table 2).

Vivid evidence of the perceived appropriateness of specific ceramic-ware types for specific vessels exists in potters' and dealers' advertisements and invoices. In 1852, the E. & W. Bennett "Domestic Queensware Pottery" advertised its "Cane or Salamander Ware" (alternate names for yellow ware) comprising "Pitchers, Mugs, Bowls, Chambers, Oval and Round Dishes, Snuff Jars, Jelly Cans, &c. &c. The assortment of Rockingham consists in part of Plain and Embossed Tea Pots, Coffee Pots, Pitchers, Bowls, Mugs, Cake Moulds, Jars, Bedpans, Spittoons." There were no tea- or coffeepots, or spittoons in yellow ware, nor was the word "embossed," i.e., decorated, included. A Baltimore importer's 1857 invoice listed edged plates and dishes; C.C. bakers, ewers, and basins; dipt bowls; yellow round milk pans; blue (transfer-printed) plates; blue handled teacups, meaning blue transfer-printed teacups with handles; and white [iron]stone chambers, pickles, plates, dishes, covered dishes, sauce tureens, cups and saucers, sugar, cream and [slop] bowl, butters, and salads. The four spittoons listed were of Rockingham ware.[9]

On a hypothetical continuum of potential for symbolic meaning in the Rockingham-ware vessels under discussion, teapots were at the top of the hierarchy. In addition to the association of tea with gentility, teapots were often elaborately decorated and were used, typically, at the front of the house in the parlor or dining room. Food preparation vessels, minimally decorated at most and used in the kitchen at the back of the house, represented the bottom of the hierarchy. This symbolic hierarchy predicated on locus of usage within the house corresponded to the middle-class Victorian conception of the house itself: "The front section was architecture as John Ruskin understood it; the rear was only building." This is not to suggest that any artifact may not be endowed with meaning beyond its strictly utilitarian function. A Rockingham-ware nappy, for example, occupies a central decorative position in the home of Alvin Rackliff, a seventy-five-year-old lobsterman of Spruce Head, Maine, because it was the "bowl" his grandfather used for the ritual Saturday night baked-bean supper. But going beyond personal associations, some artifacts are more likely than others to have meaning for the culture at large or at least for some segments of the population. If Rockingham-ware cooking vessels appeared in textual references at all, they were discussed in practical terms: They were "capable of standing the fire, and resisting changes of temperature," according to Webster's *Encyclopaedia of Domestic Economy* and Catherine E. Beecher and Harriet Beecher Stowe noted in their book of household advice: "Brown earthen pans are said to be best for milk and cooking. Tin pans are lighter, and more convenient, but are too cold for many purposes." (It is clear that Beecher and Stowe were not referring to brown-glazed redware, because there is a warning in the same paragraph not to put fluids in red earthenware "as there is a poisonous ingredient in the glazing which the acid takes off.") [10] Teapots, on the other hand, were notably charged with meaning and even power to transform: "A woman may be expected to retain and increase the womanly characteristics of gentleness, kindness, and all kinds of loveliness, who has a pretty tea-service to preside over every day . . . and men under the influence of such women, and such cheerful home associations, are always better citizens." [11]

The universality of equating tea with home life, as did Annie Trumbull Slosson, the author quoted last, above, is vividly illustrated in the recollections of Melba Hamilton Miller, born and raised in rural Maine in the early decades of the twentieth century. When asked how she spent her time as a child after school and during the summers, she remembered playing "on the edge of the woods up above my mother's there. We had playhouses made out of fir boughs. We hunted around and found old teakettles and put them in our playhouses to see who could have the best playhouse." [12]

Slosson's faith in the power of "a pretty tea-service" to influence and exert control over social action grew from the belief current throughout much of the nineteenth century that physical environment shaped moral stance. The belief is cousin to an aspect of anthropological theory today that proposes a model for the role of artifacts in culture change: "Each use of an artefact, through its previous associations and usage, has a significance and meaning within society so that the artefact is an active force in social change." [13]

For the discussions of Rockingham ware in American life that follow, the key to discovering the cultural meaning of objects and the means through which they implemented change was the linking of vessel forms, shapes, and decorative motifs to their usage contexts: to the historic consumers who chose them. Although ownership of Rockingham ware per se was too universal to be culturally diagnostic, the distribution of forms and decoration chosen in Rockingham ware differs markedly according to membership of the owners in various combinations of social groups. The social factors of gender, class, and urban or rural residence were all operative in influencing choice.

Determining the distribution of Rockingham-ware vessels demographically required a variety of approaches. For class and residence in urban or rural communities, the work of historical archaeologists was the most rewarding source of information and the only method for identifying enough Rockingham-ware owners to conduct significant quantitative analysis. However, it was little help in identifying the relationship between gender and Rockingham-ware vessels because with sites occupied by both males and females, it is impossible to determine archaeologically who used them. For research in this area and for amplifying the data on the other social factors, my major sources of information were period texts and the names on surviving Rockingham-ware presentation pieces coupled with information about their recipients gleaned from census schedules, city directories, local histories, published biographies, property deeds, and probate data.

The results of this research revealed clearly definable patterns of Rockingham-ware distribution: working-class women favored one particular design in Rockingham-ware teapots; middle-class men living in cities formed the market for another Rockingham-ware vessel; rural preference for another was marked. I will argue in the following chapters that Americans used particular examples of these Rockingham-ware vessel forms to express and to mediate deeply held cultural values.

❧ 5 ❧

Rockingham Ware and Gender Identity

In Annie Trumbull Slosson's discussion of the tea service in family life, gender specificity was as much an underlying assumption as was belief in environmental determinism. As Slosson represented it, presiding over tea was a virtual extension of one's womanhood. Textual references and images of tea drinking bear out this strong gender identification. Images of taking tea, whether they were of family tea or a tea party, and whether or not there were men in attendance, always showed women pouring. If a man is shown handling tea accoutrements, he is a servant either bringing in the tea tray or pouring hot water into the teapot from the tea kettle.[1] Moreover, depictions of the act of pouring tea would have identified the woman pouring as the female head of the household, the hostess, or an honored participant at a social event. Well into the twentieth century, newspaper society columnists reporting on teas given for fund-raising events or other public or semipublic occasions typically noted that "Mrs. So-and-So poured."

Integral to the formulation of tea service, womanhood, and the home, was the idea of serving others, an aspect of ideal womanhood as it was understood by mid-nineteenth-century Americans. Authors who wrote on the subject of women used the phrase "the cult of True Womanhood" to refer to the ideal, which incorporated also the virtues of "piety, purity, submissiveness and domesticity." They did not, however, define the phrase for their readers. According to Barbara Welter, they "used this phrase as frequently as writers on religion mentioned God. Neither group felt it necessary to define their favorite terms; they simply assumed—with some justification—that readers would intuitively understand exactly what they meant."[2]

In the Old Testament story Rebekah at the Well, Abraham's servant recognized the woman whom God had chosen to be Isaac's wife by her offer to carry water from the well until all his thirsty camels were satiated. By portraying a woman performing, in obedience to God's plan, such a prodigious act of service to man, the story seemed to symbolize the concept of ideal womanhood. Accordingly, it so captivated mid-nineteenth-century Americans that it was one of the most frequently illustrated stories in American Bibles of the period.[3]

This fact coupled with the marketing instincts of Edwin Bennett of Baltimore, who, in 1851, put out a teapot illustrating the Rebekah-at-the-Well story, may have been the single greatest contribution to the huge popularity of Rockingham-ware teapots. Rockingham-ware teapots were the most numerous vessels in this study, numbering eighty-six. They accounted for close to a third of all vessels in the study and were the most numerous on residential sites as well (sixty-five).[4] (See table 2, page 72.) The utilitarian practicality of these brown teapots was important in that, unlike light-colored ones, they did not show tea stains; but the decoration seems to have been the more influential selling point. Of the eighty-six teapots in the study, thirty-one were decorated with the Rebekah-at-the-Well motif and another seven probably were, judging from the shape of the fragments. Of the sixty-five teapots recovered from domestic sites, more than half (thirty-five) were either definitely or probably Rebekah-at-the-Well teapots. The subject matter of eighteen Rockingham-ware teapots from domestic sites and two from restaurant or tavern sites could not be determined because their fragments were too small or were from nondiagnostic parts of the vessel, but there is little doubt that some of these were also decorated with Rebekah at the Well. Of the twelve Rockingham-ware teapots on domestic sites that had recognizable decoration other than Rebekah at the Well, eight had naturalistic floral or plant designs; a classical medallion, the Holy Family, and a Chinese motif decorated three of the others; and one was undecorated.

After E. & W. Bennett introduced the Rebekah-at-the-Well teapot, nearly all the potteries in the United States copied it. (The Bennett version is illustrated in figure 38.) By the century's end, it had become such a standard that the "Rebecca Tea Pot" was advertised in four sizes in the 1897 Sears, Roebuck catalogue—although a picture of a teapot with a Chinese motif got into the ad instead of Rebekah at the Well. Remaining in production intermittently at the Edwin Bennett Pottery until the factory burned down in 1936, the Rebekah-at-the-Well teapot became the best- and longest-selling Rockingham-ware pattern in history.[5]

The Rebekah-at-the-Well teapot was a brilliant example of the adaptation of an English design for the American market. Bennett's designer, Charles Coxon, simply transferred the design from an English embossed stoneware pitcher with the exotic title "Arabic" to a Rockingham-ware teapot, changing the title to "Rebekah at the Well." The pitcher, probably by Samuel Alcock & Company, and the Minton

FIG. 38. Rebekah-at-the-Well teapot. E. & W. Bennett or Edwin Bennett Pottery, Baltimore, 1855–1870. Buff earthenware with translucent mottled brown glaze. H. 9″. (National Museum of American History, Smithsonian Institution.)

figure on which it was based were executed in the mid-1840s; the title "Arabic" was printed on the pitcher base.[6] The title "Rebekah at the Well" was inscribed on a raised rectangle on both sides of the Bennett teapot, an unusually emphatic manner of identifying a design subject inasmuch as imagery on Rockingham ware was rarely titled, even on the base of the piece.

Thus E. & W. Bennett, simply by renaming an old image and placing it on a teapot instead of a pitcher, tapped into the very core of mid-nineteenth-century domestic values. The woman at home serving liquid refreshment to others could pour from a teapot bearing the image of Rebekah, who also served liquid refreshment and who, representing submissiveness to God's will and the needs of man—and also purity, being chosen of God—was the ultimate example of the True Woman.

The fact that Rebekah at the Well was a Bible story was essential to the success of the Rebekah-at-the-Well teapot, for, as Biblical subject matter, it resonated with a dominant theme in the American discourse about ideal womanhood: the equation of women's role in maintaining the home with her responsibility for maintaining and perpetuating the sacred aspects of home and family life. Developing during the Second Great Awakening as a reaction against the harsher doctrines of Calvinism, the ideology of home religion had become integral to American Protestant Christianity by the time the Rebekah-at-the-Well teapot appeared. The theme was sounded from the pulpit, the influential Protestant theologian Horace Bushnell declaring in 1847: "Religion never thoroughly penetrates life, till it becomes domestic." Moreover, with Rebekah as symbol, the theme was turned to potent political use. In 1851, the same year E. & W. Bennett introduced the Rebekah-at-the-Well teapot, the International Order of Oddfellows, a men's secret social and benevolent society, established a "Degree of Rebekah" to be conferred on members and their wives for the purpose of defusing "the prejudice felt against the Order by many of the fairer sex in various portions of the Union." The wives, however, were not entitled to membership because, the Oddfellows manual explained, "while man is called upon to go forth into the world and fight its battles, woman's place is at the home-altar, as the high-priestess of that sacred spot; and her business—one which she well understands—is to cheer *him* in his rough journey, and to nerve him to proceed in it with faith and patience."[7]

By converting "Arabic" into "Rebekah at the Well" and placing it on a domestic artifact the same year the Oddfellows established the Degree of Rebekah, the E. & W. Bennett pottery was able to place both a reminder of woman's highest duty and a means through which to effect it in every woman's home. For the doctrine that house design and home furnishings influenced character and morality incorporated the belief that household furnishings displaying religious symbolism contributed to the religious well-being of the family.[8] In addition to the overt iconography of the Biblical story represented by the Rebekah-at-the-Well teapot, the designer went to the trouble of placing the embossed image against a paneled background instead of the plain background of the English pitcher that was the source of the design. This type of paneling, known as "gothic" during the period, appeared, with other gothic motifs, not only on Rockingham-ware vessels but on the full range of home furnishings. Flourishing along with gothic-revival domestic architecture from the 1840s until after the Civil War, they graphically associated religious edifices of the past with the home.[9]

As mentioned above, Rockingham-ware teapots with floral or foliate decoration were second in number to those decorated with the Rebekah-at-the-Well motif. Taking all vessel forms into consideration, floral or foliate motifs outnumbered by more than two to one any other relief-molded subject in this study except Rebekah at the Well. Although not as directly symbolic, it is highly probable that these also tied in with the ideology of home religion. Nature, as God's work, was part of the concept of the Christian home, whose beauty, as the literature of the period described it, came from "a close tie with the natural setting." The home was often depicted, David Handlin continues, "covered with vines," and "framed by shade trees." The mother was an essential part of these home scenes, with flowers frequently included to enhance the home associations. She cultivated the garden, tended the vines over the porch and the house plants, and was depicted wearing flowers "that came from all these places."[10] As Suzanne Spencer-Wood notes, Catharine E. Beecher and Harriet Beecher Stowe, in their widely popular domestic manual, *The American Woman's Home,* symbolized the connection between women, domesticity, nature, and morality by showing a vase of flowers with the Bible at the place that symbolized family communion: a small, round table that stood in a gothic-arched central recess in the entrance hall. Spencer-Wood points out that "both Gothic and floral designs were widely viewed in the dominant ideology as symbols of women's greater piety and morality due to their closeness to nature and God in a domestic sphere separated from men's capitalistic public sphere that was considered corrupted by usury."[11] The frequency with which gothic motifs appeared together with floral and foliate designs on Rockingham-ware vessels in this study (twelve examples—see figure 39) attests to the thoroughness with which these associations had pervaded the culture of American home life.

In 1907, an article in the *Baltimore Sunday Sun* stated that "Rebekah drawing water at the well continues to draw womankind unto her with such irresistible attraction that 100 specimens of this teapot are sold at the [Bennett] manufactory to one of any other design."[12] But what was the nature of the attraction? Was Rebekah still, in this new century, a symbol of the True Woman? For some, perhaps. For others, the teapot appears to have become simply a means of introducing an appealing touch of nostalgia into home decor. Edwin Bennett's grandson noted in a letter to a family member that because the teapot had become "an antique," the pottery had begun making and marketing it again—after 1890, according to the context of the letter. (It is not known when or why they had stopped making it.) Moreover, an early-twentieth-century writer advised putting a Rebekah-at-the-Well teapot on the mantel to achieve an "old timey look."[13] The fact that he or she chose the Rebekah-at-the-Well teapot for this purpose underscores the ubiquitousness of the piece; it was so familiar that it stood for its age.

FIG. 39. Pitcher fragment. American, 1845–1870. Buff earthenware with translucent brown glaze, H. ca. 5″. Excavated from a farm in northern Illinois. (Courtesy of the Illinois Transportation Archaelogical Research Program and the Illinois Department of Transportation.)

What had happened during the final decades of the nineteenth century and the beginning of the twentieth to transform this symbol of ideal womanhood into an icon of nostalgia? One answer, of course, is that through long familiarity, the meaning of an image can loose impact and specificity. The process is reinforced if the object has become a collectible or antique, as the Rebekah-at-the-Well teapot had according to Bennett's grandson. Analyzing the process whereby some artifacts become valued as antiques, the archaeologist Frederick Matthew Wiseman maintains that "the result of the whole process of becoming an antique is that both utility and symbolism are suppressed and the artifact acquires a new and radically different social patterning function."[14]

It is possible that, for some, the Rebekah-at-the-Well teapot's new statement, decorative and antiquarian, may have included commentary

on the old ideal. The object may have been freed from its original ide-
ological function not so much by its changed social functions as by a
developing change in cultural values. In *Disorderly Conduct: Visions of
Gender in Victorian America,* Carroll Smith-Rosenberg describes the
development during this period of the "new woman," who, in seeking
gender equality and challenging gender conventions, repudiated the
cultural norms inherent in the cult of True Womanhood.[15] As these
changes were occurring, consumers were mediating them perhaps with
such familiar and well-understood iconographic messages as the Rebekah-at-the-Well teapot. Although not necessarily with fully articulated intention, they may have been casting an affectionate (or disdain-
ful) glance backward at the old cultural values, or perhaps symbolically
preserving them.

Throughout the permutations over time of the cultural meaning and
uses of the Rebekah-at-the-Well teapot, the theme of Rebekah at the
Well always remained with the Rockingham-ware teapot or occasionally with a matching sugar bowl, sugar bowls being part of a tea service.
Even though the design in England had first appeared on a figurine and
subsequently a pitcher, potters in the United States trying to expand the
market for the overwhelmingly popular image were never able to trans-
fer it successfully to another vessel form or type of ware. There were attempts: the image of Rebekah at the Well is known on a Rockingham-
ware pitcher, but this combination is so uncommon that the effort to
branch out must have been commercially unsuccessful. The Rebekah-
at-the-Well teapot has turned up, also infrequently, in yellow ware and
in various examples of whiteware with polychrome glaze, and one notable experiment displayed Rebekah embossed on a blue battlemented
vase. But these are rare examples. Clearly not just the image of Rebekah
at the Well, but the image of Rebekah at the Well on a Rockingham-
ware teapot formed the message—a message with mutable meaning,
but always for and about women.

After teapots, pitchers were the most numerous Rockingham-ware
vessels recovered from residential sites in this study (see table 2). Pitchers, of course, were not gender-specific vessel forms, as teapots were.
Both men and woman are depicted using them. Vermeer's kitchen
scenes with women pouring from pitchers come to mind, and Rebekah,
herself, appears to be holding a pitcher or ewer at the well. However,
when women are shown with pitchers, they are using them to prepare
food or to serve—presumably to serve others, just as they are represented when shown with the teapot. When men are shown with pitchers in nineteenth-century and earlier images, they are depicted as

fulfilling their own needs, using the pitchers not as vessels for serving, but as drinking vessels. There is no chance that Toby Philpot, the jolly toper made famous in the eighteenth-century song "Little Brown Jug," and embodied in eighteenth- and nineteenth-century Toby jugs (see figure 12, page 40) is going to pour the contents of the pitcher he is holding for someone else. (The terms "jug" and "pitcher" were used interchangeably in nineteenth-century American potters' price lists and are still used interchangeably in England, although "jug" is the more common term there.)

The settings and situations depicted where men are drinking out of pitchers in nineteenth-century images that I have seen often involve the idea of excess. Toby jugs imply excessive alcohol intake. When the point of the image is that a man is performing an archetypically manly form of hard physical labor that has brought on a mighty thirst, he is shown drinking out of a pitcher, not out of a glass, mug, tankard, or any other vessel now usually associated with individual consumption. *The Thirsty Drover,* by Francis William Edmonds, depicts the drover, who has stopped at a house with a well in the dooryard, being handed a large pitcher from which to drink.[16] An illustration from *Harper's Weekly* shows a frontiersman resting from the effort of felling a Paul Bunyan–sized tree and drinking from a large pitcher that a small boy has handed him. The caption assures us that the contents are "not a 'cup of sack,' but wholesome and pure water from the neighboring spring." [17] By declaring otherwise, the caption may be suggesting that a man drinking from a pitcher might be expected to be drinking an alcoholic beverage. (See figure 40.) Supporting this interpretation are two phrases defined in the *Oxford English Dictionary*: "Pitcher-house," meaning "a room in a great house, in which the wine and ale were kept"; and "pitcher-man," meaning "a man addicted to drinking, a toper." Both phrases are given as obsolete. Women are not similarly depicted requiting excessive thirst by drinking out of pitchers.

In earlier centuries, vessels with bulbous bodies and cylindrical necks with no spout were commonly used for both pouring and drinking. There is no reason to assume that, when spouts were added to some of these vessels to facilitate pouring, the newly shaped vessels were immediately differentiated from drinking vessels. Nineteenth-century images of very thirsty men drinking directly from the pitcher might have been merely matter-of-fact depictions of ordinary behavior. Or, since the emphasis in these images was on men satisfying an elemental need or indulging in excessive alcohol intake, it is possible that the intent was to convey that concept by showing them practicing behavior considered

FIG. 40. Illustration. Reprinted from *Harper's Weekly: A Journal of Civilization*, 11 January
1868.

unrefined by the time the images were made—or if not unrefined, at
least direct and unceremonious. At the very least it seems probable that
during the last half of the nineteenth century, drinking directly from
the jug was more a male than a female prerogative.

At any rate, pitchers appeared in such images as vessels used for
personal gratification rather than as intermediate vessels for pouring
into other containers. This helps to explain a particular genre of
Rockingham-ware pitcher, the hunt pitcher, which was used frequently
as a personal item, a gift for men usually, as evidenced by the numerous
inscribed examples that survive. Hunting subjects decorated three-

quarters of the Rockingham-ware presentation pitchers I mentioned in chapter 1. All showed stag hunts and, on the opposite side, some depicted boar hunts, hunters, or examples of prey such as a dead game bird. Eight names on the presentation pitchers could not be identified as to gender, having only one or two initials preceding the surnames, but men's names outnumbered women's seventeen to four among the twenty-one identified. Three of the women, moreover, were related to owners and a workman at the Swan Hill Pottery, South Amboy, New Jersey, which produced, between the 1850s and 1890s, a popular version of the hunt pitcher decorated with an image of mounted huntsmen on the side opposite the stag hunt.[18] Personal associations rather than gender appropriateness were the operative factors in these examples. As presentation pieces, pitchers depicting hunt scenes had historical precedent, especially in England, as part of the hunt ritual. They served as trophies in which a fox hunter might receive the brush (foxtail) from the master of the hunt.

Evidence for other contents associated with Rockingham-ware hunt pitchers points toward beer. A decorative motif of hops frequently encircles the necks of Rockingham-ware pitchers embossed with the stag-hunt/boar-hunt theme, and hunt motifs make up the decoration on the majority of beer pitchers I have seen. There are beer-pitcher versions of the pitcher showing vultures picking over a carcass, as pictured in figure 6, and of the boar- and stag-hunt pitcher illustrated in figure 19; and there are beer pitchers with images of mounted riders and a stag hunt, and of a variety of game animals, including fish. Other imagery includes a smoker and snuff taker, a Renaissance-revival design of large-scale anthemia, a simple design of triple *X*'s in a medallion on the front of the pitcher, and a man in what appears to be cavalier dress sitting behind an archway and holding a foaming mug and a long smoking pipe. This beer pitcher illustrated in figure 41 (see also plate 13) is attributed to the Edwin Bennett Pottery on the basis of glaze style, quality of molding, and decorative elements that appear in known Bennett pieces, such as the bull- or steer-head spout, which Bennett used also on a beer pitcher showing herons standing in a marsh.

Beer pitchers are recognizable as such because they are constructed so that the foam stays in the pitcher when the beer or ale is poured. Their spouts, which sometimes are closed and perforated rather than fully open, are connected near the base of the interior by a

FIG. 41. Beer pitcher. Attributed to the Edwin Bennett Pottery, 1870–1885. Buff earthenware with translucent mottled brown and clear glaze, H. 11″. (Private collection; photo, Rick Echelmeyer.)

tube formed by a partition so that the liquid must enter the pouring area from the bottom. Beer pitchers (also called "ale pitchers" or "jugs") usually have covers, and they are always large, having a capacity of a gallon or a gallon and a half.

Rockingham-ware potters made the beer-pitcher form from at least the early 1850s if Edwin AtLee Barber correctly dated (about 1852) two ale pitchers that the Edwin Bennett Pottery loaned to the Pennsylvania Museum in 1914.[19] In 1861, a Peoria, Illinois, newspaper touted "a beer pitcher of brown earthen ware" introduced by that city's American Pottery Company. According to the article, the beer pitcher "differs in one respect from the common pattern, which is that the nose is covered by a strainer which holds back the froth and gives a clear stream of liquid. It is invaluable for saloons."

This beer pitcher appeared at the time when beer was becoming popular in the United States following the introduction of lager. German lager was tastier than the earlier English-style beer because its manufacturing process was better suited to the American climate. The popularity of beer "continued to rise," according to William J. Rorabaugh, author of *The Alcoholic Republic,* "especially after the Civil War, when the high taxes on spirits and nostalgic memories of wartime Union Army lager beer rations stimulated its sales."[20] Indeed this was when beer pitchers began to appear regularly on price lists that I have seen. They seem to have been a standard item on a number of price lists dating from the late 1870s to the late 1920s. They are included on the earlier of two known Edwin Bennett Pottery price lists, which dates from before 1882 and was still used after 1882, but they are not included on the 1898 price list.

Pitcher sherds with elements of hunt designs were more numerous in the archaeological excavations analyzed in this study than those with any other decorative motif. Of thirty-eight fragmentary Rockingham-ware pitchers with identifiable subject matter, fourteen were hunt pitchers. The images included four boar and stag hunts; three of hanging dead game; three of live game, including deer, boar, and small game animals such as rabbits, squirrels, doves, and other game birds; one of mounted hunters; one of a hunter kneeling ready to shoot his rifle; and two hound-shaped handles that more often than not were part of pitchers with hunting images. Nine of these hunt-theme pitchers were from residential sites, two were from restaurant sites, and three were from sites with unidentified usage. Floral designs were the only other large category of Rockingham-ware pitchers, with nine examples on residential sites and two from restaurants.

As mentioned above, pitchers with hunt scenes were a tradional fox-hunting present. A subclass of Rockingham-ware hunt pitchers connected in another way to formulaic gift giving: about one-third of the presentation hunt pitchers had large green ceramic frogs in their interior. Frog *mugs* (or toad mugs) were tavern ware that had evolved from the age-old practical joke of slipping a live toad into a fellow drinker's beer. According to D. S. Skinner, frogs, which were fertility cult objects in some ancient cultures and good-luck symbols in more recent times, came to predominate as the hidden ceramic surprise over toads, which had darker associations. As the nineteenth century progressed, potters produced painted, gilded, and inscribed presentation frog mugs. "It is evident that frogs were moving into the parlour. . . . [T]heir status changed, so that they began to be considered pleasant additions to showy presentation pottery: an accepted symbol of good luck expressed to the recipient by his friends and well-wishers." [21] The frog in the presentation hunt pitcher might have harked back to the tavern joke, or have simply meant good luck. It might have been meant to be amusing because of the "glug-glug" sound liquid makes when it is poured from pitchers with ceramic frogs in the bottom.

With or without frogs, what did the popular Rockingham-ware hunt pitchers signify? Evidence suggests that they filled gender-specific roles analogous to Rebekah-at-the-Well teapots; they were male accoutrements that expressed and reinforced the prevailing image of masculinity. Scholars who have written about images of hunting in nineteenth-century art and artifacts have stressed the symbolic relationship between hunting and the nineteenth-century concept of masculinity. "In the nineteenth century," Kenneth L. Ames writes, "man as hunter was considered as inseparable from certain conceptions of 'natural' masculinity as it is today. Men are supposed to hunt. Men are supposed to kill." Elizabeth Johns also mentions the emphasis on violence in the male-as-hunter construct. Discussing genre paintings of western trappers and hunters, she argues that the "representations preserve the illusion of masculine independence, and they construct male power as attained through violence." [22]

The context of Ames's comments on hunt imagery is discussion of the subject matter found in mid-nineteenth-century dining-room decoration, concentrated especially in the relief decoration on sideboards produced between the 1840s and 1870s. The "iconography of dining" included fruits; vegetables; attributes of the hunt, harvest, and vintage; and representations of "dead rabbits, deer and other mammals, fish, and fowl." [23] Dead game suspended by the hind legs from a branch was

FIG. 42. Sideboard. Probably New York, ca. 1855. Black walnut, marble, with tulip and white pine secondary woods, H. 106″. (Museum of Fine Arts, Houston; museum purchase with funds provided by Anaruth and Aron S. Gordon: Photo, Peter Hill, Inc.)

often the centerpiece of sideboards and constituted also the genre of Rockingham-ware pitchers called "game pitchers." These were included on Rockingham-ware manufacturers' price lists from the 1850s at least into the 1880s. Among the hunt images occurring on archaeological sites in this study, game pitchers were found at one residential site, one

restaurant or tavern site, and one site, whose historic use is unknown.

Ames interprets these images of hanging dead game as elements of the violence that was "a prime ingredient of the Romanticism of the last century," but a subdued form, "the violence occurring offstage, so to speak." He sees the images as a complex of meanings, among which were statements perhaps about "the relationship of humankind to the natural world, expressing and endorsing a highly human-centered vision," or about predation, natural and also national, as explicitly suggested by the overarching presence of the American eagle at the top of the sideboard illustrated in figure 42. (The Rockingham-ware pitcher illustrated in figure 43 bears the same messages, the American eagle under the spout being in a position of honor analogous to that of the eagle at the top of the sideboard.) Ames continues: "It is difficult . . . to speak of predation without also speaking of gender, of conventional Victorian understandings of what masculinity was all about." Ruth Irwin Weidner also discusses the gendered aspects of images of dead game in art, specifically the hunter "returning with a gift of game to a waiting woman. . . . It is at the time of the hunters' return that the archetypal gender duality between the male prowess of the hunters and the domestic sphere of the waiting females is most accentuated."[24]

Rockingham-ware hunt pitchers, then, were symbols of masculinity. As such, they defined the man's sphere of action as far from hearth and home, underscoring the separateness of male and female roles. In her discussion of the popularity of hunt-scene genre painting, Johns examines the male sense of autonomy that hunt images reinforced. Her emphasis is on male identification with *western* hunters, but I would argue that her explanation can be extended to other hunting imagery:

FIG. 43. Pitcher. (Front view of pitcher illustrated in fig. 24.) Attributed to Taylor & Speeler, Trenton, N.J., 1852–1855. Buff earthenware with translucent mottled brown and blue glaze, H. 9″. (Private collection.)

As the popularity of images of Western trappers and hunters would suggest, white American males' assumption of their absolute autonomy as *males* bolstered the justification of separate spheres for the sexes. And as a counter to the worrisome implications of class stratification in the democracy, men's devotion to the exploration of economic and political autonomy was in many ways a commitment to a self-sufficient masculinity that underlay class. Fascinated by this phenomenon, Tocqueville wrote that American men rarely enjoyed the communal sympathy with their wives typical of gender relations in Europe, in which men and women shared the circumstances of class. If American men felt any common identity, he observed, it was with other (white) men, with whom they shared the opportunity—more accurately, the fierce drive—to go for the main chance."[25]

The primary habitat of the third big-selling Rockingham-ware form, the spittoon, was probably public places—all public places.[26] Public places brought the spittoon count up from fourth place on residential sites to second place, behind the teapot, when all types of sites are included (table 2), and if 476 of the Rockingham-ware spittoons deposited at the old state capitol in Frankfort, Kentucky, had not been excluded from analysis for statistical reasons, spittoons would have vastly outnumbered all other vessels.

In residences, spittoons seem to have been the functional and culturally expressive equivalents in the nineteenth century of ashtrays in the early and middle twentieth. Supporting this observation, "china parlor spittoons" were deemed "suitable for presents," and early Rockingham-ware potters listed spittoons with other fashion-sensitive forms, those that would have been highly visible in the parlor and dining room. For example, the Phoenix Pottery, East Liverpool, Ohio, advertised: "A competent designer being constantly employed enables us to keep pace with all the new and improved styles of the day. Gorgeous patterns of Water Urns, Spittoons, pitchers, fancy toys, dessert sets, flower vases, goblets, mantle ornaments, &c., in great variety."[27] Embossed decorative motifs on spittoons drew from much of the natural world—shells, flowers, and birds being especially prevalent. Geometric designs were popular, and religious themes were not neglected. They included various examples of gothic paneling and ornament, and one model seems to represent a gothic edifice with elaborately leaded windows. (See figure 44 and plate 14.) Another, shown in figure 45, exhibited winged angels in a heaven furnished with Corinthian columns.

It is unusual for the commonplace equipage of daily life to figure much in contemporary discussion, but spittoons were an exception because foreign visitors to the United States, being repelled by the American habit of chewing tobacco, discussed them at length. "Spittoons should replace the eagle as the American national emblem," a British commentator unkindly quipped. A Russian, traveling in 1857 on one of the numerous elegantly appointed American steamships, described "the cool, eternally busy American [who] had already dragged out the newspaper just in from California, had put his feet on the marble fireplace or on its bronze grille, had pulled out some chewing tobacco from the front pocket of his waistcoat and had managed to savor its taste, spitting into spittoons placed for this noble purpose by every table, couch, and armchair."[28] Eyre Crowe, who traveled through the United

FIG. 44. Spittoon. American, 1845–1870. Buff earthenware with translucent mottled brown and clear glaze, H. 4¼″. (Private collection; photo, Rick Echelmeyer.)

FIG. 45. Spittoon. Attributed to a South Amboy, N.J., pottery, 1850–1880. Buff earthenware with translucent mottled brown glaze, H. 4½″. (Elizabeth and David McGrail collection.)

States with William Thackeray in 1852–1853, described spittoons as if they were an exotic genus. He complained about their exclusion from dictionaries:

For example, they [lexicographers] allude to pipes, they dilate upon tobacco, but the useful receptacles for the moistening results, popularly known as "spittoons," or "expectorators," or "expectaroons," are terms jealously excluded

FIG. 46. "Expectaroons, Charleston, 1852." Book illustration from Eyre Crowe, *With Thackeray in America* (New York: Charles Scribner's Sons, 1893).

from their vocabularies; yet they are palpable enough to the senses. The court-yard of the Charleston Hotel was piled with these in the morning, when the wholesome water-hose was turned upon them vigorously, a sight quite unique in its way. (See figure 46.) [29]

In the same passage Crowe offered more details: "Insufficient, strange to say, they were, for I recollect being put into a bedroom the walls of which were maculated with the bistre-coloured emissions of former slumberers on the same pillow."

Crowe's illustration shows that the spittoons in the Charleston Hotel courtyard were octagonal in shape and, although the shape was not unusual, these, in Charleston before 1852 or 1853, were probably made by E. & W. Bennett of Baltimore. The pottery did business in the South and its emphasis on octagonal vessels as early as the 1840s is noted in the Edwin Bennett Pottery letter quoted in chapter 2, page 47. Barber, writing in the 1890s, noted that the octagon-shaped spittoons were "still in demand, after fifty years of uninterrupted popularity." Crowe's comment explains the particular popularity of Rockingham-ware spittoons, which, at the Kentucky capitol, for example, outnumbered the cheaper redware or yellow-ware spittoons by 477 to 17 and 32, respectively. The color of Rockingham-ware spittoons acted as camouflage. A late-nineteenth-century housewares catalogue advertised: "These are a strong, durable article, of good size, at a very reasonable price, and as they are of a bright Brown color, they do not show the contents like white ones." [30]

American Rockingham-ware production, including vast quantities of aesthetically effective, cheap spittoons, was only at the beginning of its period of rapid expansion in 1842 when Charles Dickens, touring the United States, complained repeatedly about Americans spitting on the floor: "In every bar-room and hotel passage the stone floor looks as if it were paved with open oysters." Spittoons, known also as "cuspidors" and in a small, handled version, "spitting cups," had existed before this time, but the word "spittoon" was new: The *Oxford English Dictionary* gives an 1840 quotation as its first instance of use. The new (inelegant) word probably indicated a new clientele and a new practice for some Americans who were more accustomed to spitting on the floor. The inscription on a cube-shaped Rockingham-ware spittoon also suggests the novelty of the form. The legend, formed with embossed letters running around the top of the otherwise prettily decorated vessel, reads PLEASE SPIT IN . . . BOX." (A piece of the vessel is missing where the word "the" or "this" would have been.) (See figure 47.) Excavated at a Cincinnati archaeological site, the spittoon was discarded sometime between 1855 and 1874 but was probably in use fifteen or so years earlier, inasmuch as archaeologists have often found that much of a time lag between the dates of datable ceramics in a deposition and the dates that the actual deposition took place. (The dates of deposition are usually much closer to the dates on deposited glass bottles, particularly medicine and whiskey bottles.)[31] Given the concurrence of the new word, "spittoon," with increased spittoon production, there is every reason to think that the multitude of inexpensive, appropriately colored spittoons that Rockingham-ware manufacturers offered to the American public might have effected behavioral modification for some in the populace theretofore used to doing without receptacles.

The travel notes of Isabella Lucy Bird, an Englishwoman who toured the United States in 1854, graphically support the argument that spittoon use was a relative refinement. Her descriptions effectively rank the practice more genteel than spitting on the floor, but less genteel than not spitting at all. Forced to stay at a squalid inn in Chicago because the "best hotels" were full, she described "a large, meanly-furnished apartment, garnished with six spittoons, which, however, to my disgust, did not prevent the floor from receiving a large quantity of

FIG. 47. Spittoon fragment. American, 1845–1860. Buff earthenware with translucent mottled brown glaze. Raised letters on each of the four sides read: "Please spit in . . . box." The words "BOX" and "SPIT" are at the top and bottom, respectively, of the picture. Excavated from a Cincinnati, Ohio, site. (Courtesy, Cincinnati Museum Center.)

tobacco-juice." There, although distressed by everything she saw, she "was not at all sorry for the opportunity, thus accidentally given me, of seeing something of American society in its lowest grade." On the *Mayflower,* a luxurious steamship that carried her from Detroit to Buffalo, she "could not have believed that such magnificence existed in a ship; it impressed me much more than anything I have seen in the palaces of England." In the saloon, "porcelain spittoons in considerable numbers garnished the floor, and their office was by no means a sinecure one." Describing life in New York City, she said: "The peculiar expressions which go under the name of Americanisms are never heard in good society, and those disagreeable habits connected with tobacco are equally unknown. . . . I have frequently heard Americans speak of the descriptions given by Dickens and Mrs. Trollope of the slang and disagreeable practices to be met with in the States; and they never, on a single occasion, denied their truthfulness, but said that these writers mistook the perpetrators of these vulgarities for *gentlemen*." [32]

Usually men people the nineteenth-century images in which spittoons appear—typically barrooms, newsstands, or hotel lobbies—and one might easily think of spittoons as exclusively male accoutrements were it not for Isabella Lucy Bird's testimony, for the accommodations "garnished" with spittoons that she described in the Chicago inn and on the steamship were quarters reserved for women. The "meanly-furnished apartment" at the inn was "the so-called 'ladies' parlour'"; the saloon on the steamship was "the saloon exclusively devoted to ladies." Below the saloon was the "ladies' cabin, also very handsome, but disfigured by numerous spittoons." [33]

Unlike teapots and pitchers, spittoons do not seem to appear in images of nineteenth-century domestic interiors, but, thanks to archaeology, we know that they were there. Their noninclusion could mean that they were relatively unfreighted with cultural meaning, or it could mean that, especially as the century progressed, they carried cultural meaning their owners were not proud of. The latter interpretation would not be surprising considering that, as Bird reported, people in "good society" did not spit tobacco juice. Emulation of the behaviors of those in higher social strata was common. Especially compelling would have been the fact that Europeans were vocal in their dislike of tobacco chewing, for nineteenth-century Americans typically looked to Europe for cultural validation.

An ingenious device made in a variety of designs attests to the discomfort some Americans may have felt surrounding this issue: it was the parlor footstool—some came with upholstered lids—that opened to

FIG. 48. Advertisement in a trade journal. Killian Brothers, New York. In *American Cabinet-Maker, Upholsterer and Carpet Reporter* 13, no. 23 (Oct. 1876). (Courtesy of Strong Museum, Rochester, New York; Photo, Robert Edwards.)

reveal a spittoon inside. Quintessentially American was the offering of Kilian Brothers, of New York, "manufacturers of cabinet furniture and fancy articles." The "Kilian's Patent Spittoon-Footbench," advertised in 1876, was meant to look almost like a conventional footstool, but, being modern and mechanized, it was twice as useful. It was the picture of Victorian respectability when closed, but it popped open with a tap of the toe to provide instant physical convenience when required (figure 48).[34]

✿ 6 ✿

Rockingham Ware and Class

Determining the social class of inhabitants of the residential sites in this study was the first step toward finding out whether class was a factor in Rockingham-ware usage.[1] For most of the population I was investigating, the only data available for interpretation were the bare biographical facts from such records as the decennial census, property deeds, and city directories. These usually included age, sex, occupation, place of residence, and sometimes race. Data about wealth, ethnicity, and condition of property tenure were also obtainable at times, but what was missing was the emic information that would breathe life into these strings of facts: how did people in these times and places formulate perceptions of class from this information?

Social historians have offered answers. In *The Emergence of the Middle Class: Social Experience in the American City, 1760–1900,* Stuart M. Blumin discusses work as the primary determinant of class structure in nineteenth-century America and maintains that social identities "arose from, and were most generally framed in terms of, economic activity." Others also use occupation as a measure of class or socioeconomic status, and I have followed their lead, grouping occupations— following Theodore Hershberg and Robert Dockhorn's classification of nineteenth-century work nomenclature—into the categories "professional and high white collar," "proprietary and low white collar," "skilled craftsman," "unskilled occupations, specified as to the type of labor," and "unskilled, unspecified."[2] Additional categories are owner-operator farmer, tenant farmer, and slave. (Slaves could have performed either skilled or unskilled labor; the category is based solely on their unfree status.). I had been uneasy about trying to categorize class membership along the dimension of occupation alone until, after grouping the occupational categories into larger categories with class designations, the resultant differential in Rockingham-ware vessel distribution showed the efficacy of the approach.

In grouping occupations into larger hierarchical categories for use as the defining variable of class, Blumin argues that the pursuit of non-manual versus manual labor separated the middle from the lower class, thus placing skilled craftsmen in the lower class. However, in *The Refinement of America: Persons, Houses, Cities,* Richard L. Bushman includes "successful artisans" along with "smaller merchants and professionals, ordinary well-off farmers, schoolteachers, minor government officials, clerks, shopkeepers, industrial entrepreneurs, and managers" in his definition of middle-class status. Corroborating Bushman's categorization is John F. McClymer's finding, in "Late Nineteenth-Century American Working-Class Living Standards," that a small but significant number of skilled workers (18.7 percent of a sample of 385) were able to go beyond adequate housing and nourishment to meet consumption standards deemed necessary for middle-class status—the ability to afford presentable clothes and furnish a parlor for entertaining guests, for example.[3] Other studies of nineteenth-century earnings and living standards tend to support this finding. Moreover, in the area of perception and consciousness of class, Blumin acknowledges (although finds evidence to the contrary more compelling) that "the tendency to perceive mechanics as members of the middle class may have been widespread." Richard P. Horwitz offers corroborative evidence for this perception in his study of a nineteenth-century Maine town.[4]

Blumin does not introduce the category of lower middle class into his discussion, but I would be inclined to classify skilled craftsmen in that category were it not for an overriding complication that has become apparent in the data for my study and that Blumin discusses throughout his work: in nineteenth-century directories and census data, there is undecipherable ambiguity in artisan-level occupational terminology. Blumin wrote: "Many of the wealthier manual workers . . . were in reality manufacturers, retailers, and other nonmanual businessmen who retained artisanal occupational labels." Documents for several workers in this study of Rockingham-ware consumption identify such a pattern. Table 3, for example, gives data from the decennial census and Philadelphia business directories of 1860, 1870, and 1880 for the John Gill family of shoemakers, showing how the description of their work had advanced to "manufacturing" status by 1870, and by 1880 had included "stores." But they were still listed as shoemakers.[5]

There are seven other "skilled craftsman" sites in the Rockingham-ware study, however, that remain ambiguous. In table 4, which shows distribution of Rockingham-ware forms by occupational category, I have retained a "craftsman" category but have created also a "craftsman/proprietor" category for such situations as the Gills represent. "Craftsman/proprietor" would be classified as middle class, but since it

TABLE 3
The Gill Family Shoemaking Business, 1860–1880

Source	Family	Age	Job Description
1860 Census	John S. Ginn	48	Shoemaker
	Jacob	18	Shoemaker
1860 Business Directory	John L. Gill		Boot and shoemaker ladies
1870 Census	John Gill	58	Shoemaker
	Jasper	28	Shoemaker
1870 Business Directory	John L. Gill		Boot and shoemaker ladies also manuf
1880 Census	John Gill	68	Shoemaker
	Casper	39	Works shoemaking
1880 Business Directory	Aspar J. Gill		Boot and shoemakers plus stores

SOURCES OF THE GILL FAMILY CENSUS AND DIRECTORY DATA: Commuter Tunnel project files, John Milner Associates, Philadelphia.

is impossible to determine the exact circumstances of the occupants in the remaining craftsman sites, I have combined the categories "craftsman/proprietor" and "craftsman" into one level in table 5 (page 109), where occupational categories are consolidated into class levels. I have not defined this level as either middle or lower class. Taking out the ambiguous middle of the continuum helps to clarify the analysis of the upper and lower levels. For rural domestic sites, I placed owner-operators of farms and plantations in the upper level and tenant farmers, ranging in affluence from wage laborers and sharecroppers to cash renters, in the lower.[6]

Not all sites in this study could be ranked according to class. Thirty were primarily nonresidential, and the historical use of eight is unknown (see table 2, page 72). Nor were all the residential sites homogeneous as to class. Several households representing different classes occupied some of the sites simultaneously, and at other sites, the class membership of residents changed over the period of artifact deposition. But in nearly two-thirds of the ninety-four residential sites, class membership could be identified.

The figures in table 5 show that the lower-class category averaged slightly more Rockingham-ware vessels per site than did the middle-class category (2.3 to 2.2), but the difference is not statistically significant. Markedly significant, however, is the distribution of the two most numerous Rockingham-ware vessel forms, teapots and pitchers, on residential sites. Three-quarters of all lower-class sites had at least one teapot. As table 5 shows (see page 109), teapots accounted for almost half of all vessels occurring on lower-class sites, whereas pitchers accounted for less than one-tenth. By contrast, pitchers were the most popular form on middle-class sites, representing 27 percent of the total; teapots represented less than one-tenth. The contrast becomes more striking when one learns that of the six middle-class sites from which teapots were recovered, five were occupied by households with servants or slaves; the Rockingham-ware teapot might have been for their use.

Class-related differences in Rockingham-ware consumption are further underscored by the fact that only ten residential assemblages contained both pitchers and teapots. Not surprisingly, seven of these came from sites that were heterogeneous in class status, either because of multiple family occupation synchronically or over time or because middle-class householders with slaves or servants occupied the sites. One assemblage containing both pitchers and teapots was from a craftsman's household, and two were recovered from lower-class sites in Alexandria, Virginia. (On the majority of craftsman/proprietor and lower-class sites, I could not determine whether servants were present. Where the information was available, there were no servants.) The only Rockingham-ware pitchers found on lower-class sites were three pitchers from three sites in Alexandria within the same residential block. Two were from both households in a duplex at which artifact disposal across the boundary between the contiguous yards was possible, although unlikely; the third belonged to Charles McKinny, a mariner living at the opposite end of the block from the duplex on a parallel street where real-estate values were rising and shopkeepers and white-collar workers were taking over properties formerly occupied by unskilled workers like McKinny. There is no evidence to explain this coincidence. Possibly emulation was a factor; the hypothesized deposition periods for the duplex properties did overlap. Propinquity to higher-status neighbors may have impelled McKinny to social imitation. British archaeologist Danny Miller discusses the strategy wherein people wishing to improve their relative position within the social hierarchy "may seek to emulate the group above . . . by adopting certain of the products or styles associated with the higher group."[7] The fact that the craftsman/proprietor status level (table 4) more closely resembles the middle than the lower class in teapot and pitcher usage nicely aligns with this interpretation.

For about half the sites for which class could be determined, minimum vessel counts for ware types other than Rockingham were available. Only one lower-class site with Rockingham-ware teapots also contained teapots of other ware types: a Michigan ironworker's household had one in majolica and one in pearl- or whiteware. Minimum vessel counts were available for only one of the five lower-class sites that did not contain Rockingham-ware teapots; that site did not have teapots of

TABLE 4

Distribution of Rockingham-Ware Vessel Forms on Residential Sites by Occupational Level

Vessel form	Professional/ high white collar (5 sites)	Proprietor/ low white collar (13 sites)	Owner-operator farmer (11 sites)	Skilled craftsman/ proprietor (3 sites)	Skilled craftsman (7 sites)	Unskilled-specified (10 sites)	Unskilled-specified and unskilled-unspecified (3 sites)	Tenant farmer (4 sites)	Slave (3 sites)	Total vessels
Teapot	0	3	3	0	4	11	1	3	6	31
Pitcher	1	13	3	3	6	2	1	0	0	29
Mixing bowl	1	1	11	2	1	6	0	0	1	23
Spittoon	0	5	7	1	2	3	3	1	0	22
Baking vessel*	4	2	3	0	0	1	0	2	0	12
Serving dish	0	0	2	0	0	0	0	0	2	4
Chamber pot	0	0	1	1	0	0	0	0	0	2
Tobacco jar	0	1	0	1	0	0	0	0	0	2
Flower pot	0	0	0	2	0	0	0	0	0	2
Mug	0	0	0	0	0	0	0	1	0	1
Milk pan	1	0	0	0	0	0	0	0	0	1
Box	0	0	0	0	0	0	1	0	0	1
Bottle	0	0	1	0	0	0	0	0	0	1
Figurine	0	1	0	0	0	0	0	0	0	1
Total vessels	7	26	31	10	13	23	6	7	9	132

SOURCES: Rockingham-ware fragments and documentary data from archaeological investigations.
*Includes nappies, baking dishes, and pie plates.

any kind, but did have teacups and saucers, suggesting that teapots simply were not discarded. By contrast, there were many teapots in wares other than Rockingham on middle-class sites—notably that of Joseph Smith's summer kitchen at Nauvoo. Required to entertain many visitors to the Mormon settlement, the Smith household had discarded four transfer-printed white earthenware teapots, two of porcelain, and one in the fashionable black refined stoneware that the Wedgwood pottery had brand-named "Black Basalt." A middle-class householder's probate inventory in Paterson, New Jersey, included a metal teapot, and undoubtedly other householders in the middle-class sample also owned them. These would not have appeared in the archaeological record, however, because they were rarely discarded and, if they were, would not have lasted in the soil as long as ceramics.[8]

Both classes owned pitchers in other types of ware. Yellow ware and a range of white earthenware varieties occurred on lower-class sites; these varieties, plus redware, stoneware, and porcelain, occurred on middle-class sites.

Rockingham ware was among the least expensive ceramics of the period. This no doubt contributed to lower-class usage of Rockingham-ware teapots, and it was probably a decisive factor in middle-class consumers' *not* using them. Tea ware characteristically involved a relatively greater proportion of a family's expenditure on household goods than vessels for other purposes because of the role tea ware played in the establishment and maintenance of social status.

The practice of differentiating between tea ware and dining ware, particularly of using dark teapots, had a long history and undoubtedly contributed to the popularity of Rockingham-ware teapots over those in the cheaper yellow ware, which were made (although in fewer numbers and designs) by the same manufacturers that made Rockingham ware. Since at least the beginning of the eighteenth century, teapots in dark colors had been popular, for they were directly employed in the display of social status—among Caucasians at least. White hands were a sign that a woman had servants and did not have to work, and pouring tea from a dark teapot was an ideal means of setting them off. Thus Josiah Wedgwood, referring to his Black Basalt line, wrote to his partner Thomas Bentley in 1772: "Thanks for your discovery in favor of the black Teapots. I hope *white hands* will continue in fashion & then we may continue to make *black Teapots* 'til you can find us better employment." In the century following Wedgwood's comment, contrasting tea ware continued to be fashionable. When, in 1878, Annie Trumbull Slosson discussed the transforming power of "a pretty tea-service . . . however cheap and homely it may seem to the more wealthy," she may have been thinking about white-bodied tea wares with colored decoration in or over the glaze, or any of the tea wares on the market made from dark bodies or glazed with dark glaze. Whatever the case, she was contrasting tea ware to whiteware: "There cannot be any force exerted on a man's or a woman's mind by a lot of white crockery set out to eat from."[9]

Slosson was a member of the middle or upper class, but the practice of differentiating between tea ware and dining ware also occurred in households of lower-class status. Pamela J. Cressey found that lower-class residents of a nineteenth-century African-American neighborhood in Alexandria, Virginia, used refined redware or Rockingham-ware vessels for serving tea and coffee and whiteware for dining vessels. ("Refined redware" refers to molded or wheel-thrown redware vessels finished on a lathe and glazed with either a clear or a black glaze. They, like Rockingham ware, were among the least expensive tea wares available.) The finding supports the hypothesis, as Blumin phrased it, that "the domestic ideal influenced life within working-class homes," although the "cult of True Womanhood" or "women's sphere," as discussed by such scholars as Barbara Welter and Mary P. Ryan, has been specifically identified with the middle class. Certainly the Oddfellows, who, as mentioned earlier, incorporated "woman's place at the home-altar" into the very text of their operating principles, demonstrate the wider reaches of the cult of domesticity. The organization started as a working-class club and retained that association even though some businessmen subsequently joined.[10]

Where Rockingham teapots were associated with lower-class status from the beginning, evidence suggests that Rockingham ware in general slid down the social scale as the nineteenth century progressed. A comparison of Rockingham ware deposited before 1870 with that deposited after 1870 leads to this conclusion. Analyzing only sites where the class of the occupants was known (forty-eight sites with ninety-two vessels), 61 percent of middle-class Rockingham-ware deposition occurred before 1870 and 39 percent after. For the lower class, percentages were 42 percent early and 58 percent late. Moreover, nearly twice as many Rockingham-ware teapots, long associated with lower-class usage, were discarded after 1870 than before (forty late, twenty-three early). These data point to a shift in the popularity of Rockingham ware from the middle class to the lower class in the latter part of the nineteenth century.

If Rockingham ware in general became increasingly associated with lower-class status and Rockingham-ware teapots always had been, and the predominant image on Rockingham-ware teapots was Rebekah at the Well, one must ask why early-twentieth-century advice literature proposed decorating the home with Rebekah-at-the-Well teapots. This literature addressed readers with a more than comfortable income: those of upper-middle-class or higher status. Why was the Rebekah-at-the-Well teapot recommended as a reminder of the past to those who would not previously have used it, and was this new market actually buying the teapot? The answer to the first question is that the decorating advice falls into the category that Pierre Bourdieu calls "the 'rehabilitation' of 'vulgar' objects." Reversing Miller's emulation process described above, wherein a lower-status group copies the consumption patterns of those who rank higher, Bourdieu discusses the phenomenon of the higher-status group appropriating the lower-status group's artifact, investing it with new meaning in the process to perform a new social function. A familiar example is the practice of dining by candlelight. Photographs of middle-class or elite Victorian dining rooms do not show candles on the table, for those who could do so acquired the lighting innovations of the day: gas, then electricity.[11] When these were no longer innovations, and the avant-garde were ready to move on to a new mode, only those who could never be mistaken for members of social groups still having to use more primitive forms of lighting could risk using candlelight.

Candlelight dining was one of a congeries of behaviors and attitudes that constituted the colonial revival—that turning to an American past the establishment perceived as simple and wholesome compared to the urbanizing, industrializing, ethnically diversifying present. Decorating the home to achieve an "old-timey look" with artifacts such as the Rebekah-at-the-Well teapot was an integral part of the colonial-revival impulse, as was a growing interest in the subject of antiques in general. (The concept of "colonial" was vague enough chronologically to include almost anything perceived as in the past.) Books and magazine articles about collecting included Rockingham ware: "The exhibition of Vermont [Bennington] pottery at the Pan-American Exposition last year [1901], has aroused a wide interest in this new subject for the collector." Such interest quickly stimulated Rockingham-ware potters to make reproductions of early pieces—as the Edwin Bennett Pottery had done with the Rebekah-at-the-Well teapot, and the Vance Faience Company had done with their reissue of the Daniel Greatbach hunt-scene pitcher. By 1906, antiques writers were warning Rockingham-ware collectors to be wary. In an article entitled "Frauds in Old China," the author cautioned that "some of the reproductions of the cheaper grades of pottery now on the market are made from the original moulds," citing Rockingham-ware cow creamers and a Toby jug.[12]

It is my contention that the Rebekah-at-the-Well teapot would not have been put forth as a "rehabilitated" artifact if there had not been several ranks in the social hierarchy between the group to whom it was recommended and the group with whom it was formerly associated. Additionally, enough time had to have elapsed since the object was introduced not only to make it seem quaint, but also, as Bourdieu puts it, to make it "sufficiently dated to cease to be 'compromising.'" For, he adds, "the 'rehabilitation' of 'vulgar' objects is more risky . . . the smaller the distance in social space or time."[13] The Rebekah-at-the-Well teapot had been introduced more than fifty years earlier, making it "sufficiently dated," and the Edwin Bennett Pottery had stopped producing it sometime before the 1890s, according to Bennett's grandson. But many other American potteries made it, and it was advertised as late as 1897 in the Sears, Roebuck catalogue. It had not disappeared from the market except, perhaps, from the market its new customers knew. The demarcation in class-associated usage of Rockingham ware that had occurred by the last few decades of the nineteenth century may have provided sufficient perception of distance to allow the Rebekah-at-the-Well teapot to function as a humble but charming reminder of the past.

In answer to the second question posed above (namely, were middle-class people buying this teapot?), evidence of middle-class or elite ownership of the Rebekah-at-the-Well teapot is scanty but does exist. An example in my database belonged to a plantation owner of elite status and could have been discarded around the turn of the century, but since there were servants in the household, the status of those who used the teapot cannot be identified. Anecdotal evidence exists, however, that is unambiguous. Mary Lucy Macon Michaux Harvie, born in 1855 on her father's plantation, "Beaumont," in Powhatan County, Virginia, lived on the plantation until about 1890, when she moved to Richmond with her husband and children. Her granddaughter, Mary Michaux Graves Danzoll, born in Richmond in 1904, remembered as a child having tea with her grandmother every afternoon "up in her room." There was a Rebekah-at-the-Well teapot in the house, but they did not use it for tea, nor did she ever remember seeing it in use. There were servants: a cook, a housemaid, and a chauffeur or horse driver, but the teapot was not for their use either; "it belonged to the family." The teapot remained in Mary Harvie's possession until she died in 1945, when her granddaughter incorporated it into her own household.[14]

The author of a review of the Bennington, Vermont, United States Pottery Company's exhibit of Rockingham ware at the New York Crystal Palace exposition in 1853 might have been surprised to learn that Rockingham-ware pitchers acquired popularity with the middle class. Mentioning "candlesticks, pitchers, spittoons, picture-frames, teapots,

TABLE 5

109

Rockingham Ware
and Class

Distribution of Rockingham-Ware Vessel Forms on Residential Sites by Class

Vessel form	Class and Number of Sites			
	Middle class (29)	Craftsman or craftsman/ proprietor (10)	Lower class (20)	Total vessels
Teapot	6	4	21	31
Pitcher	17	9	3	29
Mixing bowl	13	3	7	23
Spittoon	12	3	7	22
Baking vessel*	9	0	3	12
Serving dish	2	0	2	4
Chamber pot	1	1	0	2
Tobacco jar	1	1	0	2
Flower pot	0	2	0	2
Mug	0	0	1	1
Milk pan	1	0	0	1
Box	0	0	1	1
Bottle	1	0	0	1
Figurine	1	0	0	1
Total vessels by class	64	23	45	132

SOURCES: Rockingham-ware fragments and documentary data from archaeological investigations.
*Includes nappies, baking dishes, and pie plates.

etc.," the reviewer wrote: "This ware has become a favorite article in New England, and deserves much merit as cottage furniture." The term "cottage" at that time in the United States meant specifically working-class housing.[15] The class-related prediction proved to be accurate for teapots, as we have seen, but wrong for pitchers. As shown in table 5, pitchers outnumbered all other vessel forms on middle-class sites, and there were more pitchers on middle-class sites than on craftsman/proprietor and lower-class sites put together.

Before considering the implications of this finding, it is necessary to confirm that in households occupied by members of more than one class, such as middle-class households with servants, the heads of the household were the ones using the Rockingham-ware pitchers. (Households from two of the fourteen middle-class sites that had pitchers are known to have employed servants and others undoubtedly did also.) For this purpose, we have the evidence of some of the presentation pitchers mentioned in chapter 5. For twenty of the thirty-seven Rockingham-ware presentation pitchers, documentary information about the owners' occupation, wealth level, or both was available. All were of the middle class or higher. More than half belonged to the professional/high-white-collar or wealthy landowner group.

Considering the generally held belief that there is a positive correlation between the cost of a commodity and its role in status establishment or maintenance, one must ask how it is possible that Rockingham ware, cheaper by half than the white ceramics that filled the needs of most middle-class householders, fitted into the middle-class menage without upsetting what Grant McCracken has intriguingly named the "Diderot unity"—the manner in which "consumer goods in any complement are linked by some commonality or unity." (In an essay entitled "Regrets on Parting with My Old Dressing Gown," Diderot recounts how the gift of a sumptuous red dressing gown had compelled him to redecorate his shabby and comfortable old study to match the elegance of the gown.) I maintain that the presence of Rockingham-ware pitchers in middle-class houses illustrates the role that fashion, fundamentally capricious, had begun to play in consumer choice after the middle of the eighteenth century, when, Dell Upton observes, "status was no longer a stable condition, but had to be maintained constantly by a quick grasp and speedy adoption of the newest material goods."[16]

The outstanding eighteenth-century parallel to the nineteenth-century use of Rockingham ware by the middle class was the social position of creamware, which was inexpensive compared to porcelain. Having obtained royal patronage, Wedgwood, as mentioned in the introduction, had managed to make his creamware, brand-named "Queensware," chic enough to be used for dessert—customarily the fanciest course—even when porcelain was used for the main course. The parallel is not exact; I know of no evidence that American Rockingham-ware manufacturers tried for high-status patronage. In fact, the Crystal Palace review suggests otherwise. However, if Rockingham-ware pitchers had initially found acceptance at the "cottage" level, it is doubtful that the middle class would have taken to them, at least during their first generation of usage. Both Miller and Bourdieu stress the perceived need of upper-status groups to maintain the contrast in consumer choices between themselves and lower-status groups.[17]

What then was the appeal of Rockingham-ware pitchers to middle-class consumers? Color and theme coordination with fashionable interiors may have contributed. Brown harmonized with the rustic decor that was a component of the rococo revival, and branch handles, flowers, and trailing vines were stock elements in Rockingham-ware pitcher decoration. Rockingham ware subsequently blended with the brown interiors that, as Lewis Mumford pointed out, dominated the American scene for thirty years following the Civil War.[18] But the striking prevalence of hunt subjects, especially in pitchers that were presents for middle-class recipients, suggests that there was a more specifically class-related meaning to this particular genre.

In all variations of the Rockingham-ware pitcher depicting a hunt in progress, there were images of the stag hunt. Kenneth Ames points out that stag-hunt references carry class allusions, referring to royal game preserves of the Middle Ages and, later, to deer parks of the wealthy. "Throughout, the possession of deer and the right to hunt them were identified with royalty, power, status," and during the nineteenth century, for "much of white, urbane Western society, the vision of the good life was derived largely from European monarchical and aristocratic lifestyles of the past." Having established that hunting was a key ingredient in the nineteenth-century concept of masculinity, Elizabeth Johns links hunt images to the middle class by explaining how the concept of masculinity served middle-class requirements: "This ideology of masculinity—and with it the ideology of the domestic sphere—was particularly useful to men of the new urban middle classes, who wished to be at once essentially male (independent and strong) and successful in the social world of the city. To assume this identity, they needed the 'natural' arrangements of urban middle-class gender definitions." In limiting her discussion to *middle-class* gender definitions, Johns explains that gender definitions were proposed as universal, but observes that women laboring in industry or as domestic servants could hardly exercise "sweet domestic influence in the parlor," nor could "women who did half the outdoor work on a farm." [19]

Johns is specifically discussing here the "new *urban* merchants, professionals, bankers, clerks, and publishers," many of whom were "new to the social requirements of middle-class status." (Emphasis added.) In that light, it should be noted that all but one of the hunt pitchers in the archaeological database for this study occurred on urban sites; the other was excavated from the DuPont Powder Plant's industrial village near Wilmington, Delaware, a context that was culturally closer to an urban than a rural setting. [20] Moreover, the identified owners of the presentation hunt pitchers lived for the most part in cities or towns near large metropolitan areas, mostly in northern New Jersey. The next chapter will discuss the reasons for this and other differences between urban and rural Rockingham-ware distribution.

♔ 7 ♔

Rockingham Ware in Rural America

The distribution of Rockingham-ware vessel forms in this study shows that class was the most influential factor in form selection. But within the pattern of distribution described in the previous chapter—teapots in lower-class households and pitchers in middle-class households—factors other than class also produced distinct differences in Rockingham-ware usage. This chapter will consider differences between urban and rural patterns.

The most pronounced difference between urban and rural Rockingham-ware distribution is the preponderance of food preparation vessels, especially mixing bowls, on rural sites and the relative paucity on those sites of two of the most numerous forms found on urban sites, the teapot and the pitcher. (See table 6.) What is the explanation for this? And can explaining such minor details of everyday life tell us anything of interest or importance about the similarities or differences between rural and urban America of the past? The answer to the second question, I believe, is yes, for the results of myriad small choices such as these produced much of the color and texture of past cultures. The answer to the first question follows.

Before examining and attempting to explain these patterns of Rockingham-ware distribution, I will describe the categories that make up the rural to urban continuum, as is outlined in table 1, chapter 1 (page 21). The rural sites were mostly farms and plantations located in Massachusetts, New York, New Jersey, Pennsylvania, Maryland, Georgia, Tennessee, Ohio, Illinois, and Texas, but also included a small house on a rural estate in New Jersey, an island belonging to lobstermen in coastal Maine, an abbey in Maryland, and an inn at a crossroads in Tennessee. The city sites are located in Lowell, Massachusetts; New York City; Paterson and Trenton, New Jersey; Philadelphia and Pittsburgh, Pennsylvania; Dover and Wilmington, Delaware; Washington, D.C.; Alexandria, Virginia; Ashville, North Carolina; Charleston, South Carolina; Covington, Frankfort, and Lexington, Kentucky;

TABLE 6

Distribution of Selected Rockingham-Ware Vessel Forms by Community Type

Vessel Form	Urban sites (91)	% of urban vessels	Rural sites (23)	% of rural vessels	Village sites (17)**	% of village vessels	Total vessels
Teapot	66	33	9	18	11	28	86
Spittoon	50	25	8	16	6	15	64
Pitcher	47	23	4	8	8	21	59
Mixing bowl	13	6	14	28	10	26	37
Baking vessels*	6	3	6	12	3	8	15
Other forms	21	10	9	18	1	3	31
Total vessels	203	100%	50	100%	39	101%	292

SOURCES: Rockingham-ware fragments and documentary data from archaeological investigations.
*Includes nappies, baking dishes, and pie plates.
**The category "army post" is included in the village designation along with mining and industrial village sites.

Cincinnati, Ohio; New Albany, Indiana; Alton, Bloomington, Galena, and Springfield, Illinois; St. Louis, Missouri; and Sacramento and San Francisco, California.

Considering population alone, some of the smaller of these communities might be defined as towns rather than cities at the time the artifact depositions were made. Galena, Illinois, for example, where deposition could have taken place as early as 1845, had a population of about 2,000 in 1840, 6,000 in 1850, and 12,000 to 14,000 in 1860. By comparison, Chicago had populations of about 4,500, 30,000, and 93,000 in those years, respectively; and Cincinnati, the most populous city in the Midwest region at midcentury, had 46,000 (1840), 115,000 (1850), and 174,000 (1860). It is quibbling, however, to insist on deciding which of the communities should be called towns and which, cities. The spatial and functional complexity of the least populous of them distinguish them from small towns or villages.

In Galena, for example, by the mid-1840s, the commercial district had already segmented into specialized zones. Near the wharf there were warehouses, forwarding and commission merchants, lawyers' offices conveniently near their shipping clients, a mining office to serve the nearby lead mines, a dry-goods store, grocery stores, coffeehouses, gambling and drinking establishments, boardinghouses and hotels, a cigar shop, and a barbershop. Moving progressively further from the wharf were increasingly elite business areas, one centering on the stage office and post office; the next on the newspaper office; and following that was the commercial core of the town where the best retail establishments, business and professional offices, and hotels were located. Residential areas on the bluffs above the town were connected to the commercial areas by sets of stairs. North of the commercial part of town, manufacturing of goods such as wagons, furniture, leather goods, guns, tin, iron, and sheet metal took place.[1]

The category "village" in table 6 is artificial, as it was based on population concentration only. The category comprises several different kinds of communities that had spatially concentrated populations but not the spatial or functional configuration of large towns or cities. Of the thirteen communities included in the category, three were small country towns or villages: Dummerston, Vermont; Upper Lisle, New York; and Everett Village, Ohio. They provided limited commercial, business, and professional services and such light industrial services as blacksmithing, milling, and tanning to the surrounding, mostly agricultural, countryside; they were reliant upon larger urban entrepots to provide most of their consumer goods both for use within the village and for trade with the countryside. Two communities, Richmondtown and Sandy Ground on Staten Island, New York, were located close to New York City. Harpers Ferry, West Virginia, was an industrial town, the site of a United States armory that had been in operation since 1801. Numerous other industries operated in Harpers Ferry by the 1850s, which was the period of Rockingham-ware deposition there (approximately 1850–1865). Still, an 1855 report referred to the community as a "village."[2] Nauvoo, Illinois, was a religious settlement on the Mississippi River founded in 1839 by the Mormon leader Joseph Smith. Large numbers of Mormon converts rapidly swelled the town's population, but after a mob murdered Smith in 1844, population dwindled as members of the community left to follow the new Mormon leader, Brigham Young, ultimately to the Great Salt Lake. Four of the communities are industrial sites that included housing for employees. At each of these sites, the artifacts were excavated from the residential areas. The one-company communities—Allaire Village, an ironworks in Monmouth County, New Jersey; the DuPont Powder Works near Wilmington, Delaware; a blast furnace at Fayette, Michigan and the Reward Mine, on the Papago Reservation in Southwest Arizona—are included in the "village" category because of their population density, but, lacking the occupational diversity of villages, towns, or cities, their social dynamics would have been different.

Because of the disparate nature of the communities that make up the "village" category, treating it as an explanatory entity for interpreting Rockingham-ware distribution would be meaningless. It is included in table 6 to account for the location of all vessels in the study, but I have used only the rural and urban groups of sites in analyzing Rockingham-ware distribution along the urban to rural continuum.

Vessels from the functional category "food preparation" turned up on more than half the rural sites and constituted 39 percent of all rural Rockingham-ware vessels. In this study, the category includes bowls and baking vessels, which were nappies, pie plates, and baking dishes. Bowls alone accounted for 28 percent of rural vessels. (See table 6.) In marked contrast, Rockingham-ware food-preparation vessels turned up on only one in seven urban sites and constituted 9 percent of urban Rockingham ware. Bowls made up only 6 percent of urban Rockingham ware.

Not only were Rockingham-ware food preparation vessels primarily a rural consumer item, Rockingham-ware bowls in particular were distinctly a choice of the rural middle class. Of the twelve bowls from rural sites where I could identify the class membership of the site occupants, all but one belonged to families of middle-class status. The twelfth is from the slave row of a long-staple cotton and rice plantation in Georgia that had possible sporadic occupation after the war. No Rockingham-ware bowls were found on tenant farms. There is less documentation about the few city sites with Rockingham-ware food preparation vessels, but where class membership could be determined, the owners were members of the craftsman or craftsman/proprietor class. Why did these vessels in Rockingham ware catch the fancy particularly of middle-class country dwellers?

Unlike teapots and pitchers, for which period images and textual references provide some context for understanding their meanings and uses, food preparation vessels, unsurprisingly, did not appear to carry sufficient symbolic weight to have appeared in texts or images. Indirect evidence from a variety of sources, rather, converged to provide a plausible answer to the question. Among the sources that gave up bits of relevant information were period references to rural practices and characteristics, scholarly studies of rural life of the past, the physical characteristics of the vessels themselves, and potters' price lists, which sometimes contained sizes and one-word descriptions of the vessels.

Rockingham-ware food preparation vessels did not appear on the earliest Rockingham- and yellow-ware makers' price lists; the forms were listed only in yellow ware. Having been at first associated with fancy English teapots, Rockingham ware may have been considered inappropriate and, with the additional cost of the glaze, unnecessary for such a strictly utilitarian function as cooking. However, Rockingham-ware manufacturers soon extended the use of the popular glaze to include baking dishes and bowls, for they appeared on price lists by the late 1850s. The Rockingham-ware versions generally cost between 10 and 30 percent more than yellow ware for identical sizes, shapes, and embossed decoration, and the cost differential continued throughout the period of Rockingham- and yellow-ware production.[3] Yet since all the baking vessels and all but two of the bowls on rural sites came from farm sites, it appears that farmers purchased them at four times the rate of city dwellers.

Scholars have discussed the differences between rural and urban culture. In their studies, the qualities of practicality and thrift emerge as characteristic of rural values. As the authors of one study of rural life observed, "The concerns of countryside dwellers were more immediate and pragmatic than were those of residents of the center villages, and they were less consciously provoked or constrained by the neighborhood gazes of those who set social standards or monitored the norms of propriety."[4] In this light, it seems surprising that farm families would have spent extra money on Rockingham-embellished food preparation vessels when the same forms were available in equally strong, heat resistant, serviceable, and cheaper yellow ware. The explanation, I believe, is that middle-class farm families used these vessels for serving food at the table. Rockingham-ware nappies and especially the mixing bowls served as capacious serving vessels for the farm table. The choice of the more expensively decorated Rockingham-ware nappies and large bowls over the equally large yellow-ware examples would have conformed to that aspect of middle-class respectability that dictated the use of specialized utensils for the ritual of dining. Specialization and hierarchical distinction in household organization, as in most other cultural matters, were hallmarks of the latter half of the nineteenth century. As Kenneth L. Ames observes, "[S]pecialization produced objects that could with propriety serve only one purpose or a closely related set of purposes. These were appropriate only in designated spaces, which they in turn helped to define and distinguish." [5]

What evidence supports the theory that Rockingham-ware vessels were used for dining? Unequivocal evidence for the use of at least one nappy at table lies in the comments of the rural New Englander Alvin Rackliff about his grandfather's baked-bean bowl (chapter 4, p. 78). (Whether the beans were also baked in the nappy is unknown.) Another nappy from the same period was unearthed from an island near Mr. Rackliff's property, the island having been inhabited by two lobster-fishing families. [6] In that close-knit community, where most families had lived for generations and were often related, it is probable that both families used the nappies for the same purpose.

No such direct evidence exists for Rockingham-ware bowls, but several factors suggest that table use might be the explanation for their great popularity in the country. If farm families dined in the "old English" style (serving dishes placed on the table, diners helping themselves)—instead of either *à la Russe* (food brought to the table from the kitchen served onto individual plates) or the modification of *à la Russe* called "American" style (food served onto individual plates by a host or hostess working either at or near the dining table)—and if large numbers of people were at the table, then large serving vessels would have been required. [7] Evidence from a variety of sources suggests that farm families did typically dine in the old English style and that on average more people were gathered around the farm table than its urban counterpart.

Addressing the issue of dining style, a mid-nineteenth-century cooking and housekeeping guide stated that a meal of two courses wherein "the head and side dishes are served at the same time" and "the second service is dessert" was "the favorite style in the country." A farm boy's recollection colorfully confirms that the dining style with which he was familiar was self-service from vessels on the table: "Man and boy went to the table as they came from the field, wet with sweat. . . . The farmwife's universal greeting to her ravenous workers was, 'Now boys, help yourselves. What you can't reach, yell for.'" Concerning the number of diners at table, farm families tended to be larger than urban families, and farmhands as well as the farm family probably swelled the ranks of diners at meals. The farm boy's allusion to the "ravenous workers," "man and boy" at table hints at this arrangement, and a study by Sally McMurry of farmhouse plans submitted to agricultural publications by farmers and their wives lends further support. McMurry quotes intriguing commentary accompanying a farm woman's ideal farmhouse plan in which a sink was situated in the rear entranceway for "preventing the necessity of farm hands, and others, going to the kitchen to wash." McMurry conjectured that "this measure precluded congestion in the kitchen, where continual preparations were made to feed the farmhands, who probably ate in the dining room."[8]

The presence of hired farmhands is documented at two of the six farm sites where Rockingham-ware bowls were recovered. (These two farm sites accounted for four bowls.) The presence or absence of farmhands is not documented at the other four farm sites (eight bowls), but, where one site is entirely undocumented, the other three were owned by high-status farmers, one having other farms and a house in town. Probably these farm owners would have had hired hands. The other two Rockingham-ware bowls on rural sites were from a crossroads inn in Tennessee and the slave row mentioned above.

Were the fourteen Rockingham-ware bowls on rural sites in this study big enough to have served large groups of people? The size of seven bowls is unknown; five bowls were between eleven and fourteen inches in diameter; two were nine inches. A Rockingham- and yellow-ware potter's price list from the 1880s provided information about capacities, specifying that eleven-inch bowls held one gallon, fourteen-inch bowls held three gallons.[9] In contrast, available potters' price lists reveal that the largest Rockingham vessels designated by their names specifically for food service, "rice dishes" and "oyster dishes," came in sizes no larger than nine inches in diameter. A vessel of that size, using the price list cited above as a guide, would hold, at most, two quarts. In whiteware, the largest "covered dishes" were also nine inches, the largest "soup tureens" were ten inches.[10] The largest of the Rockingham- or yellow-ware bowls, then, were the best containers for feeding a lot of hungry farmers at one sitting.

Evidence from Rockingham-ware distribution reinforces the theory that Rockingham-ware bowls were used as serving vessels for large groups. Three Rockingham-ware bowls were excavated from the sites of two boardinghouses: two from a boardinghouse for miners at a turn-of-the-century mining camp in Arizona (included in the "village" category, table 6), and one from the novelist Thomas Wolfe's home in Ashville, North Carolina, which his mother, Julia Wolfe, ran as a boardinghouse from about 1906 to 1945. (The period of artifact deposition on the site was estimated to be 1910–1920.) Wolfe described the boardinghouse in his novel *Look Homeward, Angel.*

The well-known phrase "boardinghouse reach" identifies the style of dining associated with boardinghouses. Substantiating material evidence comes from Michael T. Lucas's analysis of archaeological data from a boardinghouse in Harpers Ferry, West Virginia. Lucas discusses ceramic findings that suggest that "boarders helped themselves to food items placed before them." The artifacts included large plates (at a time when, with the popularization of *à la Russe* and American dining styles, smaller plates had become more fashionable and were more available) and four "undecorated bakers, which could be used for vegetables and placed on the table." Lucas excludes "food preparation" wares, specifically mixing bowls, from analysis because "they do not apply specifically to the consumption of food at the table." [11] I would argue, however, that mixing bowls should have been included for the same reason that they would have been used for food consumption on farms: they were vessels of a convenient size for serving large quantities of food from which diners could help themselves.

My argument that Rockingham-ware bowls were used to serve large groups of diners at table is based thus far on the circumstance that they were found in places where large groups of people would have been dining together in the old English style and on the improbability of country people spending extra money on Rockingham-embellished vessels for cooking when, as the paucity of Rockingham-ware food preparation forms on city sites suggests, city dwellers did not. This argument is strengthened by evidence embedded in the price lists of the Rockingham- and yellow-ware potters. From about 1853, "lipped" bowls began appearing in yellow ware. They were listed usually in four (occasionally five) sizes, from eight to twelve or thirteen inches in diameter, and were exactly the same shape and design as plain-rimmed bowls except that the rim was shaped with a pouring spout. Lipped bowls facilitated the pouring of ingredients from one vessel to another, an important procedure in cooking, but not relevant at the dining table except where small lipped bowls might be used to pour sauce or gravy. Lipped bowls were not, however, made in Rockingham ware. If Rockingham-ware bowls had been made primarily for culinary purposes, they would have been offered in lipped versions as well as plain, for they were made by the same potters who made yellow-ware bowls, both lipped and plain.

Rockingham-ware bowls were not offered in the specialized lipped cooking shape and they were more fancily glazed and more expensive than yellow-ware bowls. These distinctions signified that in the minds of the manufacturers (and presumably their customers) Rockingham-ware and yellow-ware bowls served different purposes. The Rockingham-ware bowls met the all-important criterion of specialization in dining utensils. Ames noted in his discussion of specialization that "to many Victorians, the concepts of specialization and refinement were inseparable."[12]

The large body of household advice and etiquette literature published and sold during the nineteenth and early twentieth century confirms that the practice and display of refinement and civilized behavior were high-stakes issues. The venues for these undertakings were primarily the parlor and dining room of middle-class houses, the "public" rooms of the house, where visitors were entertained. For demonstrating "refinement, character, and (to use the catch-all term so dear to the hearts of nineteenth-century advisers) 'good breeding,'" John Kasson notes, the dining table was considered the supreme testing and proving ground.[13] Objects that played a role in such consequential matters, the objects used in dining, had to be different from objects that merely functioned in a production capacity. Not only did they have to be different, they had to be higher on the decorative scale of values. Stripped-down functionality was only appropriate for the behind-the-scenes artifacts that facilitated the important work going on at the dining table.

Through interpretation of correspondence, household records, wills, inventories, diaries, excavated artifacts, and pictorial material, scholars have been able to make some assessment of the degree to which the prescribed dining standards were actually practiced. They have found evidence of considerable compliance at all levels of the middle class. Working with letters and pictures from the 1880s and 1890s, Clifford E. Clark concludes that, "following the lead of the magazine and plan book promoters, the dining room had become a central symbol for the attainment of middle-class status. Linen, silver, and china which accompanied elaborate meals and stylized dining room etiquette were now widely accepted as signs of having entered the ranks of the middle-class consumer society."[14]

Data from a study of the material culture of late-nineteenth- and early-twentieth-century urban working-class homes reveal interestingly that, in contrast to urban middle-class culture— where the dining room and its furniture and accoutrements used together in the ritual of dining made up the expression of status—the dining room and its artifacts were indeed symbols of status, but they were unrelated to the act of dining, which occurred in the kitchen. In a 1910 study of mill-town households, the author found that five-room houses contained "an anomaly known as the 'dining room,'" which was furnished with a sideboard, table, and dining chairs, but was used not for meals but as a room for sewing or ironing. One immigrant woman, for whom dining-room furniture represented assimilation of American customs, explicitly expressed its importance as a symbol: waving her hand toward a huge, newly acquired buffet and large cut-glass punch bowl, she proudly told a visiting settlement worker, "And so I become American."[15]

The studies cited above were of city, town, and suburban domestic practices. Did farmers hold the same values? Specifically, were there indications, in addition to their use of Rockingham-ware bowls, that middle-class farmers also perceived specialization as an element of refinement and genteel behavior? One need look no further than the numerous objections of farm reformers to the inclusion of parlors in farmhouses to know that they did. Specialization of both space and artifacts in the form of formal parlors with appropriate furnishings had taken root firmly in rural soil, even though the active role of women in farm production and the necessity of following agriculturally dictated work schedules—not to mention the traveling distance from farm to farm—proscribed many of the social uses assigned to city parlors such as the practice of social calling. Farm reform writers cited parlors as examples of urban overrefinement and excessive formality, yet farmers in significant numbers retained the parlor: as a space, as a style of furnishing, and as a behavioral system. At odds with the rest of farm life, the parlor was used rarely, being opened only for such formal occasions as weddings and funerals, the minister's call, or visits from other persons of elevated rank. In a memoir of life in her family farmhouse, built in 1868 in Onondaga County, New York, Anne Gertrude Sneller documented this usage of the parlor, noting that "more impressive and less intimate callers were guided to the back parlor," while "neighbors visited in the dining room." Sally McMurry, author of "City Parlor, Country Sitting Room," the source of some of this information about rural parlors, argues convincingly that the issues discussed in the article were relevant to farm families of a socioeconomic status comparable to the urban middle class.[16]

While confirming the quasi-ceremonial use of the parlor, Sneller's characterization of the farmhouse dining room as a gathering place for neighbors is in striking contrast to the urban concept of the dining room as a venue for the practice of "stylized etiquette." Nineteenth-century room nomenclature (as it appears in farmhouse plans such as those illustrated in McMurry's studies and in publications like Andrew Jackson Downing's *The Architecture of Country Houses*) shows, however, that, far from being peculiar to Sneller's family, such informal use of the dining room was characteristic of farm life. Relatively few farmhouse plans even showed rooms labeled "dining room." More showed rooms labeled "sitting room" or "living room," and one had a room designated "dining & sitting room." McMurry illustrated an 1881 plan of a room labeled "living room" in which there was a cook stove and a dining table, but which also contained such amenities as corner and side cupboards, a bookcase, and a greenhouse.[17]

The substitution of such informal, multipurpose rooms for dining rooms in farmhouses would seem to have been culturally distant from the urban middle-class concept of dining rooms, where the most ritualized practices of specialization in space and artifacts, thus of gentility, took place. They also differed in concept from the working-class immigrant's dining room described above, where the furnishings alone, unincorporated into the act of dining, made a statement about status. Unlike urban middle-class dining, moreover, which gathered the diners together in an event separate in time and space from work activities and was thus capable of being compartmentalized and ritualized, dining was an integral part of the farm workday in which the entire workforce participated. Nevertheless, as the middle-class farmwife's choice of fancy Rockingham-ware bowls over plain yellow ware demonstrates, the accoutrements by which a middle-class table could be recognized were not overlooked.

This nuanced view of farm dining would be unrecoverable from documents alone. For documents such as house plans, household-advice literature, diaries, or memoirs like Anne Gertrude Sneller's deal typically with large units and comprehensive concepts such as whole rooms and room usage. Even household inventories of the mid- and late nineteenth century and the twentieth century tend not to itemize household objects at this level. These lost, broken, or discarded things are the data sets unique to archaeology. Thanks to historical archaeology, we can reconstruct the multiple contexts in which they were used. Such evidence as the occurrence on middle-class farm sites of the large Rockingham-ware bowl—distinguished from plain cooking ware by more elaborate decoration and greater cost—corrects the impression given by documents alone; it demonstrates that just as farm families participated in middle-class parlor culture, they also, within the constraints of practicality, participated in middle-class dining-room culture through the ritualization of dining by the use of specialized artifacts.

If middle-class farmwives ornamented their dining tables with Rockingham-ware serving bowls, did they differentiate dining from cooking by using the less expensive yellow ware in preparing meals? Or did they make the Rockingham ware do for both? As Karin Calvert has pointed out, where the simple definition of specialization may be "a multiplicity of objects, each serving a single function," the Victorians also delighted in objects especially made to serve two different purposes: highchairs that folded into strollers, canes that held a whiskey flask, or the upholstered footstool (figure 48, page 99), whose top popped open to expose a spittoon. Seen from this point of view, large Rockingham-ware bowls would have been a highly specialized form; practical in the kitchen, but made with no lip and glazed ornamentally so as to be suitable for the dining table.[18] Indeed, the distribution of Rockingham-ware bowls in this study indicates that they served a discrete segment of the population: households or boarding establishments needing to serve large numbers of diners.

To answer the question of whether middle-class farm families observed a hierarchy in their cooking and serving vessels, one would need to know whether or not those who used Rockingham-ware bowls also used large yellow-ware bowls. Before describing my attempt to find the answer, I should emphasize that it isn't possible to confirm archaeologically that someone *did not* use something. Occupants of a site might have used the objects in question but discarded them elsewhere. Or, as the historical archaeologist George L. Miller points out, they might have discarded the objects on the site, but the objects might not have turned up in the excavated sample since often only 10 percent of a given site is excavated. Additionally, in many yard-scatter contexts, a vessel may be represented by less than 5 percent of its sherds.[19] Inevitably, then, the excavation process will miss some of the vessels discarded on the site. However, even if underrepresentative, the vessel fragments that are recovered give us interpretable information.

I was able to reexamine the ceramic fragments from five of the six farm sites where Rockingham-ware bowl fragments were found. On two prosperous farm sites yellow-ware bowls were present. One was the house site of Charles C. Munro, a wealthy farmer of Dresden, Ohio, where there was a yellow-ware bowl twelve inches in diameter and a Rockingham-ware bowl about eleven inches in diameter. Munro, the son of a pioneer trading-post owner, had lived in the fourteen-room brick "mansion," as it was known, on his family's 500-acre farm until he built a new farmhouse on the 265 acres he had inherited at the time of his father's death in 1847. In the 1860 census, Charles Munro's real estate was appraised at $13,480. Upon his mother's death in 1864, he inherited such luxuries as a tall-case clock and mahogany bureau. "One corn shelling machine" along with other farming utensils in the bequest indicates that Munro was actively farming.[20]

The ceramic vessel count at the site of the other prosperous farm, the Drake farm site in Silver Creek Township, northwestern Illinois, revealed no fewer than three yellow-ware and four Rockingham-ware bowls. The yellow-ware bowls measured six to seven inches, fifteen to sixteen inches, and fourteen inches or greater in diameter. One Rockingham-ware bowl was eleven inches in diameter; the size of the rim fragments of the other three was insufficient to estimate their diameters accurately. No pouring lips were in evidence on any of the yellow-ware bowls. That does not necessarily mean that they were unlipped bowls; with the small size of the rim fragments and the large circumferences, most of each bowl was missing. Chauncey and Roxanna Stebbins owned the farm, and by the time of Chauncey's death in 1857, they had acquired several other farms as well as a house in town. (The site acquired its name from Roxanna Stebbins's second husband, Lloyd Drake, whom she married in 1859.)[21]

Although the sample size is small, the above archaeological findings suggest that farm families who could afford to duplicate forms in order to meet the middle-class requirement of separate cooking and serving vessels did so, and that the thrift ascribed to farm culture may not necessarily have applied where the economic status of the family did not require it.

As to whether the other farm households that used Rockingham-ware bowls also had yellow-ware bowls, the evidence is inconclusive. Two sites had yellow-ware fragments that might have been from bowls, but the fragments were too small to identify them positively as such even though rim fragments were present. On one of these sites, which was an owner-occupied as opposed to a tenant farm, there were two Rockingham-ware bowls, nine to ten and fourteen to fifteen inches in diameter; the other site, which was undocumented, had a Rockingham-ware bowl greater than twelve inches in diameter. A third farm site had one yellow-ware fragment that might have been a nappy, chamber pot, or milk pan, but was not a bowl. The two Rockingham-ware bowls on that site were nine and twelve inches in diameter. The evaluation of this farm, also owner occupied, was less than one-third of that of Charles

Munro, but still substantially middle class by nineteenth-century standards. The farmer, J. W. Drews (or Drewes), owned eighty acres in 1863 and probably an additional twenty-four acres in 1874. According to the 1870 census, his real estate was worth four thousand dollars.[22]

Although we cannot know whether or not the owners of the last three farms mentioned had yellow-ware bowls, the presence of Rockingham-ware bowls, which were more expensive than like bowls in yellow ware and met the culturally prescribed requirements for tableware, tells us that their occupants were probably cognizant of and willing to conform to the rules of middle-class respectability by acquiring more expensive vessels for dining.

As mentioned at the beginning of this chapter, the distribution of Rockingham-ware teapots and pitchers in the country followed urban usage patterns in terms of class. Table 7, which includes only sites where class membership of occupants has been identified, shows teapots accounting for a larger percentage of rural lower-class than rural middle-class vessels. The class-relatedness of the teapot distribution is underscored by the fact that two of the three teapots on middle-class sites were from farms with resident servants—housekeepers and nurses—and the third was from a Maryland plantation that had slaves before and servants after the Civil War.[23]

Only middle-class rural sites in this study included Rockingham-ware pitchers, which appear to have been altogether less popular in the country than they were in the city. Table 6 shows them constituting only 8 percent of rural Rockingham-ware vessels, compared to 23 percent of the urban assemblage. What was particularly missing in the country were pitchers with hunting images: boar and stag hunts, hunters on horseback or kneeling with rifles ready to fire, various game animals, or the images of hanging, dead game like those on mid-nineteenth-century sideboards. Availability was not an issue; dates of Rockingham-ware deposition in rural and urban areas were similar. Nevertheless, although pitchers with hunting images made up the largest subject-matter group on urban sites in this study, they seem not to have interested country dwellers. If hunt pitchers were "guy things" for men living in the city, they may well have seemed irrelevant for men living on the farm.

Rockingham-ware hunt pitchers may also have represented a touch of country life for city dwellers, particularly the life of a country gentleman. In *Pastoral Inventions: Rural Life in Nineteenth-Century American Art and Culture,* Sarah Burns analyzes American artists' depictions of rural life in pictorial art and the reasons these works appealed to the American public. The reasons involved the idealization of rural life as a

TABLE 7

Distribution of Selected Rockingham-Ware Vessel Forms by Community Type and Class

Community Type/Class/Number of Sites	Teapot	Pitcher	Bowl	Spittoon	Baking vessels*	Other	Total vessels
Urban Middle (13 sites)	2	11	1	3	4	3	24
Urban Craftsman/proprietor (10 sites)	4	9	3	3	0	4	23
Urban Lower (12 sites)	15	3	0	5	0	1	24
Total urban vessels	21	23	4	11	4	8	71
Rural Middle (11 sites)	3	3	11	7	3	4	31
Rural Craftsman/proprietor (0 sites)	0	0	0	0	0	0	0
Rural Lower (7 sites)	4	0	1	1	3	3	12
Total rural vessels	7	3	12	8	6	7	43
Village middle (5 sites)	1	3	1	2	2	0	9
Village Craftsman/proprietor (0 sites)	0	0	0	0	0	0	0
Village Lower (1 site)	2	0	6	1	0	0	9
Total village vessels	3	3	7	3	2	0	18
Total vessels	31	29	23	22	12	15	132

SOURCES: Rockingham-ware fragments and documentary data from archaeological investigations.
*Includes nappies, baking dishes, and pie plates.

simple, natural existence, a metaphor for healthy mental and physical life and moral rectitude. With increasing urbanization and industrialization during the nineteenth century, images of rural life came to symbolize what was perceived to have been lost of these cultural values. Allied to the nostalgia for an idealized rural existence was a movement Burns calls "the middle-class retreat to Arcadian rusticity," which gained momentum in the 1840s and spawned the body of country-house literature exemplified by Andrew Jackson Downing's *Architecture of Country Houses,* first published in 1850 and reprinted throughout the nineteenth and early twentieth centuries.[24] The activities depicted on the Rockingham-ware pitchers—hunting, riding, and shooting—were emblematic of country villa life. They were perhaps analogous in a small way to the painted landscapes recommended by an American Art Union catalogue (circa 1840s) for city dwellers "who cannot afford a seat in the country to refresh their wearied spirits."[25]

In the context of urban nostalgia for country life, it is worth noting that in all the hundreds of different images on Rockingham ware, I know of only one identifiably urban scene. It shows firemen running with a hose to douse flames shooting from the third-story windows of a narrow, stone building at least four stories high. The Salamander Works, located (probably significantly) in New York City, introduced this pitcher, called "Fire Engine," on their 1837 price list. The urban scene must have been a commercial failure because—with the exception of one close copy of the Salamander Works's Fire Engine made at Abraham Cadmus's Congress Pottery, South Amboy, New Jersey, between 1848 and 1854—other potters did not follow Salamander's lead in showing city buildings and city streets. (Cadmus also was a New Yorker, having been a ship chandler in Manhattan when he first purchased the pottery.)[26]

Burns observes that the works of art discussed in *Pastoral Inventions* were generally produced in "east coast cultural centers or oriented toward culture consumers of those regions." These were the business and professional classes concentrated in eastern cities and suburbs.[27] Rockingham-ware hunt pitchers followed this pattern as well. Not only were they confined to urban settings, they were mostly confined to the older eastern cities—where nostalgia for the rural life was well rooted in the culture. Except for two excavated from sites in Sacramento, California, the excavations included in this study turned up no Rockingham-ware hunt pitchers in cities west of the Alleghenies. The Sacramento examples emphasize the easternness of the genre, for the gold rush–fueled population explosion that made instant cities of San Francisco and Sacramento made it economically feasible for eastern

TABLE 8

Distribution of Selected Rockingham-Ware Vessel Forms on Urban Sites by Region

| | Region and Number of Sites | | | |
| | Eastern Cities (70) | | Midwestern Cities (10) | |
Vessel Form	Number	Percent	Number	Percent
Teapot	52	37	1	4
Spittoon	30	21	2	8
Pitcher	40	28	4	16
Mixing bowl	6	4	7	28
Baking vessel*	1	1	4	16
Other forms	12	9	7	28
Total	141	100	25	100

SOURCES: Rockingham-ware fragments and documentary data from archaeological investigations.
*Includes nappies, baking dishes, and pie plates.

merchants to ship goods by water directly from the East Coast to these California port cities.[28] Rockingham ware made at the United States Pottery Company, Bennington, Vermont, was found in pre-railroad contexts in both Sacramento and San Francisco, and while it could conceivably have jounced overland in wagons, it is far more probable that the popular new ware was part of the East to West Coast shipping trade.

Table 8 compares the distribution of Rockingham-ware vessel forms between cities in the Midwest and the East, showing that the distribution configuration in midwestern cities more closely resembles that of the rural than the urban distributions shown in table 6. (All urban excavations between the eastern states and the West Coast in this study were in the Midwest.) I suggest that an explanation for this may be that those aspects of the eastern urban discourse that involved regret for the loss of country life and country values may not have inhered in the culture of midwestern cities because of the demographics of midwestern city formation. The midwestern cities in this study were established in the early nineteenth century, but, discussing the settlers of midwestern urban centers at mid-nineteenth century, the authors of *The Midwest and the Nation* noted that "many, if not most, were migrants from rural to urban areas."[29] While the urban inhabitants of both regions had access to the same Rockingham-ware forms and designs at the same time and Rockingham-ware deposition took place at about the same time in both regions—mostly in the second half of the nineteenth and early part of the twentieth centuries—city dwellers in the East and the Midwest chose differently. It appears that Rockingham-ware pitchers and teapots were not popular items in midwestern cities but big mixing bowls were. The migrants would undoubtedly have brought their household goods from the farm to the city with them, including their large Rockingham-ware bowls. These, unearthed more than a century later, give material testimony to their owners' move to the city, and they give substance and form to observations about the Middle West published in *Century Magazine* early in the twentieth century:

But what of mining, logging, and manufacturing, all told? Islets of exception in an ocean of rule. Corn is king. The hog, a corn-field on legs, made Chicago. Scratch a Middle-Westerner, and you find a farmer. Either he lives on a farm or in a farming village or in a city that was a farming village only yesterday.[30]

Conclusion

Rockingham ware was of its time. Speaking eloquently of that time, the embossed pictorial images that decorated Rockingham-ware vessels constituted a catalogue of Victorian themes. The image of Rebekah at the Well on Rockingham-ware teapots so embodied the cult of True Womanhood flourishing at mid nineteenth century that it became an icon of that time and that culture to a subsequent generation. The profusion of gothic motifs and floral images on Rockingham-ware pitchers, spittoons, bowls and other forms signified home religion deeply rooted in the culture. Images of hunting and game animals on Rockingham-ware pitchers spoke of urbanization and a concomitant nostalgia for country life. They spoke also of men's role in the business and professional world, increasingly separate from the domestic sphere, and of masculinity itself in its association with hunting.

In such small details as these pictorial images from the past repeating their messages over and over again in daily use, we discover the depth to which the cultural issues they represented penetrated domestic life. The Rebekah at the Well teapot is not our only source of information about the cult of True Womanhood, and the hunt pitcher is not our only clue to the cultural changes that occurred as the population of America shifted from the farm to the city. But the ubiquity of these vehicles of expression—their very ordinariness—speaks to the pervasiveness of their messages. In their ordinariness also lies their power to convey symbolic meaning.

Identifying the symbolic meaning of these images by situating them in their cultural context is half the job. The other, vital half is the task of identifying the people to whom they were meaningful. For this purpose, especially with commonplace objects of everyday use, historical archaeology is the most effective resource. Historical archaeology is the only resource for discovering even the existence of symbolic meaning in the use of such workaday vessel forms as large Rockingham-ware bowls.

Vessel forms such as these were simply not mentioned in documents relating to domestic life. Only their different patterns of distribution—not explainable by utilitarian function—signal symbolic meaning. And only historical archaeology, through systematic excavation of rim fragment after rim fragment, painstaking research into the records that identify their users, and careful synthesis of these data can uncover the patterns.

With such small details of domestic life gleaned from archaeological investigation, we may understand the often subtle manner in which people employed artifacts to communicate meaning and implement both cultural continuity and cultural change. Moreover, with actual fragments of historical domestic artifacts in hand, we are able to visualize the material life of the past with an immediacy rarely present in other sorts of data. Literature about house design generally dealt with issues on a larger scale than the artifacts used in keeping house—exteriors, room designs, or floor plans. Likewise, memoirs of home life sometimes depict the shape and size of rooms, describe the ways in which people used them and perhaps the furniture, but rarely do they touch upon the small objects of household use. Anne Gertrude Sneller wrote that neighbors visited in the dining room. But as she wrote, the color, shape, texture, and associations of small, familiar objects would have brought that room to life in her memory. She may have thought them too commonplace to write about; she may not even have articulated the memory. Yet these objects that were used day in and day out and are now brought to light again help to flesh out the bare bones of floor plans and fill in the outlines of recorded memory.

APPENDIX

Archaeological Database

Northeast

Archaeologist (see notes, pp. 162–165)	Site	Community type	Historical use	Occupational level (see table 4)	Servants	Form	Deposition date	Glaze: Rockingham or variegated	Embossed decoration	Identification/attribution
Maine Jane Perkins Claney	Calf Island, St. George	Rural	Residence	Unskilled-specified	Unknown	Nappy	1884–1960	Rock	None	
Vermont Suzanne W. Elliott	Asa Knight Property, Dummerston[1]	Village	Residence	Proprietor	Unknown	Pitcher Pitcher Spittoon	1850–1900	Var Var Rock	Beaded Beaded Floral / octagonal	
Massachusetts Jed Levin	Merrimac Mfg. Co., Lowell; workers' houses.	Urban	Residence	Craftsman	Unknown	Teapot	1847–1865	Var	Paneled	Bennington, Vt.
	Boardinghouse for (mostly female) workers.	Urban	Boarding house	Unskilled-specified	NA	Teapot	1840–1865	Rock	Unknown	
John Foster Cheney III, Greg Laden, Nancy S. Seasholes	Weston Farmstead, Windsor[2]	Rural	Farmstead	Tenant farmer	Unknown	Teapot Baking pan Baking pan	1890–1919	Rock Rock Rock	Octagonal Unknown Unknown	

Continued on next page

New York

Investigator	Site	Setting	Use	Status		Vessel	Date	Material	Motif
Lou Ann Wurst and Randall H. McQuire	John Burghardt House, Upper Lisle, Broome County[3]	Village	Residence	Proprietor	Unknown	Pitcher	1850–1870	Rock	Diamond
						Spittoon		Rock	Gothic windows
						Pie Plate		Rock	
Sherene Baugher-Perlin	Arthur Kill and Richmondtown Rd., Richmondtown, Staten Island[4]	Village	1830–1879: Hotel; 1890–1953: Parish house	Multiple levels	NA	Pitcher	1840–1920	Rock	Unknown
						Teapot		Rock	Rusticated
						Spittoon		Rock	Unknown
	Lot 11, Richmondtown Rd., Richmondtown, Staten Island[4]	Village	Residence	Unknown	Unknown	Teapot	ca. 1930	Rock	Rebekah at Well
Nancy Waters	Perine House, Richmondtown, Staten Island	Rural	Farmstead	Farm owner	Yes	Teapot	1840–1913	Rock	Unknown
						Bowl		Rock	Unknown
William V. Askins	Sandy Ground, Staten Island[5]	Village	Residence	Unknown	Unknown	Teapot	ca. 1913	Rock	Rebekah at Well
						Teapot	ca. 1895	Rock	Rebekah at Well
						Teapot		Rock	Rebekah at Well
Karen S. Rubinson	210 East 54th St., New York[6]	Urban	Residence/ Business	Multiple levels	Unknown	Teapot	1878–1950	Rock	Unknown
						Teapot		Rock	Rebekah at Well
						Tumbler		Rock	Unknown
	205 East 53rd St.[6]	Urban	Residence	Proprietor	Yes	Teapot	1875–1902	Rock	Decagonal
New York University (archaeologists)	West 4th St. betw. McDougal & Thompson (Washington Square South)[7]	Urban	Residence	Professional	Unknown	Pitcher	ca. 1860	Rock	Boar/stag hunt
	93 W. 3rd St.[7]	Urban	Multiple residence	Multiple levels	Unknown	Teapot	1870–1900	Rock	Rebekah at Well
						Spittoon		Rock	Unknown
						Teapot		Rock	Unknown

Archaeologist (see notes, pp. 162–165)	Site	Community type	Historical use	Occupational level (see table 4)	Servants	Form	Deposition date	Glaze: Rockingham or variegated	Embossed decoration	Identification/attribution
Middle Atlantic										
New Jersey Lu Ann De Cunzo										
	9 Ellison St., Paterson[8]	Urban	Residence	Craftsman	No	Pitcher Teapot	1855–1865	Var Rock	Unknown Decagonal	
	1 to 4 Van Houten St., Paterson[8]	Urban	Residence Res./tavern	Low white collar NA	Unknown NA	Pitcher Teapot	1845–1855 1872–1885	Rock Rock	Boar/stag hunt Rebekah at Well	
	15 Ellison St., Paterson[8]	Urban	Residence	Craftsman	No	Pitcher Spittoon	1850s	Rock Var	Boar/stag hunt Lobed	Attr. Taylor & Speeler, Trenton, N.J.
	12 Mill St., Paterson[8]	Urban	Residence	Unskilled-specified	No	Teapot Spittoon Spittoon	1880–1895	Rock Rock Rock	Rebekah at Well Unknown Unknown	
Louis Berger and Assoc. Inc.	Charles Moore Farm[9]	Rural	Farmstead	Proprietor/farm owner	Yes	Teapot Spittoon Nappy	1857–1905	Rock Var Rock	Unknown Scalloped/fluted None	
Hunter Research, Inc.	Thomas Olden House, Princeton[10]	Rural	Residence	Unknown	Unknown	Spittoon	1840–1850	Rock	Unknown	
	Allaire Mansion[11]	Industrial village	Residence/boarding house/hotel	NA	NA	Pitcher Teapot	1840–1880	Rock Rock	Unknown Prob. Rebekah at Well	
	12 N. Warren St., Trenton[12]	Rural	Residence/business	Unknown	Unknown	Teapot Spittoon Bowl	1895–1905	Rock Rock Rock	Prob. decagonal Unknown Lobed, 4" high	

Site					Form	Date	Ware	Decoration	Maker
18–22 North Warren St., Trenton[13]	Urban	Hotel	NA	NA	Spittoon	ca. 1890	Rock	Medallion	
Pennsylvania									
John Milner Assoc. Inc.									
John Quincy Adams Public School. 451–457 Darien St., Philadelphia[14]	Urban	School	NA	NA	Spittoon / Spittoon	1860–1880	Rock / Rock	Unknown / Unknown	
North of Brown St., betw. 8th and 9th, Philadelphia[14]	Urban	Unknown	Unknown	Unknown	Pitcher / Spittoon / Soap dish	1880–1900	Rock / Var / Rock	Hound handle / Fluted / Unknown	
249 Schell St., Philadelphia[14]	Urban	Residence	Unskilled-specified and unskilled-unspecified	Unknown	Spittoon / Small box (probably sugar)	1850–1860	Rock / Rock	Unknown / Unknown	
809 Depot St., Philadelphia[14]	Urban	Residence	Multiple levels	No	Teapot	1870–1900	Rock	Medallion	J. E. Jeffords, Philadelphia
802 Depot St. Philadelphia[14]	Urban	Residence/ business	Proprietor	No	Pitcher / Pitcher / Spittoon	1875–1900	Rock / Rock / Rock	Putto / Live game / Unknown	
806 Depot St., Philadelphia[14]	Urban	Residence	Professional	No	Pitcher / Pitcher	1876–1900	Rock / Rock	Beading / Medallion	
813 & 815 Buttonwood St., Philadelphia[14]	Urban	Residence/ business	Multiple levels	No	Pitcher / Pitcher / Pitcher / Spittoon / Jardiniere	1848–1860	Rock / Rock / Rock / Rock / Rock	Floral / Mask at spout / Floral / Diamond pattern / Unknown	

Continued on next page

135

Archaeologist (see notes, pp. 162–165)	Site	Community type	Historical use	Occupational level (see table 4)	Servants	Form	Deposition date	Glaze: Rockingham or variegated	Embossed decoration	Identification/attribution
	Darien & Callowhill Sts., Philadelphia[14]	Urban	Residence/business	Craftsman/proprietor	No	Pitcher	1880–1910	Rock	Undecorated	
	226 Darien (Chester) St., Philadelphia[14]	Urban	Residence	Multiple levels	No	Pitcher	1840–1860	Rock	Rouletted banding	
	829 Wood St., Philadelphia[14]	Urban	Residence	Craftsman	No	Pitcher Pitcher Pitcher Spittoon	1840–1860	Rock Rock Rock Var	Live game Floral & paneled Paneled Vertical reeding	
	Frankford Arsenal residential quarters[15]	Urban	Residence	Unknown	Unknown	Teapot	1840–1900	Rock	Unknown	
	Steel Farmstead[16]	Rural	Farmstead	Multiple levels	Yes	Pitcher Teapot Teapot Marble	1870–1920	Rock Rock Rock Rock	Medallion Rebekah at Well Rebekah at Well	
Barbara Liggett	17–19 Hudson (now Orianna) St., Philadelphia[17]	Urban	Restaurant	NA	NA	Pitcher Pitcher Pitcher Pitcher Pitcher Pitcher Teapot Spittoon	1869–1880	Rock Rock Rock Rock Rock Rock Rock	Mask, octagonal Octagonal Floral Floral Live game Hanging game Unknown Diamond design	
B. Bruce Powell	Carpenters' Company, 320 Chestnut St., Philadelphia[18]	Urban	Clubhouse	NA	NA	Spittoon	1840–1861	Dark and opaque Rock	Gothic	American Pottery Co., Jersey City, N.J.

Continued on next page

Source	Location	Urban	Site type			Vessel form	Date	Material	Decoration
	Independence Hall yard[19]	Urban	Public gatherings and traffic	NA	NA	Teapot	1851–1920	Rock	Rebekah at Well
	309 Walnut St., Philadelphia[20]	Urban	Bus. office	NA	NA	Teapot	1873–1900	Rock	Figures seated at tea table
Lee Nelson, Architectural historian	Tower of Independence Hall; beneath floor boards of closet under stairs[21]	Urban	Government building	NA	NA	Spittoon	1850–1920	Rock	Unknown
Louis Berger and Assoc. International	83 (747) Swanson St., Philadelphia	Urban	Residence	Multiple levels	Unknown	Pitcher	1850–1870	Rock	Figures smoking; classical motifs; octagonal shape
						Teapot		Rock	Unknown
Verna L. Cowin, the Carnegie Museum of Natural History	82, 84 or 86 Third St., Pittsburgh[22]	Urban	Commercial/ residential	NA	NA	Bowl / Nappy	1865–1890	Rock / Rock	Gothic & floral
	Prob. 37 Market St., Pittsburgh[22]	Urban	Saloon/ restaurant	NA	NA	Pitcher / Teapot / Spttoon / Spittoon	1850–1890	Rock / Rock / Rock / Rock	Putti with goat / Unknown / Gothic & paneled / Floral & paneled
	Betw. 4th, 3rd, Market, & Wood Sts., Pittsburgh[22]	Urban	Commercial/ residential	NA	NA	Bowl / Canning jar	1850–1890	Rock / Rock	Geometric
	Market near 2nd, Pittsburgh[22]	Urban	Commercial/ residential	NA	NA	Bowl	1850–1890	Rock	None
	Betw. 3rd, 4th, Market & Wood Sts., Pittsburgh[22]	Urban	Commercial/ residential	NA	NA	Pitcher / Pitcher	1850–1890	Rock / Rock	Kneeling hunter / Tulip

Archaeologist (see notes, pp. 162–165)	Site	Community type	Historical use	Occupational level (see table 4)	Servants	Form	Deposition date	Glaze: Rockingham or variegated	Embossed decoration	Identification/attribution
	Betw. 2nd, 3rd, Market & Wood Sts., Pittsburgh[22]	Urban	Unknown	Unknown	Unknown	Spittoon	1850–1890	Rock	Lobed	
	Near corner Market & 2nd, Pittsburgh[22]	Urban	Commercial/residential	NA	NA	Mug	1850–1890	Rock	Footed, cuplike	
	Betw. 3rd & 4th, Market & Wood Sts., Pittsburgh[22]	Urban	Commercial/Residential	NA	NA	Spittoon	1850–1890	Rock	Unknown	
	Betw. 2nd, 3rd, Market, & Wood Sts., Pittsburgh[22]	Urban	Unknown	NA	NA	Mug	1850–1890	Rock	Footed, cuplike	
NPW Consultants, Inc.	McCrory site No. 1, California, Washington County[23]	Rural	Farmstead	Farm owner	Unknown	Nappy or pie plate	1840–1970	Rock	None	
Delaware										
Louis Berger and Assoc. International	615 Church St., Wilmington[24]	Urban	Residence	Proprietor	No	Pitcher	1861–1872	Rock	Putti & floral	
The Hagley Museum	Gibbons House and Burns, McPherson, Cheney Houses, DuPont Powder Works, near Wilmington[25]	Industrial village	Residence	Multiple levels	Unknown	Pitcher / Teapot / Teapot / Nappy	1851–1906	Rock / Rock / Rock / Rock	Hound handle / Rebekah at Well / Unknown	
	Gibbons House, etc. (as above); Foreman's house[25]	Industrial village	Residence	Low white collar		Pie plate		Rock		

Cara L. Wise	Old State House, Dover[26]	Urban	State Capitol	NA	NA	Spittoon Spittoon	1873	Rock Rock	Unknown Unknown	
District of Columbia										
John Milner Associates	133 Quander Alley, Washington[27]	Urban	Residence	Unskilled-specified and unskilled-unspecified	Unknown	Teapot	1898–1942	Rock	Unknown	
	1359 Ohio St.[28]	Urban	Residence/brothel	Unskilled-specified	Unknown	Teapot Teapot	1894–1910	Rock Rock	Rebekah at Well Floral	Attributed to E. & W. Bennett, Baltimore, Md.
	317 13½ St.[28]	Urban	Residence/poss. brothel	Unskilled-specified	Unknown	Teapot	1880–1910	Rock	Rebekah at Well	E. & W. Bennett, Baltimore
	1353 Ohio St.[28]	Urban	Residence/brothel	Unskilled-specified	Unknown	Teapot	1860–1880	Rock	Rebekah at Well	E. & W. Bennett, Baltimore
Soil Systems	942 I St., NW[29]	Urban	Prob. residence	Unknown	Unknown	Teapot Teapot	1855–1857	Rock Rock	Unknown Unknown	
Maryland										
Saint Mary's City Commission	Tolle Tabb's site[30]	Rural	Farmstead	Tenant farmer	Unknown	Teapot Mug	1848–1860	Rock Rock	Multisided Beaded	Attributed to E. & W. Bennett, Baltimore
Henry M. Miller	Brome Plantation, St. Mary's City[31]	Rural	Plantation	Plantation owner	Yes	Pitcher Teapot Spittoon Bottle	1840–1950	Rock Rock Rock Rock	Unknown Rebekah at Well Shells, beading None	

Continued on next page

Archaeologist (see notes, pp. 162–165)	Site	Community type	Historical use	Occupational level (see table 4)	Servants	Form	Deposition date	Glaze: Rockingham or variegated	Embossed decoration	Identification/attribution
Julia A. King	Susquehanna[32]	Rural	Farmstead	Tenant farmer	Unknown	Teapot	1893–1940	Rock	Rebekah at Well	
Katherine J. Dinnel	St. Inigoes Manor House[33]	Rural	Jesuit plantation manor house	Professional	Unknown	Mug	1840–1872	Rock	Unknown	
Southeast										
Virginia										
Alexandria Archaeology	407 South Fairfax St., Alexandria[34]	Urban	Residence	Unskilled-specified	Unknown	Pitcher / Teapot	1900–1910	Rock / Rock	Mounted hunters / Rebekah at Well	
	209 Wolfe St., Alexandria[34]	Urban	Residence	Multiple levels	Unknown	Teapot	Post 1900	Rock	Figural: Chinese motif	
	316 South Alfred St., Alexandria[34]	Urban	Residence	Unskilled-specified	Unknown	Teapot	1875–1910	Rock	Rebekah at Well	Attributed to E. & W. Bennett, Baltimore
	318 South Alfred St., Alexandria[34]	Urban	Residence	Unskilled-specified	Unknown	Teapot	1875–1910	Rock	Multisided	
	Samuel Lindsay House, 104 South St. Asaph St., Alexandria[35]	Urban	Residence	Low white collar / Proprietor	Unknown / Unknown	Pitcher / Teapot	1843–1864 / 1850–1900	Rock / Rock	Floral / Floral & paneled	
	916 Gibbon St., Alexandria[35]	Urban	Residence	Multiple levels	Unknown	Teapot	1850–1862	Rock	Floral & octagonal	
	114 South St. Asaph St.,	Urban	Residence	Owner: low white collar;	yes	Teapot	1849–1860	Rock	Floral	Attr. E. & W. Bennett,
						Teapot		Rock	Floral	Attr. as above

Site	Setting	Context	Occupant	Vessel	Form	Date	Material	Decoration
Alexandria[36]			resident: slave		Teapot		Rock	Rebekah at Well
					Teapot		Rock	Unknown
					Teapot		Rock	Unknown
Coleman site, 417 South Fairfax St., Alexandria[36]	Urban	Residence	Multiple levels	Yes	Teapot	1830–1860	Rock	Unknown
418 South Royal St., Alexandria[37]	Urban	Residence	Multiple levels	Unknown	Pitcher	1860–1882	Rock	Unknown
					Teapot		Rock	Unknown
					Teapot		Rock	Unknown
					Spittoon		Rock	Shell
422 South Royal St., Alexandria[37]	Urban	Residence	Unskilled-specified and unskilled-unspecified	Unknown	Pitcher	1860–1910	Rock	Unknown
					Spittoon		Rock	Unknown
					Spittoon		Rock	Unknown
420 South Royal St., Alexandria[37]	Urban	Residence	Unskilled-specified	Unknown	Pitcher	1860–1870	Rock	Figural: "Idle Apprentices"
			Multiple levels		Teapot	1860–1905	Rock	Rebekah at Well
					Spittoon		Rock	Unknown
West Virginia								
Philip Coon House, Harper's Ferry[38]	Village	Residence	Proprietor	Yes	Teapot	1850–1865	Rock	Unknown
National Park Service, Eastern Team, United States Department of the Interior								
North Carolina								
Thomas Wolfe House, 48 Spruce St., Ashville	Urban	Boarding-house	NA	Unknown	Teapot	1910–1920	Rock	Undecorated
					Bowl		Rock	Unknown
Linda F. Carnes-McNaughton and Terry M. Harper								

Continued on next page

South Carolina

Archaeologist (see notes, pp. 162–165)	Site	Community type	Historical use	Occupational level (see table 4)	Servants	Form	Deposition date	Glaze: Rockingham or variegated	Embossed decoration	Identification/attribution
Elaine Bitterold	Hayward-Washington House, 87 Church St., Charleston[39]	Urban	Business & residence	Multiple levels	Unknown	Pitcher	After 1880	Rock	Boar/stag hunt	E. & W. Bennett
						Pitcher	1880–1930	Rock	Flower on handle	Attr.
						Teapot	1851–1900	Rock	Rebekah at Well	E. & W. Bennett
						Teapot		Rock	Rebekah at Well	Attr. as above
						Teapot		Rock	Rebekah at Well	Attr. as above
						Teapot		Rock	Floral	Attr. as above
						Teapot		Rock	Floral	Attr. as above
								Rock	"Holy Family"	
Martha Zierden, the Charleston Museum	King, Hasell, Meeting, and Market Sts. block, Charleston[40]	Urban	Commercial/residential	NA	Unknown	Teapot	1851–1860	Rock	Rebekah at Well	E. & W. Bennett
						Teapot	1890–1900	Rock	Rebekah at Well	E. & W. Bennett
						Teapot	1846–1860	Rock	Floral	Attributed to Edwin Bennnett
						Spittoon		Rock	Floral	
	66 Society St., Charleston[41]	Urban	Residence	Unknown	Unknown	Teapot	1839–1890	Rock	Reeded lid	

Georgia

Archaeologist (see notes, pp. 162–165)	Site	Community type	Historical use	Occupational level (see table 4)	Servants	Form	Deposition date	Glaze: Rockingham or variegated	Embossed decoration	Identification/attribution
Lawrence E. Babits	Slave row, McIntosh County	Rural	Plantation	Enslaved laborers	Unknown	Bowl	1840s–1860s	Rock	Unknown	

Tennessee

Joseph L. Benthall	Netherland Inn, Kingsport[42]	Rural	Inn	NA	NA	Bowl	1840–1906	Rock	Unknown
Samuel D. Smith	South Cabin, the Hermitage, Davidson County (near Nashville)[43]	Rural	Slave quarters	Enslaved laborers	Unknown	Teapot Bowl Bowl	1830–1860	Rock Rock Rock	Unknown Scalloped rim
Kentucky									
Robert P. Fay	Liberty Hall, Montgomery & Wilkinson Sts., Frankfort[44]	Urban	Residence	Professional	Unknown	Milk pan	1840–1900	Rock	None
W. Stephen and Kim A. McBride	Farrow site, High St., Lexington[45]	Urban	Residence	Craftsman	Unknown	Pitcher Bowl	1855–1865	Rock Rock	Paneled gothic
	McCormick site, High St., Lexington[45]	Urban	Residence	Unskilled Proprietor	Unknown	Teapot Pitcher Spittoon	1860–1895 1850–1865 1860–1865	Rock Rock Rock	Unknown Floral Wide ribbing at top
			After 1871, prob. boarding house	Unknown	Unknown	Marble	1860–1895	Rock	Unknown
Robert A. Genheimer	54–56 East Second St., Covington[46]	Urban	Residence/saloon	NA	No	Pitcher Pitcher Pitcher Spittoon Crock Bowl	1873–1890	Rock Rock Rock Rock Rock Rock	Hexagonal Gothic/geometric Acanthus Unknown
Ronald W. Deiss	State capitol building[47]	Urban	Government	NA	NA	477	1846–1920	Rock	Unknown

Continued on next page

Archaeologist (see notes, pp. 162–165)	Site	Community type	Historical use	Occupational level (see table 4)	Servants	Form	Deposition date	Glaze: Rockingham or variegated	Embossed decoration	Identification/ attribution
			building			Spittoons				
						Mug	1846–1897	Rock	Beaded	

Midwest

Ohio

Archaeologist (see notes, pp. 162–165)	Site	Community type	Historical use	Occupational level (see table 4)	Servants	Form	Deposition date	Glaze: Rockingham or variegated	Embossed decoration	Identification/ attribution
Jeff Carskadden	Charles C. Munro House[48]	Rural	Farmstead	Farm owner	Unknown	Bowl	1851–1913	Rock	Unknown	
Miami Purchase Assoc. for Historic Preservation—Artifacts in collection of the Cincinnati Museum of Natural History	425 (23) Chestnut St., Cincinnati[49]	Urban	Residence	Multiple levels	Unknown	Chamber pot	1855–1880	Rock	Unknown	
						Flowerpot		Rock	Unknown	
						Flowerpot		Rock	Unknown	
	427 (25) Chestnut St., Cincinnati[49]	Urban	Residence	Proprietor	Yes	Figurine	1840–1875	Rock	Dog	
						Tobacco jar	1855–1874	Rock	Reeding	
						Spittoon		Rock	Floral & inscription: "Please spit in [the or this] box"	
						Pitcher	1869–1900	Rock	Floral	
						Bowl	1874–1876	Rock	Unknown	
William J. Hunt, Jr.	Matthews House[50]	Village	Residence	Unknown	Unknown	Bowl	1840–1920	Rock	Unknown	

Continued on next page

Indiana

Trina C. Maples, University of Louisville

Gregory House site, 911 East Market St., New Albany	Urban	Residence	Unknown	Unknown	Teapot	1901–1920	Rock	Plain—pineapple shape

Illinois

Leslie A. Perry

520 South Eighth St., Springfield[51]	Urban	Residence	Multiple levels	Unknown	Bowl	1854–1904	Rock	Scallop rim
David Davis House, Bloomington	Urban	Residence	Professional	Yes	Baking dish Baking dish	1871–1935	Rock Rock	None None

Floyd Mansberger, Fever River Research

Bartlett House site, Pike County	Rural	Farmstead	Farm owner	Unknown	Bowl	1860–1915	Rock	Lobed

Midwest Archaeological Research Center

Smiling Hog site, Scott County	Rural	Farmstead	Farm owner	Unknown	Bowl Bowl	1870–1890	Rock Rock	Unknown Unknown
Fall Creek site	Rural	Farmstead	Unknown	Unknown	Bowl	1840–1865	Rock	Unknown
Biesmann site, 618 South Bench St., Galena[52]	Urban	Residence	Unknown	Unknown	Pitcher Pitcher Pitcher Spittoon	1845–1930	Rock Rock Rock Rock	Floral Floral Lambrequins and floral Open mouthed
510 East Grove St., Bloomington[53]	Urban	Residence	Professional	Yes	Nappy Nappy	1880–1890	Rock Rock	None None
Drews site, St. Clair County[54]	Rural	Farmstead	Farm owner	No	Pitcher Bowl Bowl Bowl	1860–1930	Rock Rock Rock Rock	Unknown Unknown Unknown Unknown
Droit site, St. Clair County[55]	Rural	Farmstead	Farm owner	Unknown	Spittoon Spittoon Baking pan	ca.1900	Rock Rock Rock	Fluting Unknown

Archaeologist (see notes, pp. 162–165)	Site	Community type	Historical use	Occupational level (see table 4)	Servants	Form	Deposition date	Glaze: Rockingham or variegated	Embossed decoration	Identification/ attribution
	Drake site, Stephenson County[56]	Rural	Farmstead	Farm owner	Unknown	Pitcher	1838–1896	Rock	Floral & Gothic	
						Bowl		Rock	Unknown	
						Bowl		Rock	Unknown	
						Bowl		Rock	Unknown	
						Bowl		Rock	Unknown	
						Chamber pot		Rock	Unknown	
	Thomas Hyndman Residence[57]	Urban	Residence	Multiple levels	Unknown	Bowl	ca. 1895	Rock	Gothic Lambrequins	
						Bowl		Rock	Gothic Lambrequins	
	Mitchell House site, Scott County[58]	Rural	Farmstead	Farm owner	Yes	Spittoon	1840–1867	Rock	Floral octagonal	
						Spittoon		Rock	Floral octagonal	
						Spittoon		Rock	Floral octagonal	
						Dish		Rock	Prob. octagonal	
U. of Missouri Archaeological Field School	Joseph Smith Homestead summer kitchen, Nauvoo[59]	Village	Residence	Professional	Unknown	Bowl	1839–1846	Rock	Unknown	
	Smith Mansion Hotel latrine, Nauvoo[60]	Village	Hotel	NA	NA	Pitcher	1843–1875	Rock	Octagonal	
						Pitcher		Rock	Octagonal	
Missouri										
M. Colleen Hamilton	Carr & 21st Sts., St. Louis[61]	Urban	Residences	Unknown	Unknown	Bowl	1850–1890	Var	Gothic lambrequins & beaded	
						Mug		Rock	Unknown	

Continued on next page

Investigator	Site	Settlement	Structure	Occupation		Vessel Form	Date	Ware	Decoration
	Lot 286, Broadway, Collins, & Ashley, North St. Louis[61]	Urban	Residences	Unknown	Unknown	Bowl Bowl Bowl	1880–1900	Rock Rock Rock	Beaded Unknown Unknown
Michigan									
Patrick E. Martin	House II[62]	Industrial village	Residence	Unskilled-specified	Unknown	Teapot Teapot Spittoon Bowl Bowl Bowl Bowl Bowl	1867–1891	Rock Rock Var Rock Rock Rock Rock Rock	Unknown Unknown Unknown Unknown Unknown Unknown Unknown Unknown
Gulf States									
Texas									
Johnney Pollan	Eagle Island Plantation, Lake Jackson	Rural	Plantation	Tenant farmer	Unknown	Spittoon	1865–1900	Rock	Unknown
Charles D. Cheek	Fort Concho, West Texas[63]	Army Post	Army fort	NA	NA	Jar	1867–1889	Rock	Unknown
Southwest									
Arizona									
Robert M. Herskovitz	Army Post at Apache Pass between Dos Cabezas and Chiricahua Mts[64]	Army post	Guardhouse	NA	NA	Spittoon	1862–1894	Rock	Unknown

Archaeologist (see notes, pp. 162–165)	Site	Community type	Historical use	Occupational level (see table 4)	Servants	Form	Deposition date	Glaze: Rockingham or variegated	Embossed decoration	Identification/ attribution
George A. Teague	Reward Mine, southern Arizona[65]	Mining camp	Boarding-house	NA	NA	Bowl Bowl	1885–1915	Rock Rock	Unknown Unknown	
West Coast										
California										
Jeanette Schulz	Hotel de France, 915 Front St., Sacramento[66]	Urban	Hotel	NA	NA	Teapot Teapot Teapot Teapot Teapot Spittoon Spittoon Spittoon Jar	1864–1905	Rock Rock Rock Rock Rock Rock Rock Rock Rock	Floral Unknown Unknown Unknown Unknown Unknown Unknown Unknown Floral	
Adrian and Mary Praetzellis	Unspecified site in Sacramento[67]	Urban	Unknown	Unknown	Unknown	Pitcher	Unknown	Var	Diamond pattern	Attr. the United States Pottery, Bennington, Vt.
	Front Street, Sacramento[67]	Urban	Unknown	Unknown	Unknown	Pitcher Spittoon	1848–1863 1848–1900	Rock Rock	Hound handle Vertical panels	
	Hastings Bank, 2nd & J Sts., Sacramento[67]	Urban	Government and business	NA	NA	Spittoon	Unknown	Rock	Unknown	
	Budd Building, 903 Front St., Sacramento[66,67]	Urban	Unknown	Unknown	Unknown	Pitcher Spittoon	After 1906	Rock Rock	Hanging game Floral & paneled	

					Vessel	Date	Paste	Pattern	Manufacturer
	"Hannum" saloon, 325 K St., Sacramento[66,67,68]	Urban	Saloon/residence	NA	NA	Tobacco jar	1866–1884	Rock	Horizontal linear	Lyman & Fenton, Bennington, Vt.
						Baking dish		Var	Octagonal	
	"Gruhler" saloon, 325 K St., Sacramento[66,67,68]	Urban	Saloon/residence	NA	NA	Spittoon	1884–1888	Rock	Vertical linear	
						Spittoon		Rock	Medallion	
	1020 Fourth St., Sacramento[66,67,68]	Urban	Saloon	NA	NA	Spittoon	1881–1885	Rock	Lozenge	First two attr. to Lyman & Fenton, Bennington, Vt.
						Spittoon		Rock	Lozenge	
						Spittoon		Rock	Beaded	
						Spittoon		Rock	Unknown	
C. Lynn Furnis	City Hotel, Sacramento[67]	Urban	Hotel & subsequent residences	Unknown	Unknown	Teapot	1851–1878	Rock	Rebekah at Well	
						Teapot		Rock	Rebekah at Well	
						Teapot		Rock	Rebekah at Well	
						Teapot		Rock	Rebekah at Well	
						Teapot		Rock	Unknown	
						Teapot		Rock	Unknown	
						Spittoon		Rock	Unknown	
						Spittoon		Rock	Unknown	
						Spittoon		Rock	Unknown	
						Spittoon		Rock	Unknown	
Archeo-Tec	505 Montgomery St., San Francisco	Urban	Unknown	Unknown	Unknown	Teapot	1851–1853	Rock	Unknown	
						Spittoon		Rock	Unknown	
						Spittoon		Rock	Unknown	
	Pan Magna Plaza	Urban	Residence & business	Craftsman	Unknown	Teapot	ca. 1847	Rock	Unknown	

Notes

Preface: Rockingham Ware in the United States

1. Barber, *Pottery and Porcelain.*

Introduction: The Role of Context in Artifact Interpretation

1. Morris, *Home Place,* 132, 25.
2. Deetz, "Archaeologists as Storytellers," 95.
3. Csikszentmihalyi and Rochberg-Halton, *The Meaning of Things,* 17.
4. Deetz, "Material Culture and Archaeology," 9–10.
5. Deetz, *In Small Things Forgotten,* 35–37. Herman, *The Stolen House,* 5. George L. Miller, "Classification and Economic Scaling," 1–41.
6. For discussions of contextual archaeology, see Beaudry, "Reinventing Historical Archaeology," 473–97; De Cunzo, "People, Material Culture, Context, and Culture," 1–17; Herman, "Historical Archaeology," 19–31; and Mrozowski, "Nature, Society, and Culture," 447–72.
7. Prown, "The Truth of Material Culture," 20, 21, 11.
8. Prown, unpublished essay quoted in Haltman, Introduction to Prown and Haltman, *American Artifacts,* 2.
9. Prown, "The Truth of Material Culture," 16–19. Deetz, *In Small Things Forgotten,* 4.
10. George L. Miller, "'The Market Basket,'" 3–4.
11. Yentsch, "Minimum Vessel Lists," 27.
12. Mayhew and Myers, *A Documentary History of American Interiors,* 69.
13. Buten, *18th-Century Wedgwood,* 19–20.
14. For a discussion of poverty and gentility, see Bushman, *The Refinement of America,* esp. 182–83.
15. Csikszentmihalyi and Rochberg-Halton, *The Meaning of Things,* 57, 82.
16. Miller, "Classification and Economic Scaling"; Miller, "Revised Set of CC Index Values," 1–25. For studies using Miller's indices, see Spencer-Wood, *Consumer Choice in Historical Archaeology.*
17. McEwan, "The Archaeology of Women," 33–41; Groover, "Evidence for Folkways and Cultural Exchange," 41–64; Wall, "Examining Gender, Class, and Ethnicity," 102–17; Reckner and Brighton, "'Free from All Vicious Habits,'" 63–86; Lucas, "A la Russe, à la Pell-Mell," 80–93; Wall, "Sacred Dinners and Secular Teas," 69–81.
18. Yentsch, "Minimum Vessel Lists," 24–53; Fitts, "The Archaeology of Middle-Class Domesticity and Gentility," 39–62; Crass, Penner, and Forehand, "Gentility and Material Culture," 14–31; and Zierden, "A Trans-Atlantic Merchant's House in Charleston," 73–87.
19. Yentsch, "Minimum Vessel Lists," 27. Yentsch refers to Beaudry et al.,

"A Vessel Typology for Early Chesapeake Ceramics" (1983),18–42. R. Holme, *The Academy of Armoury* (Chester, England, n.p., 1688), cited in Beaudry et al., "A Vessel Typology" (1993), 56–57.

20. The sites were the Robson site in Wall's "Examining Gender, Class, and Ethnicity" and "Sacred Dinners and Secular Teas"; and the Aiken-Rhett, Heyward-Washington, and 66 Society Street sites in Zierden's "A Trans-Atlantic Merchant's House."

21. Roberts and Cosans, *The Archeology of the Nineteenth Century*, 119.

22. Among misleading statements in Brewer's work is her assertion that Orcutt (spelled "Oncutt" by Brewer) & Thompson, in Poughkeepsie, worked between 1860 and 1870 (pp. 36, 44). Orcutt & Thompson produced the first datable prototypical Rockingham ware and worked in 1830/1831.

23. Sotheby Park Bernet, *Jacqueline D. Hodgson Collection*, 22 Jan. 1974. Bourne, *Bennington Pottery*, 26 April 1988.

1. Reading Historical Artifacts

1. De Cunzo, "People, Material Culture, Context, and Culture," 16. De Cunzo cites Barrie Reynolds, "Material Systems: An Approach to the Study of Kwandu Material Culture," in *Material Anthropology: Contemporary Approaches to Material Culture*, ed. Barrie Reynolds and Margaret A. Stott (Lanham, Md.: University Press of America, 1987), 155–87.

2. The retailer was John Collamore, Jr. & Co. The Richard M. Tucker, Jr., papers are in the collection of the Margaret Woodbury Strong Museum, Rochester, N.Y.

3. The eighteenth-century reference is from Stone, "Artifacts Are Not Enough," 74.

4. Martin, *The Standard of Living in 1860*, 45.

5. Glaser and Strauss, *The Discovery of Grounded Theory*.

6. Twain, *Life on the Mississippi*, 188. Williamson, *The Growth of the American Economy*, 168.

7. Deetz, "American Historical Archeology," 363.

8. Darnton, *The Great Cat Massacre*, 262.

9. Ames, *Death in the Dining Room*, 68–73.

10. For a discussion of the organization and perception of reality in nineteenth-century literature, pictorial arts, and the theater, see Meisel, *Realizations*. See also Hadfield, *Every Picture Tells a Story*.

11. Houghton, *The Victorian Frame of Mind*, and Miyoshi, *The Divided Self*. Carroll, *Through the Looking Glass*, 175.

12. Brusewitz, *Hunting*, passim.

2. Defining Rockingham Ware

1. Barber, *Pottery and Porcelain*, 18. Langenbeck, *The Chemistry of Pottery*, 72, 66.

2. "Fenton's Patent Flint Enamel and Parian Ware," Boston, 16 Sept. 1853;

"U. S. Pottery Co., Bennington, Vt. Manufacturers of the Patent Flint, Enameled, Parian, Agate, Yellow and other Wares," Boston, 17 Nov. 1854. Invoices are in the collection of the Bennington Museum, Bennington, Vt.

3. Cox and Cox, *Rockingham Pottery and Porcelain,* 108–9. Jewitt, *The Ceramic Art of Great Britain,* 283–84.

4. Jewitt, *The Ceramic Art of Great Britain,* 281.

5. Cox and Cox, *Rockingham Pottery and Porcelain,* 109, 34, 60.

6. Cox and Cox, *Rockingham Pottery and Porcelain,* 108. For information on imitators, see Cox and Cox, *Rockingham Pottery and Porcelain,* 110–13; Philip Miller, "What's in a Name?" 18. See esp. Cox, "The Analysis of Rockingham," 40–58.

7. Undated letter from J. Walker, Utica, N.Y., to John Howson, published in the Staffordshire weekly newspaper, *Potters' Examiner and Workman's Advocate,* 17 Feb. 1844, quoted in Goodby, "'Our Home in the West,'" 15. Information on Wedgwood Rockingham-ware production from Lynn Miller, the Wedgwood Museum, personal communications, 20 Sept. 1990, and 13 Feb. 1991.

8. Cox and Cox, *Rockingham Pottery and Porcelain,* 73.

9. Cox and Cox, *Rockingham Pottery and Porcelain,* 112–13; Cox, "The Analysis of Rockingham," 46, 48–49, 54–55, 57. The marked Podmore & Walker pitcher is in the collection of Diana and J. Garrison Stradling; personal communication, 13 Oct. 1998. The invoice to A. Southern is in the Warshaw Collection of Business Americana, National Museum of American History, Smithsonian Institution, Washington, D.C. *M'Elroy's Philadelphia Directory for 1842* (Philadelphia: Orrin Rogers, 1842) lists Adam Southern as a "crockeryware" merchant, 251. For the Rockingham Works rental notice, which appeared June 10, 1842, in the *Doncaster Nottingham and Lincoln Gazette,* see Cox and Cox, *Rockingham Pottery and Porcelain,* 73.

10. Jewitt, *The Ceramic Art of Great Britain,* 281.

11. See Jewitt, *The Ceramic Art of Great Britain,* 27, 30, 348–59; Henrywood, *An Illustrated Guide to British Jugs,* 203–9; Henrywood, *Relief-Moulded Jugs,* 14–15.

12. For a succinct discussion of early-nineteenth-century molding in America, see Myers, *Handcraft to Industry,* 32.

13. Henrywood, *Relief-Moulded Jugs,* 53–56. The *Commercial Advertiser,* 16 Oct. 1829, quoted in *Niles' Weekly Register* 37, no. 946 (Oct. 1829): 154. The pitcher is in the collection of Alexandria Archaeology, Alexandria, Va. "List of Prices of Fine Flint Ware, Embossed and Plain, Manufactured by D. and J. Henderson, Jersey City, N.J. . . . 1830," reprinted in *Antiques* 26, no.3 (Sept. 1934): 109. *Directory of Jersey City.*

14. Lardner, *A Treatise,* 51. Lardner discussed earthenware as well as porcelain in this work.

15. Ketchum, *Potters and Potteries of New York State,* 191, 115, 189–191.

16. See Newark Museum, *The Pottery and Porcelain of New Jersey,* 34–35. Examples are illustrated in Stradling and Denker, *Jersey City,* figs. 2, 3, 6, 7, 15; and Watkins, "Henderson of Jersey City and His Pitchers," 388. Quote is in Watkins, "Henderson of Jersey City," 389–90.

17. Barber, *Pottery and Porcelain,* 119–20.

18. The pitcher is marked "SALAMANDER/WORKS/54 CANNON ST/NEW

YORK CITY/NEW YORK" (impressed) and "F3" (raised letters). Collection, Henry Ford Museum, Dearborn, Mich.; J. Disturnell, *New York as It Is, in 1835 . . . Also the Hudson River Guide;* "Salamander Works, 62 Cannon St., New York. Flint and Fire Proof Ware Manufactory. . . . April, 1837." "F" designated the "Steam Boat" design and "3" indicated the size. Five sizes were offered; "3" (the pitcher under discussion) is just under 8″ high. The price list is in the Bella Landauer Collection, New York Historical Society.

19. *Washington, D.C. Daily National Intelligencer,* 16 July 1833, item no. 72 in Karen D. Boring, "A Survey of Ceramic Advertisements in *The National Daily [sic] Intelligencer, 1827–1837* (1973, typescript), in the collection of National Museum of American History, Smithsonian Institution. The 1835 advertisement is mentioned in the exhibition checklist for Stradling and Denker, *Jersey City,* 8. Carr, "Reminiscences of an Old Potter," 27–28. Ketchum, *Potters and Potteries of New York State,* 33–34, 200–3.

20. R. J. C. Hildyard, personal communication, 20 Feb. 1989. *Fifteenth Exhibition of American Manufactures . . . 1845 . . . the Franklin Institute.* Records at the Franklin Institute, Philadelphia, Pa.

21. The advertisement appeared in the *Mercantile Register,* 1846, reprinted in *Antiques* 28, no. 4 (Oct. 1935): 168–69. *Sixteenth Exhibition of American Manufactures . . . 1846 . . . the Franklin Institute.* Records at the Franklin Institute, Philadelphia, Pa. Barber, *Pottery and Porcelain,* 196.

22. Zusy, *Norton Stoneware and American Redware,* 15. Price list headed "Fenton's Crockery Works, Bennington, Vermont"; price list headed "East Bennington, 1848, Bought of Lyman, Fenton & Park," Bennington Museum, Bennington, VT. Wood, "Memories of the Fentons," 153.

23. See Myers, *Handcraft to Industry,* 18–19.

24. *Seventeenth Exhibition of American Manufacturers . . . 1847 . . . the Franklin Institute.* Records at the Franklin Institute, Philadelphia, PA.

25. Barber, *Pottery and Porcelain,* 194–195, 423. Riles, "Biography of James Bennett."

26. Barber, *Marks of American Potters,* 75.

27. William Vodrey to Barber, 9 May 1892. Diana Stradling kindly provided me with a copy of this letter. Barber, *Pottery and Porcelain,* 201. *Wellsville Patriot* (Wellsville, Ohio), July 11, 1854, cited in Gates and Ormerod, "East Liverpool, Ohio, Pottery District," 4.

28. Barber, *Pottery and Porcelain,* 196; Barber to the Edwin Bennett Pottery Company, 1 Nov. 1912; ser. 2, Edwin AtLee Barber Records, Philadelphia Museum of Art, Archives.

29. Gates and Ormerod, "East Liverpool, Ohio, Pottery District," 3–5; Barber, *Pottery and Porcelain,* 192, 194.

30. Cox and Cox, *Rockingham Pottery and Porcelain,* 34,

31. Brunt to Barber, 7 Feb. 1914; ser. 2; Edwin AtLee Barber Records; Philadelphia Museum of Art, Archives.

32. Barber, *Pottery and Porcelain,* 196; Barber, "Recent Accessions of Pottery and Porcelain," in *Bulletin of the Pennsylvania Museum,* 22–25.

33. Letter from Bernard Howson to Staffordshire, England, 1843, published in the *Potter's and Workman's Advocate,* 16 March 1844; quoted in Goldberg, "Charles Coxon," 62.

34. Price lists shown in Branin, *The Early Makers of Handcrafted Earthenware and Stoneware,* 200, and Leibowitz, *Yellow Ware,* 45.

35. Middleton quoted in Frelinghuysen, "Paris Porcelain in America," 562. Robert Leith noted in "Conspicuous Consumption: Ceramics in the Carolina Low Country, 1700–1820," a paper presented at the Forty-fifth Annual American Ceramic Circle Symposium, Nov. 1998, that Mary Helen Hering Middleton was Henry Middleton's mother. Tunnicliffe quoted in Norris F. Schneider, "Staffordshire Potters," *Zanesville (Ohio), Zanes Times Signal,* 17 Nov. 1957.

36. Savage and Newman, *An Illustrated Dictionary of Ceramics,* 56, 246; Josiah Wedgwood & Sons, Ltd., sales catalog (1886), price list (1919), and traveling salesman's catalog, ca. 1930; collection, the Wedgwood Museum, Barlaston, Stoke-on-Trent, England; personal communication, R. J. C. Hildyard, Department of Ceramics, Victoria & Albert Museum, London, 20 Feb. 1989.

37. Verna L. Cowin, Pittsburgh Plate Glass Site report, in preparation; see also Cowin, *Pittsburgh Archaeological Resources. Rockingham Register,* 11 Oct. 1866, cited in Mullins, "Negotiating Industrial Capitalism," 167.

38. For the American Pottery Company pitcher, see Schwartz, *Collectors' Guide,* 66; for the tobacco jars, see Barret, *Bennington Pottery and Porcelain,* 94.

39. Family provenance provides a late-nineteenth- or early twentieth-century date for the Rebekah-at-the-Well teapot (discussed in chap. 6, p. 108, which has a plain dark glaze. Accession information about the bulldog pitcher is from the Monmouth County Historical Association; Branin, *The Early Makers of Handcrafted Earthenware and Stoneware,* 227. A pitcher from the same mold, made by the Haig Pottery, Philadelphia, is cataloged in the accession files of the Philadelphia Museum of Art (1893) as a bulldog growler. "Growler" was a slang term for a beer container.

40. *Philadelphia City Register.*

41. Invoice headed "Bought of Charles Fish & Co., Manufacturers of Rockingham and Yellow Ware," 1 May 1875, New Jersey State Museum, Trenton, N.J.

42. Ketchum, *American Country Pottery,* 11, 10.

3. The Americanization of Rockingham Ware

1. Wedgwood to Sir William Meredith, 2 Mar. 1765, quoted in *The Selected Letters of Josiah Wedgwood,* ed. Finer and Savage, 29. George L. Miller, "Marketing Ceramics in North America," 3.

2. Barber, *Pottery and Porcelain,* 59–63; Thistlethwaite, "The Atlantic Migration," 269–70.

3. Zusy, *Norton Stoneware and American Redware,* 15; Myers, *Handcraft to Industry,* 12, 32. Thistlethwaite, "The Atlantic Migration," 265.

4. Barber, *Pottery and Porcelain,* 158–59, 192–94.

5. "Pioneer Potting," *East Liverpool, Ohio, Tribune,* 18 Mar. 1876.

6. Riles, "James Bennett," 6–7. Bennett was Riles's great-great-grandfather.

7. Harris, *General Business Directory,* 267, 17.

8. Gates and Ormerod, "East Liverpool, Ohio, Pottery District," 4–5, 79, 52, 38, 339–42, 46, 95, 18. Quote on 4–5.

9. Letter from George Garner, quoted in Gates and Ormerod, "East Liverpool, Ohio, Pottery District," 4.

10. Riles, "James Bennett," 7. Lucille T. Cox, "Salamander Pottery Built in 1848," *East Liverpool, Ohio, Potters' Herald,* 20 May 1937. "Pioneer Potting," *East Liverpool, Ohio, Tribune,* 25 Mar. 1876.

11. Riles, "Biography of James Bennett," 7. Tunnicliffe quote in Norris F. Schneider, "Staffordshire Potters," *Zanesville (Ohio) Zanes Times Signal,* 17 Nov. 1957. Lucille T. Cox, "Wages? The Early Potters Never Were Certain," *East Liverpool (Ohio) Review,* 10 Jan. 1941.

12. Gates and Ormerod, "East Liverpool, Ohio, Pottery District," 4. *Augusta (Ga.) Daily Chronicle and Sentinel,* 26 June 1849, bound vol. Mar. 23–Dec. 31, 1849, Library of Congress.

13. *Transactions of the American Institute . . . New York . . . 1851,* 628, III, 110.

14. See Jewitt, *The Ceramic Art of Great Britain,* 160–66.

15. The *Pittsburgh Gazette* reported 8 potteries in 1849, and 11 were operating in 1853. See Gates and Ormerod, "*East Liverpool, Ohio, Pottery District,*" 4. Branin, *The Early Makers of Handcrafted Earthenware and Stoneware,* 197–98, 179; Myers, "Edwin Bennett," 35; Ketchum, *Potters and Potteries of New York State,* 118, 212–14, 241–44.

16. Barber, *Pottery and Porcelain;* Frelinghuysen, *American Porcelain;* Stratton, "American Pottery Industry"; Barber, *Historical Sketch of the Greenpoint [N.Y.] Porcelain Works;* Barret, *Bennington Pottery and Porcelain;* Curtis, "Production of Tucker Porcelain," 339–74; Springsted, "A Delftware Center in Seventeenth-Century New Jersey," 9–46; J. Garrison Stradling, "The Southern Porcelain Company," 1–39; Myers, *Handcraft to Industry;* Stradling, "A Dream of 'Porcellain' in Cincinnati," 74–90.

17. Barber, *Pottery and Porcelain,* 120, 440; *Directory of Jersey City;* Young, *The Ceramic Art,* 455. See also Stradling and Denker, *Jersey City: Shaping America's Pottery Industry.* Barret, *Bennington Pottery and Porcelain;* Myers, *Handcraft to Industry,* 32–35, 51–52, 74.

18. Young, *The Ceramic Art,* 455.

19. Myers, *Handcraft to Industry,* 33–35, 51–52, 103; Barber, *Pottery and Porcelain,* 176–77, 552–54. Miller's whiteware is mentioned in a report of the 1845 Franklin Institute Exhibition of American Manufactures and compared to an earlier example. Quoted in Myers, *Handcraft to Industry,* 102. Barber, *Marks of American Potters,* 25.

20. U.S. Geological Survey, *Mineral Resources of the U.S. 1883,* sec. 13, p. 544; quoted in Stratton, "American Pottery Industry," 5.

21. Information about Elsmore & Forster from Wetherbee, *White Ironstone,* 90–94. Stephen Theiss information from Spargo, *Early American Pottery and China,* 307.

22. Jewitt, *Ceramic Art of Great Britain,* 380.

23. Invoice of Atkins, Stedman & Co., "Importers of Earthen, China and Glass Ware," Boston, 8 Jan. 1853, collection of the Winterthur Museum. Invoices of Stillwell, Sawyer & Company, Chicago, 1856, and C. Hennecke &

Company, Milwaukee, 1873; and advertisement of William Grange & Company, Philadelphia, 1870, pottery section, Warshaw Collection of Business Americana, Archives Center, National Museum of American History, Smithsonian Institution, Washington, D.C. Rogers, *The Crockery Companion.*

24. Stratton, "American Pottery Industry," 319–20.

25. Ibid., 312–14.

26. Barber, "Early Ceramic Printing and Modeling," 51. The Dudson and Ridgway pitchers are illustrated and discussed in Henrywood, *Relief-Moulded Jugs,* 146–47, 65–68. Goldberg, "Charles Coxon," 32, 43, 57–58.

27. Barber, *Pottery and Porcelain,* 442–51; Frelinghuysen, *American Porcelain,* 21–23, 33, 25–26, 116–17; J. Garrison Stradling, "The Southern Porcelain Company," 16–17.

4. The Niche Market for Rockingham Ware

1. Herskovitz, *Fort Bowie Material Culture.* Information on Independence Hall from Steven Patrick, 18 May, 1987. Deiss, *Archaeological Investigations at Kentucky's Old State Capitol,* 170. DeBarthe, *The Smith Mansion Hotel Latrine.* Background information for the Hermitage site from Smith, *An Archaeological and Historical Assessment of the First Hermitage.*

2. Price lists headed "Fenton's Crockery Works, Bennington, Vermont" and "East Bennington, 1848, Bought of Lyman, Fenton & Park," Bennington Museum, Bennington, Vt. Price list headed "East Liverpool, Ohio, 1850. John Goodwin presents this as the lowest list of Quee[n]sware prices in America," Ohio Historical Society, East Liverpool, Ohio. "A List of Prices of Earthenware, &c manufactured at Swan Hill Pottery, South Amboy, N.J.," reproduced in Branin, *The Early Makers,* 200, 198–99. "Fenton's Patent Flint Enamel Ware, Manufactured in Benington [*sic*], Vermont," price list/invoice dated 20 July, 1852; pottery section, Warshaw Collection of Business Americana, Archives Center, National Museum of American History, Smithsonian Institution, Washington, D.C. Moore, "Bennington Ware," 22; Tower, "The Quaint Old Ware of Bennington," 226.

3. Evans, *Art Pottery of the United States,* 304.

4. Stratton, "American Pottery Industry," 6–7, 13.

5. Gates and Ormerod, "East Liverpool, Ohio, Pottery District," 184–85; Stratton, "American Pottery Industry," 13–14.

6. My observation about changing Rockingham-ware production patterns is based on examination of the price lists cited above plus those of Nichols & Boynton, 1854, Burlington, Vt; J. L. Rue & Company, ca. 1860–1870, South Amboy, N.J.; Douds & Moore, 1860s, S. & W. Baggott's Eagle Pottery Works, 1862, Vodrey Pottery Works, 1864–1865 and 1868, all East Liverpool, Ohio; E. & L. P. Norton, 1865, Bennington, Vt.; William Brunt, Jr., & Company's Phoenix Pottery Works, 1865–1866, Morley, Godwin & Flentke's Salamander Pottery Works, 1868, Agner & Foutts' American Pottery Works, 1868, Isaac W. Knowles's East Liverpool Pottery Works, 1868, all East Liverpool, Ohio; J. A. & C. W. Underwood, 1868, Fort Edward, N.Y.; A. K. Ballard, 1871, Burlington, Vt.; Haxston, Ottman & Company, 1872, Fort Edward, N.Y.; F. A. Plaisted & Son, 1873, Farmingdale, Maine;

Ottman Bros. & Company, 1876, Fort Edward, N.Y.; F. Woodworth, 1876, Burlington, Vt.; A. J. Russell & Company, 1878, West Troy, N.Y.; H. V. Colsten & Company, wholesale dealers, 1878, Great Bend, Pa.; Bulger & Worcesters' Star Pottery, 1879, McDevitt & Moore's California Pottery, 1880, both East Liverpool, Ohio; Edwin Bennett Pottery, ca. 1882, Baltimore, Md.; Agner & Gaston's American Pottery Works, 1883–1884, C. C. Thompson & Company, ca. 1886, C. C. Thompson Pottery Company, ca. 1889–1917, J. W. Croxall & Sons, 1891–1892, the D. E. McNicol Pottery Company, ca. 1892–1928, all East Liverpool; and E. Norton & Company, 1893, Bennington, Vt. Price lists are in the collections of the Ohio Historical Society, East Liverpool, Ohio; Winterthur Museum, Winterthur, De.; and the Warshaw Collection, Smithsonian Institution, Washington, D.C. Some price lists are published in Barret, *Bennington Pottery and Porcelain;* Branin, *The Early Makers;* Broderick, "A Survey of the Pottery Industry"; Ketchum, *Potters and Potteries of New York State;* and Leibowitz, *Yellow Ware.*

7. George L. Miller, "The 'Market Basket,'" 8.

8. Spencer-Wood and Heberling, "Consumer Choices in White Ceramics," 79. See also Wall, "Sacred Dinners and Secular Teas," 79; George L. Miller, "Classification and Economic Scaling," 14.

9. Fagan, *Baltimore Wholesale Business Directory,* 98. Invoice of Shirley & Cook, china, glass and queensware importers, 1857; Pottery section, Warshaw Collection of Business Americana, National Museum of American History, Smithsonian Institution, Washington, D.C.

10. Ames, "Meaning in Artifacts," 213. Ames took his information on John Ruskin, the nineteenth-century art critic and sociologist, from Ruskin's, *Seven Lamps of Architecture* (New York: Cassell, 1909), 13–16. Conversation with Alvin Rackliff, Spruce Head, Maine, August 1993. Webster, *An Encyclopaedia of Domestic Economy,* 320. Beecher and Stowe, *The American Woman's Home,* 374.

11. Slosson, *China Hunters Club,* 255, quoted in Stillinger, *The Antiquers,* 64.

12. Damon, "Hard Times, Good Times," 43.

13. Hodder, "Theoretical Archaeology," 10.

5. Rockingham Ware and Gender Identity

1. See Williams, introduction to *Dining in America,* 3–14.

2. Welter derives her evidence for the most part from fiction and prescriptive literature that was written for the middle class. Welter, "The Cult of True Womanhood," 151–52.

3. Karin Calvert, personal communication, 3 March 1987.

4. The 477 spittoons found at the state legislature site, Frankfort, Kentucky, make spittoons the most numerous form in actuality, but, as mentioned in chap. 1, I have counted them as one spittoon in the vessel counts so as not to skew the statistics.

5. Barber, *Pottery and Porcelain,* 196–97; Clarke, "Rebekah at the Well Teapots," 20; *1897 Sears Roebuck Catalogue,* 686; J. Garrison Stradling. "Puzzling Aspects," 332–37.

6. Henrywood, *Relief-Moulded Jugs,* 233–34; Myers, "Edwin Bennett," 31–35.

7. For a succinct discussion of home religion and home as a moral force, see Handlin, *The American Home,* 4–26. Bushnell quoted in McDannell, *The Christian Home,* 19. Donaldson, *The Odd-Fellows' Text-Book,* 214, 217–18.

8. McDannell, *The Christian Home,* 16–51.

9. Williams, *Savory Suppers,* 65–67; Wall, "Sacred Dinners and Secular Teas," 78–79.

10. Handlin, *The American Home,* 17.

11. Spencer-Wood, "Feminist Historical Archaeology," 419.

12. *Baltimore Sunday Sun,* quoted in Myers, "Edwin Bennett," 33.

13. George Bennett Filbert to B. Floyd Bennett, 29 Jan. 1962, Edwin Bennett Pottery Company Records, Archive Center, National Museum of American History, Smithsonian Institution. I do not have the citation for the interior decorator's advice. Robert L. Edwards, editor and publisher of *Tiller,* read the quotation to me from an early-twentieth-century home-decorating or possibly antiques-collecting book or magazine about ten years ago. I wrote down the quotation but neglected to record the citation. Mr. Edwards has been unable to find it again.

14. Wiseman, "Folk Art and Antiques," 28B.

15. Smith-Rosenberg, *Disorderly Conduct,* 173–78.

16. The painting, in the collections of the Nelson-Atkins Museum of Art, Kansas City, Mo., is illustrated in Edwards, *Domestic Bliss,* 71.

17. *Harper's Weekly: A Journal of Civilization,* (11 Jan. 1868): 18, illus., p. 1.

18. See Branin, *The Early Makers,* 203, 205.

19. Barber to Edwin H. Bennett, president, Edwin Bennett Pottery Company, 6 Feb. 1914; ser. 2; Edwin AtLee Barber Records, Philadelphia Museum of Art Archives. Bennett was the son of the Baltimore pottery's founder; Barber, *Bulletin of the Pennsylvania Museum,* 22–25.

20. The American Pottery Company of Peoria opened in 1861 under the management of Christopher Webber Fenton and Decius Clark, former proprietors of the recently defunct United States Pottery Company in Bennington, Vermont. They produced Rockingham ware, presumably, for marked pieces made by the Peoria Pottery, successor to the American Pottery Company in 1863, were of Rockingham and yellow ware, some from United States Pottery molds. *Peoria Daily Transcript,* Jan. 1861, quoted in Mansberger, *Historic Illinois Potteries,* 4, 12. Rorabaugh, *Alcoholic Republic,* 109. See also Rorabaugh, "Beer, Lemonade, and Propriety," 24–46.

21. Skinner, *Hops and Venom,* 2.

22. Ames, *Death in the Dining Room,* 73–74. For sources on nineteenth-century perceptions of masculinity, Ames cites John D'Emilio and Estelle B. Freedman, *Intimate Matters: A History of Sexuality in America* (New York: Harper & Row, 1988); Shere Hite, *The Hite Report on Male Sexuality* (New York: Ballantine Books, 1981); and Michael S. Kimmel, ed., *Changing Men: New Directions in Research on Man and Masculinity* (Newbury Park, Calif.: Sage, 1987). Johns, *American Genre Painting,* 77–78.

23. Ames, *Death in the Dining Room,* 44.

24. Ames, *Death in the Dining Room,* 68–73. Weidner, "Gifts of Wild Game," 341.

25. Johns, *American Genre Painting,* 141–42.

26. For illustrations of spittoons in public places, see Gale Research Company, *Currier and Ives,* fig. 10, and no. 0929; Maass, "Foreign Travellers and American Hotels," 22; Crowe, *With Thackeray in America,* 22.

27. Catalogue of the Progressive Mfg. Co., of Trenton, N.J., ca. 1895, Hagley Museum, Wilmington, Del. Phoenix Pottery Works advertisement in the *Wellsville (Ohio) Patriot,* 29 July 1851, 3.

28. The anonymous British commentator was quoted in a display label at the East Liverpool, Ohio, Museum of Ceramics; Schrier and Story, *A Russian Looks at America,* 60.

29. Crowe, *With Thackeray in America,* 32–33.

30. Barber, *Pottery and Porcelain,* 194. Catalogue of the Progressive Mfg. Co.

31. Dickens quoted in Maass, "Foreign Travellers and American Hotels," 23. Cinadr and Genheimer, *Queensgate II,* 1983; Gartley and Carskadden, "Marbles from an Irish Channel Cistern," 113. See also Worthy, "Classification and Interpretation," 344–45, 350–53.

32. Bird, *The Englishwoman in America,* 147–49, 168–71, 366.

33. Bird, *The Englishwoman in America,* 147, 68.

34. Advertisement in *The American Cabinet-Maker, Upholsterer and Carpet Reporter* 13, no. 21 (Oct. 1876), xxii. Five different spittoon footstools, all with upholstered tops, one pedal-operated, are illustrated in *Maine Antique Digest* (Jan. 1992), 42-F.

6. Rockingham Ware and Class

1. For this chapter I have consulted scholarship about "socioeconomic status" as well as "class" because, as the terms are used, their meanings overlap. But I have chosen to use the broader term, "class," because it incorporates cultural issues that related to Rockingham-ware vessel choice as much as the social or economic aspects of "socioeconomic status."

2. Blumin, *The Emergence of the Middle Class,* 11. Spencer-Wood summarizes precedent for using occupational categories as an indicator of class in "Miller's Indices and Consumer-Choice Profiles," 324; Hershberg and Dockhorn, "Occupational Classification," 59–77.

3. Blumin, *The Emergence of the Middle Class,* 121–33; Bushman, *The Refinement of America,* xiii; McClymer, "Late Nineteenth-Century American Working Class Living Standards," 379–98.

4. See Edgar Martin, *The Standard of Living in 1860;* and Rorabaugh, "Beer, Lemonade, and Propriety." For an extensive discussion of what were and were not considered decent standards of living, see Cowan, *More Work for Mother,* 152–73. Blumin, *The Emergence of the Middle Class,* 247. Horwitz, *Anthropology toward History.*

5. Blumin, *The Emergence of the Middle Class,* 119. The Gill family census and directory data is from the Commuter Tunnel project files, John Milner Associates, Philadelphia.

6. For rural class divisions, see Blumin, *The Emergence of the Middle Class,* 308; and Holland, "Tenant Farms," 61–62, 66.

7. Cressey, "The Alexandria, Virginia, City-Site," 148–49; John F. Stephens, "Vertical Integration Study by Year and Occupation Rank," City Survey Socioeconomic Data, Alexandria Archaeology, Alexandria, Va.; "Alexandria Archaeology Street Profile," Alexandria Urban Archaeology Program, City of Alexandria, 1983; McCord, *Across the Fence, but a World Apart,* 46–48. Danny Miller, "Structures and Strategies," 89.

8. Patrick E. Martin, *Archaeological Investigation at Fayette State Park,* 25–26, 29; Gregory Waselkov, Robert T. Bray, and Linda Waselkov, *Archaeological Investigations of the Hyrum Smith Site* (Columbia: University of Missouri,1974); De Cunzo, "Economics and Ethnicity," 507; Ann Smart Martin, "The Role of Pewter as Missing Artifact," 1.

9. Buten, *Eighteenth-Century Wedgwood,* 90; Gaye Blake-Roberts, lecture, Hagley Museum, 30 October 1989. Slosson, quoted in Stillinger, *The Antiquers,* 64.

10. Cressey, "The Alexandria, Virginia, City-Site," 245–47. Blumin, *The Emergence of the Middle Class,* 188–89. See esp., Welter, "The Cult of True Womanhood," 168; Ryan, *Cradle of the Middle Class.* Blumin, *The Emergence of the Middle Class,* 221–29.

11. Bourdieu, *Distinction,* 61. See, for example, Grover, ed., *Dining in America;* and Williams, *Savory Suppers.*

12. Moore, "Bennington Ware," 22; Barber, *Marks of American Potters,* 152; Jones, "Frauds in Old China," 196.

13. Bourdieu, *Distinction,* 61–62.

14. Conversation with Mary Michaux Graves Danzoll, Bryn Mawr, Pa., 27 Dec. 1987.

15. "Specimen of Flint Ware," *Gleason's Pictorial* 5, no. 17 (Oct. 1853), 1. The reviewer uses the terms "enamel ware" or "flint ware" or "enamel flint wares," but the ten-foot-high centerpiece of the exhibit, now housed in the Bennington Museum, is of plain Rockingham ware as were, probably, some of the smaller pieces in the exhibit. See Downing, *The Architecture of Country Houses,* esp. p. 40.

16. McCracken, *Culture and Consumption,* 118–19. Upton, *Holy Things and Profane,* 229.

17. Danny Miller, "Structures and Strategies," 89–90; Bourdieu, *Distinction,* 58–60.

18. Mumford, *The Brown Decades,* 2–4.

19. Ames, *Death in the Dining Room,* 74–75. See also Bushman, *The Refinement of America,* 33–38. Johns, *American Genre Painting,* 142.

20. Samuel W. Shogren, "Lifeways of the Industrial Worker: The Archaeological Record (A Summary of Three Field Seasons at Blacksmith Hill)," 1986; Hagley Museum and Library research files, Wilmington, Del.

7. Rockingham Ware in Rural America

1. Information about Galena from Mahoney, *River Towns in the Great West,* 285–86, 109, 254–58.

2. Atherton, *Main Street,* passim. Winter, "Social Dynamics and Structure in Lower Town Harpers Ferry," 16–17.

3. Price lists consulted are listed in the notes for chapter 4, nn. 2 and 6.

4. See McMurry, "City Parlor, Country Sitting Room," 261, 270, 272; McMurry, "Progressive Farm Families,"; Sutherland, *The Expansion of Everyday Life,* 42, 56, 77. Quote is from Worrell, Stachiw, and Simmons, "Archaeology from the Ground Up," 47.

5. Ames, *Death in the Dining Room,* 238.

6. McLane and McLane, *Islands of the Mid-Maine Coast,* 99.

7. For descriptions of dining styles, see Williams, *Savory Suppers,* 151–53; Lucas, "A la Russe, à la Pell-Mell," 82–83.

8. A Practical Housekeeper, *American Practical Cookery-Book; or, Housekeeping Made Easy* (Philadelphia: J. W. Bradley, 1861), quoted in Williams, *Savory Suppers,* 151. Sutherland, *The Expansion of Everyday Life,* 41, 53, see quotation on 72. McMurry, "Progressive Farm Families," 341–42.

9. "Revised American Standard Price List. American Pottery Works. (Established 1863.) Agner & Gaston, Manufacturers of Rockingham & Yellow Ware, Terra Cotta Hanging Baskets and Flower Pots. East Liverpool, Ohio," ca. 1883–1884, Ohio Historical Society, East Liverpool, Ohio.

10. Price lists of "Salamander Pottery Works, Morley, Godwin & Flentke, Rockingham, Yellow and Variegated Queensware, East Liverpool, O.," 1868; "James Carr, Prices Current for 1872"; "The California Pottery, McDevitt & Moore, Yellow and Rockingham Queensware, East Liverpool, O.," 1880; and "C. C. Thompson & Co., Manufacturers of Cane-Colored and White Lined Ware, Rockingham and Terra Cotta Ware, Black Stamped Decorated & Plain C. C. Ware, East Liverpool, Ohio," ca. 1886.

11. Lucas, "A la Russe, à la Pell-Mell," 83–90.

12. Ames, *Death in the Dining Room,* 238.

13. For a succinct discussion of parlor usage and etiquette, see McMurry, "City Parlor, Country Sitting Room," 265–68. Kasson, "Rituals of Dining," 131. For other discussions of dining as a social ritual and specialization as a concomitant element, see Williams, *Savory Suppers,* esp. chap. 1–3; Williams, introduction to *Dining in America,* 22; Clark, "The Vision of the Dining Room," 142–72; Ames, *Death in the Dining Room,* 4, 67–8, 76, 209–13, 238; Lucas, "A la Russe, à la Pell-Mell" 80–90; and Lucas and Shackel, "Changing Social and Material Routine in Nineteenth-Century Harpers Ferry," 29–34.

14. See Fitts, "Archaeology of Middle-Class Domesticity and Gentility in Victorian Brooklyn," 39–62, esp. 55–59; see also Lucas, "A la Russe, à la Pell-Mell" 83–90; Williams, *Savory Suppers,* 27–8, 33, 36, 44, 47–48, 52–53; and Clark, "The Vision of the Dining Room," 163–72; quote on 171.

15. Margaret Byington, *Homestead: The Households of a Mill Town* (New York: Russell Sage Foundation, 1910), 56; Esther Barrows, *Neighbors All: A Settlement Notebook* (Boston: Houghton Miflin, 1929), 70; both quoted in Cohen, "Embellishing a Life of Labor," 301–2.

16. McMurry, "City Parlor, Country Sitting Room" 268–71. See also Larkin, *The Reshaping of Everyday Life,* 125–26.

17. McMurry, "Progressive Farm Families," 340–44; Downing, *The Architecture of Country Houses;* McMurry, "City Parlor, Country Sitting Room" 275–79.

18. Karin Calvert, personal communication, 20 Dec. 1997.

19. George L. Miller, personal communication, 12 Nov. 2000.

20. Carskadden, "Historic Ceramics from the Cass House and Munro Trading Post," 34–40, 50–51.

21. Phillippe, "The Drake Site," (1988), 321–23.

22. Smith and Bonath, "Phase I and Phase II Historic Archaeological Investigations." Esarey, "The Drews Site."

23. The farms were in Somerset County, N.J. and Staten Island, N.Y. Louis Berger and Associates, "1984 Phase II Archaeological Investigations, Isaac Clark Site . . . Haviland Site . . . and Kingston Grid Site . . . South Brunswick Township, Middlesex County, New Jersey, and the Charles Moore Site . . . Franklin Township, Somerset County, New Jersey." Information on the Perine Farm, Richmondtown, Staten Island, New York, from Nancy Waters, personal communication, 1987; Henry M. Miller, with contributions by Alexander H. Morrison II, and Gary Wheeler Stone, *A Search for the "City of Saint Maries": Report on the 1981 Excavations in St. Mary's City, Maryland.* St. Maries Citty Archaeology Series 1. St. Mary's City Commission, St. Mary's City, 1983.

24. Burns, *Pastoral Inventions,* 89, 241–45. See also Foster, *The Civilized Wilderness.*

25. Burns, *Pastoral Inventions,* 77–78.

26. An example of the pitcher is in the collection of the Brooklyn Museum. Branin, *The Early Makers,* 79–80.

27. Burns, *Pastoral Inventions,* 7.

28. Mayer, *San Francisco: A Chronological and Documentary History,* 10–11.

29. Cayton and Onuf, *The Midwest and the Nation,* 58, 53.

30. Rollin L. Hartt, "Middle-Westerners and That Sort of People," *Century Magazine* 93 (1916), 173, cited in Shortridge, *The Middle West: Its Meaning in American Culture,* 35.

Appendix

1. "Historical Archaeology and the National Market: a Vermont Perspective, 1795–1920," 1977.

2. "Phase II Archaeological Site Examination; Weston Farmstead and Nichols Blacksmith Shop, Windsor, Massachusetts."

3. "Class in the Country," Society for Historical Archaeology Conference, 1990.

4. "The Prall Site: A Case Study in Historical Archaeology," 1978.

5. "Sandy Ground: Historical Archaeology of Class and Ethnicity in a Nineteenth-Century Community on Staten Island, N.Y."

6. "53rd. at Third Project for Gerald D. Hines Interests," 1984.

7. Sullivan Street site.

8. "Economics and Ethnicity: an Archaeological Perspective on Nineteenth-Century Paterson, New Jersey," 1983.

9. "Phase II Archaeological Investigations, and the Charles Moore Site (28S094), Franklin Township, Somerset County, NJ. Prepared for the Fed-

eral Highway Admin. and the N.J. Dept. of Transportation," 1984.

10. "Preliminary Archaeological investigations at the Thomas Olden House, Princeton, N.J., 1988."

11. "Allaire Mansion, Allaire Village, Monmouth County, N.J.," 1990.

12. "Archaeological Investigations Within the Durhams Block in Connection with the Capital Center Project, Trenton, N.J."

13. "Brick Tavern House, Stables, Sheds, and Lot of Land Called the Trenton House."

14. Betty Cosans-Zeebooker and David Barrett, "Archaeological Investigations in Association with the Center City Commuter Rail Connector: A Study of Nineteenth Century Urban Development in Philadelphia and Spring Garden," 1985.

15. "Historical and Archaeological Survey of Frankford Arsenal, Philadelphia, Pa.," 1979.

16. Mid County Expressway.

17. "Archaeological Investigations at Franklin Court, Independence National Historical Park, Philadelphia, Pa.," 1971.

18. "Archaeological Investigation of Carpenters' Court, Independence National Historical Park," 1958.

19. Pennsylvania State House (Independence Hall) yard, Philadelphia, Pa., 1957.

20. "Historic Structures Report on Bishop White House in Independence National Historical Park," 1959.

21. Independence National Historical Park, Philadelphia, Pa., 1963.

22. Pittsburgh Plate Glass project.

23. "Executive (Management) Summary, Phase II Archaeological Testing of Seven Areas Along the Man Valley Expressway, California Borough, Washington County, Pa."

24. Wilmington East Project.

25. Samuel W. Shogren, "Lifeways of the Industrial Worker. The Archaeological Record (A Summary of Three Field Seasons at Blacksmith Hill)," 1986.

26. "Excavations at Delaware's State House: A Study in Cultural Patterning in Eighteenth-Century Delaware," 1978.

27. Charles D. Cheek and Amy Friedlander, "Pottery and Pig's Feet: Space, Ethnicity, and Neighborhood in Washington, D.C., 1880–1940," *Historical Archaeology*, 24, no. 1 (1990): 34–60.

28. Federal Triangle III project.

29. Patrick Garrow, ed., "Archaeological Investigations in the Washington, D.C. Civic Center Site," 1982.

30. George L. Miller, "A Tenant Farmer's Tableware: Nineteenth-Century Ceramics from Tabb's Purchase," *Maryland Historical Magazine,* 69, no. 2, (Summer 1974): 197–210.

31. Henry M. Miller, with contributions by Alexander H. Morrison II, and Gary Wheeler Stone, "A Search for the 'Citty of Saint Maries': Report on the 1981 Excavations in St. Mary's City, Maryland."

32. "Archaeological Investigations at Susquehanna: A 19th Century Farm Complex Aboard Patuxant River Naval Air Station, St. Mary's County, Md."

33. "Archaeological Investigations at St. Inigoes Manor House, St. Mary's County, Md."

34. City Survey Project. Pamela J. Cressey, Barbara H. Magid, and Steven J. Shepherd, "Urban Development in North America: Status, Distance, and Material Differences in Alexandria, Va.," 1984.

35. Steven Judd Shepherd, "An Archaeological Study of Socioeconomic Stratification: Status Change in Nineteenth-Century Alexandria, Va.," 1985.

36. T. B. McCord, Jr., "Across the Fence, But a World Apart: The Coleman Site, 1796–1907," 1985.

37. Pamela J. Cressey, "The Alexandria, Va., City Site: Archaeology in an Afro-American Neighborhood, 1830–1910."

38. John F. Pousson, "Archaeological Investigations, Harpers Ferry National Historical Park, Package No. 110-A, Wager Block Back Yards."

39. "Preliminary Report on the Research at the Hayward Washington House."

40. Martha Zierden and Debi Hacker, "Charleston Place: Archaeological Investigations of the Commercial Landscape," 1987.

41. Martha Zierden, Kimberly Grimes, David Hudgens, and Cherie Black, "Charleston's First Suburb: Excavations at 66 Society Street," 1988.

42. "Archaeological Investigations at the Netherland Inn Complex," 1973.

43. "An Archaeological and Historical Assessment of the First Hermitage," 1976.

44. "Archaeological Investigations at Liberty Hall, Frankfort, Ky.," 1986.

45. Lextran Project.

46. "Archaeological Testing, Evaluation, and Final Mitigation Excavations at Covington's Riverfront Redevelopment Phase 2 Site, Kenton County, Ky.," 1987.

47. "Archaeological Investigations at Kentucky's Old State Capitol," 1988.

48. "Historic Ceramics from the Cass House and Munro Trading Post, Dresden, Ohio," *Muskingum Annals, No. 5* (1989).

49. Thomas Cinadr and Robert A. Genheimer, "Queensgate II: An Archaeological View of Nineteenth-Century Cincinnati," 1983.

50. "An Assessment of Archeological Resources Associated with Several Structures in Historic Everett Village, Cuyahoga Valley National Recreation Area, Ohio," 1986.

51. "1981 Archeological Testing at the Henson Robinson House Site, Lincoln Home National Historic Site," 1984.

52. Floyd R. Mansberger, "Report of the Galena-U.S. Route 20 Bridge Replacement Archaeological Study, Jo Daviess County, Illinois," 1984.

53. David Alan Welitschek, "Historic Archaeological Investigations at the Reuben Benjamin House," 1988.

54. Mark E. Esarey, "Report of Reconnaissance Survey and Testing of the Drews Site, 11-S-701, FAI-255 Borrow Pit 6, Extension 1, St. Clair County, Ill.," 1981.

55. Mark E. Esarey and David C. Dycus, "Report of Reconnaissance Survey and Testing for Illinois Department of Transportation Project FAI-255 Borrow Pit 29, St. Clair County, IL," 1981.

56. Joseph S. Phillippe, "Archaeological and Historical Investigations at the Drake Site: a Nineteenth Century Farmstead in Northern Illinois," 1988.

57. Frederick Thomas with a contribution by Jerry J. Moore, "Socioeco-nomic Differentiation of Late Nineteenth-Century Lower Class Households in the Little Piasa Valley, Alton, Illinois," 1990.

58. Charles R. Smith and Shawn K. Bonath, "A Report on Phase I and Phase II Historic Archaeological Investigations in Three Segments of the F.A.P. 408 Highway Corridor, Adams, Pike, and Scott Counties, Ill., 1979–1981."

59. Gregory Waselkov, Robert T. Bray, and Linda Waselkov, "Archaeolog-ical Investigations of the Hyrum Smith Site," 1978.

60. Paul DeBarthe, "The Smith Mansion Hotel Latrine and Other Dis-coveries of the 1978 Archaeological Project," Robert T. Bray, editor, 1979.

61. Meiners Collection.

62. "Archaeological Investigations at Fayette State Park," 1986.

63. "The Fort Concho Trash Dump: an Archaeological Analysis," 1977.

64. "Fort Bowie Material Culture," Tucson, Ariz.: The University of Ari-zona Press, 1978.

65. "Reward Mine and Associated Sites: Historical Archaeology on the Papago Reservation," 1980.

66. Peter D. Schulz and Betty J. Rivers, "Papers on Old Sacramento Archeology, Department of Parks & Recreation," 1980.

67. Adrian and Mary Praetzellis, "Ceramics from Old Sacramento," 1979.

68. Peter D. Schulz and Sherri M. Gust, "Faunal Remains and Social Sta-tus in 19th Century Sacramento," *Historical Archaeology* 17, no. 1 (1983).

Bibliography

All archaeological site reports that relate to the excavated artifacts used as data in this study are arranged geographically and listed in the appendix. City directories cited are listed at the end of the bibliography.

Ames, Kenneth L. *Death in the Dining Room and Other Tales of Victorian Culture.* Philadelphia: Temple University Press, 1992.

————. "Meaning in Artifacts: Hall Furnishing in Victorian America." In *Material Culture Studies in America,* edited by Thomas J. Schlereth. Nashville: The American Association for State and Local History, 1982.

Atherton, Lewis. *Main Street on the Middle Border.* Bloomington: Indiana University Press, 1954.

Barber, Edwin AtLee. "Early Ceramic Printing and Modeling in the United States." *Old China* 3, no. 2 (December 1903).

————. *Historical Sketch of the Greenpoint [N.Y.] Porcelain Works of Charles Cartlidge & Co.* Indianapolis, n.p., 1895.

————. *Marks of American Potters.* 1904. Reprint in combined edition with Barber's *Pottery and Porcelain of the United States.*

————. *The Pottery and Porcelain of the United States,* 3d ed., 1909. Reprint with Barber's Marks of American Potters and foreword by Diana and J. Garrison Stradling. New York: Feingold & Lewis, 1976.

————. "Recent Accessions of Pottery and Porcelain." *Bulletin of the Pennsylvania Museum,* no. 46 (April 1914): 20–25.

Barret, Richard Carter. *Bennington Pottery and Porcelain: A Guide to Identification.* New York: Crown Publishers, 1958.

————. *How to Identify Bennington Pottery.* Brattleboro, Vt.: Stephen Greene Press, 1964.

Battie, David, and Michael Turner. *The Price Guide to Nineteenth and Twentieth Century British Pottery.* 1979. Reprint, Woodbridge, Suffolk, England: Antique Collector's Club, 1982.

Beaudry, Mary C. "Reinventing Historical Archaeology." In *Historical Archaeology and the Study of American Culture,* edited by Lu Ann De Cunzo and Bernard L. Herman, 473–97. Winterthur, Del.: Winterthur Museum, 1996.

Beaudry, Mary C., Janet Long, Henry Miller, Fraser Neiman, and Garry Wheeler Stone. "A Vessel Typology for Early Chesapeake Ceramics: The Potomac Typological System." *Historical Archaeology* 17, no. 1 (1983): 18–42.

————. "A Vessel Typology." In *Documentary Archaeology in the New World.* 1988. Reprint, Cambridge: Cambridge University Press, 1993.

Beecher, Catherine E., and Harriet Beecher Stowe. *The American Woman's Home.* New York: J. B. Ford & Co., 1869.

Bird, Isabella Lucy. *The Englishwoman in America.* Madison: University of Wisconsin Press, 1966.

Blumin, Stuart M. *The Emergence of the Middle Class: Social Experience in the American City, 1760–1900*. Cambridge: Cambridge University Press, 1989.

Bourdieu, Pierre. *Distinction: A Social Critique of the Judgement of Taste*. Translated by Richard Nice. Cambridge: Harvard University Press, 1984.

Bourne, Richard A. *Bennington Pottery: The Robert B. and Marie P. Condon Collection*. Hyannis, Mass.: Richard A. Bourne, 1988.

Branin, M. Lelyn. *The Early Makers of Handcrafted Earthenware and Stoneware in Central and Southern New Jersey*. Rutherford, N.J.: Fairleigh Dickinson University Press, 1988.

———. *The Early Potters and Potteries of Maine*. Augusta: Maine State Museum, 1978.

Brewer, Mary. *Collector's Guide to Rockingham the Enduring Ware: Identification and Values*. Paducah, Ky.: Collector Books, 1996.

Broderick, Warren F. "The Potters of Mechanicville and Their Unusual Wares." *The Hudson Valley Regional Review* 6, no. 1 (March 1989).

———. "A Survey of the Pottery Industry of Fort Edward and Sandy Hill." *The Hudson Valley Regional Review* 8, no. 1 (March 1991).

Brusewitz, Gunnar. *Hunting*. New York: Stein and Day, 1969.

Burns, Sarah. *Pastoral Inventions: Rural Life in Nineteenth-Century American Art and Culture*. Philadelphia: Temple University Press, 1989.

Bushman, Richard L. *The Refinement of America: Persons, Houses, Cities*. 1992. Reprint, New York: Vintage Books, 1993.

Buten, David, with Jane Perkins Claney, and contributions by Patricia Pelehach. *Eighteenth Century Wedgwood: A Guide for Collectors and Connoisseurs*. New York: Main Street Press, 1980.

Carr, James. "Reminiscences of an Old Potter." *Crockery and Glass Journal* 53 (March 1901): 27–28.

Carroll, Lewis. *Through the Looking Glass and What Alice Found There: The Annotated Alice*. Edited by Martin Gardner. New York: Clarkson N. Potter, 1960.

Carskadden, Jeff. "Historic Ceramics from the Cass House and Munro Trading Post, Dresden, Ohio." *Muskingum Annals Number Five*. Zanesville, Ohio: Muskingum Valley Archaeological Survey, 1989.

Cayton, Andrew R. L., and Peter S. Onuf. *The Midwest and the Nation: Rethinking the History of an American Region*. Bloomington: Indiana University Press, 1990.

Cheek, Charles D., and Amy Friedlander. "Pottery and Pig's Feet: Space, Ethnicity, and Neighborhood in Washington, D.C., 1880–1940." *Historical Archaeology* 24, no. 1 (1990): 35–60.

Cinadr, Thomas, and Robert A. Genheimer. "Queensgate II: An Archaeological View of Nineteenth-Century Cincinnati." Cincinnati: Miami Purchase Association for Historic Preservation, 1983.

Clark, Clifford E., Jr. "The Vision of the Dining Room, Plan Book Dreams and Middle-Class Realities." In *Dining in America, 1850–1900*, edited by Kathryn Grover, 142–72. Amherst: University of Massachusetts Press, 1987.

Clarke, J. F. Gates. "Rebekah at the Well Teapots." *Spinning Wheel*, pts. 1–4 (July–December 1978).

Clement, Arthur W. *Our Pioneer Potters*. New York: Arthur W. Clement, 1947.

Cohen, Lizabeth A. "Embellishing a Life of Labor: An Interpretation of the Material Culture of American Working-Class Homes, 1885–1915." In *Material Culture Studies in America,* edited by Thomas J. Schlereth. Nashville: American Association for State and Local History, 1982.

Collard, Elizabeth. *Nineteenth-Century Pottery and Porcelain in Canada.* 2d ed. Kingston, Ont., Canada: McGill-Queen's University Press, 1984.

Cowan, Ruth Schwartz. *More Work for Mother: The Ironies of Household Technology from the Open Hearth to the Microwave.* New York: Basic Books, 1983.

Cowin, Verna L. *Pittsburgh Archaeological Resources and National Register Survey.* Pittsburgh: Carnegie Museum of Natural History, 1985.

Cox, Alwyn. "The Analysis of Rockingham and Rockingham-Type Brown-Glazed Earthenwares." *English Ceramic Circle Transactions* 15, pt. 1 (1993): 40–58.

Cox, Alwyn, and Angela Cox. *Rockingham Pottery and Porcelain, 1745–1842.* London: Faber and Faber, 1983.

Crass, David Colin, Bruce R. Penner, and Tammy R. Forehand. "Gentility and Material Culture on the Carolina Frontier." *Historical Archaeology* 33, no. 3 (1999): 14–31.

Cressey, Pamela J. "The Alexandria, Virginia, City-Site: Archaeology in an Afro-American Neighborhood, 1830–1910." Ph.D. diss., University of Iowa, 1985.

Crowe, Eyre. *With Thackeray in America.* New York: Charles Scribner's Sons, 1893.

Csikszentmihalyi, Mihaly, and Eugene Rochberg-Halton. *The Meaning of Things: Domestic Symbols and the Self.* Cambridge: Cambridge University Press, 1981.

Curtis, Phillip H. "The Production of Tucker Porcelain, 1826–1838: A Reevaluation." In *Ceramics in America,* edited by Ian M. G. Quimby, 339–74. Charlottesville: The University Press of Virginia, 1973.

Damon, Donna. "Hard Times, Good Times, and the Seat of the Pants." *Island Journal* 16 (1999): 42–47.

Darnton, Robert. *The Great Cat Massacre and Other Episodes in French Cultural History.* New York: Vintage Books, 1985.

DeBarthe, Paul. "The Smith Mansion Hotel Latrine and other Discoveries of the 1978 Archaeological Project." Columbia: University of Missouri, 1979.

DeCunzo, Lu Ann. "Economics and Ethnicity: An Archaeological Perspective on Nineteenth Century Paterson, New Jersey." Ph.D. diss., University of Pennsylvania, 1983.

————. "People, Material Culture, Context, and Culture in Historical Archaeology." Introduction to *Historical Archaeology and the Study of American Culture,* edited by Lu Ann De Cunzo and Bernard L. Herman, 1–17. Winterthur, Del.: Winterthur Museum, 1986.

Deetz, James F. "American Historical Archeology: Methods and Results." *Science* 239 (January 1988): 362–67.

————. "Discussion: Archaeologists as Storytellers," *Historical Archaeology* 32, no. 1 (1998): 94–96.

————. *In Small Things Forgotten.* New York: Doubleday, 1996.

————. "Material Culture and Archaeology—What's the Difference?" In

Historical Archaeology and the Importance of Material Things, edited by Leland Ferguson. Society for Historical Archaeology, Special Publications Series, no. 2 (1977).

Deiss, Ronald W. Archaeological Investigations at Kentucky's Old State Capitol. Frankfort: Kentucky Historical Society, 1988.

Denker, Ellen Paul. "Ceramics at the Crossroads: American Pottery at New York's Gateway, 1750–1900." *Staten Island Historian* 3, nos. 3–4 (winter–spring 1986).

Denker, Ellen Paul, and Bert Denker. *The Warner Collector's Guide to North American Pottery and Porcelain.* New York: Main Street Press/Warner Books, 1982.

Disturnell, J. *New York as It Is, in 1835 . . . Also the Hudson River Guide.* New York: J. Disturnell, 1835.

Donaldson, Paschal. *The Odd-Fellows' Text-Book; an Elucidation of the Theory of Odd-Fellowship: Embracing a Detail of the System, in All Its Branches; with Forms, Ceremonies, and Odes with Music, for Important Occasions, and a Manual of Practice for the Guidance of Officers and Lodges.* Philadelphia: Moss & Brother, 1852.

Downing, Andrew Jackson. *The Architecture of Country Houses, including Designs for Cottages, and Farm-Houses, and Villas.* 1850. Reprint, New York: Dover Publications, 1969.

Earle, Alice Morse. *China Collecting in America.* 1892. Reprint, Rutland, Vt.: Charles I. Tuttle, 1973.

Edwards, Lee M. *Domestic Bliss: Family Life in American Painting, 1840–1910.* Yonkers, N.Y.: The Hudson River Museum, 1986.

Esarey, Mark. E. "Report of Reconnaissance Survey and Testing of the Drews Site, 11-S-701, in FAI Borrow Pit 6, Extension 1, St. Clair County, Illinois." Normal, Ill.: Midwest Archaeological Research Center, Illinois State University, 1981.

Evans, Paul. *Art Pottery of the United States.* 2d ed., rev. and enl. New York: Feingold & Lewis, 1987.

Finer, Ann, and George Savage, eds. *The Selected Letters of Josiah Wedgwood.* London: Cory, Adams and Mackay, 1965.

Fitts, Robert K. "The Archaeology of Middle-Class Domesticity and Gentility in Victorian Brooklyn." *Historical Archaeology* 33, no. 1 (1999): 39–62.

Foster, Edward Halsey. *The Civilized Wilderness: Backgrounds to American Romantic Literature, 1817–1860.* New York: Free Press, [1975].

Frelinghuysen, Alice Cooney. *American Porcelain, 1770–1920.* New York: The Metropolitan Museum of Art, 1989.

———. "Paris Porcelain in America." *Antiques* 153, no. 4 (April 1998): 554–63.

Gale Research Company. *Currier & Ives: A Catalogue Raisonne.* Vol. 1. Detroit: Gale Research, 1984.

Gallo, John. *Nineteenth and Twentieth Century Yellow Ware.* Oneonta, N.Y.: John Gallo, 1985.

Gartley, Richard, and Jeff Carskadden. "Marbles from an Irish Channel Cistern, New Orleans, Louisiana." In *Proceedings of the Symposium on Ohio Valley Urban and Historic Archaeology,* edited by Donald B. Ball and Philip J. DiBlasi. Louisville, Ky.: University of Louisville, 1987.

Gates, William C., Jr., and Dana E. Ormerod. "The East Liverpool, Ohio,

Pottery District: Identification of Manufacturers and Marks." *Historical Archaeology* 16, nos. 1–2 (1982).

Glaser, Barney G., and Anselm L. Strauss. *The Discovery of Grounded Theory: Strategies for Qualitative Research.* Hawthorne, N.Y.: Aldine de Gruyter, 1967.

Goldberg, David J. "Charles Coxon: Nineteenth-Century Potter, Modeler-Designer, and Manufacturer." *American Ceramic Circle Journal* 9 (1994): 28–64.

Goodby, Miranda. "'Our Home in the West': Staffordshire Potters and their Emigration to America in the 1840s." In *Ceramics in America,* edited by Robert Hunter, 1–25. Milwaukee, Wisc.: Chipstone Foundation, 2003.

Groover, Mark D. "Evidence for Folkways and Cultural Exchange in the Eighteenth-Century South Carolina Back Country." *Historical Archaeology* 28, no. 1 (1994): 41–64.

Grover, Kathryn, ed. *Dining in America, 1850–1900.* Amherst: University of Massachusetts Press, 1987.

Hadfield, John. *Every Picture Tells a Story: Images of Victorian Life.* New York: Facts on File Publications, 1985.

Haltman, Kenneth, Introduction to *American Artifacts: Essays in Material Culture,* edited by Jules David Prown and Kenneth Haltman. East Lansing: Michigan State University Press, 2000.

Handlin, David P. *The American Home: Architecture and Society, 1815–1915.* Boston: Little, Brown, 1979.

Henrywood, R. K. *An Illustrated Guide to British Jugs.* Shrewsbury, England: Swan Hill Press, 1997.

————. *Relief-Moulded Jugs, 1820–1900.* Woodbridge, Suffolk, England: The Antique Collectors' Club, 1984.

Herman, Bernard L. "Historical Archaeology and the Search for Context." Introduction to *Historical Archaeology and the Study of American Culture,* edited by Lu Ann De Cunzo and Bernard L. Herman. Winterthur, Del.: The Winterthur Museum, 1996.

————. *The Stolen House.* Charlottesville: University Press of Virginia, 1992.

Hershberg, Theodore, and Robert Dockhorn. "Occupational Classification." *Historical Methods Newsletter* 9, nos. 2/3 (March/June 1976): 59–77.

Herskovitz, Robert M. *Fort Bowie Material Culture.* Tucson: University of Arizona Press, 1978.

Hodder, Ian. "Theoretical Archaeology: A Reactionary View." In *Symbolic and Structural Archaeology,* edited by Ian Hodder. Cambridge: Cambridge University Press, 1982.

Holland, Claudia C. "Tenant Farms of the Past, Present, and Future: An Ethnoarchaeological View." In *Historical Archaeology on Southern Plantations and Farms,* edited by Charles E. Order, Jr. Published as *Historical Archaeology* 24, no. 4 (1990): 60–69.

Horwitz, Richard P. *Anthropology toward History: Culture and Work in a Nineteenth-Century Maine Town.* Middletown, Conn.: Wesleyan University Press, 1978.

Houghton, Walter E. *The Victorian Frame of Mind, 1830–1870.* New Haven, Conn.: Yale University Press, 1957.

James, Arthur W. *The Potters and Potteries of Chester County, Pennsylvania.* Exton, Pa.: Schiffer Publishing, 1978.

Jewitt, Llewellynn. *The Ceramic Art of Great Britain.* 1883. Reprint; Poole, Dorset, England: New Orchard Editions, 1985.

Johns, Elizabeth. *American Genre Painting: The Politics of Everyday Life.* New Haven: Yale University Press, 1991.

Jones, Reginald. "Frauds in Old China." *House and Garden* (October 1906).

Kasson, John F. "Rituals of Dining, Table Manners in Victorian America." In *Dining in America, 1850–1900,* edited by Kathryn Grover, 114–41. Amherst: University of Massachusetts Press, 1987.

Ketchum, William C., Jr. *American Country Pottery: Yellowware and Spongeware.* New York: Alfred A. Knopf, 1987.

———. *The Knopf Collectors' Guides to American Antiques: Pottery and Porcelain.* Alfred A. Knopf, 1983.

———. *Potters and Potteries of New York State, 1650–1900.* Syracuse, N.Y.: Syracuse University Press, 1987.

Langenbeck, Karl. *The Chemistry of Pottery.* Easton, Pa.: Chemical Publishing Co., 1895.

Lardner, Dionysius. *A Treatise on the Progressive Improvement and Present State of the Manufacture of Porcelain and Glass.* Vol. 26 of the *Cabinet Cyclopaedia.* London: Longman, Rees, Orme, Brown, and Green, 1832.

Larkin, Jack. *The Reshaping of Everyday Life, 1790–1840.* New York: Harper & Row, 1988.

Leibowitz, Joan. *Yellow Ware: The Transitional Ceramic.* Exton, Pa.: Schiffer Publishing, 1985.

Lucas, Michael T. "A la Russe, à la Pell-Mell, or à la Practical: Ideology and Compromise at the Late Nineteenth-Century Dinner Table." *Historical Archaeology* 28, no. 4 (1994): 80–93.

Lucas, Michael T., and Paul A. Shackel. "Changing Social and Material Routine in Nineteenth-Century Harpers Ferry." *Historical Archaeology* 28, no. 4 (1994): 29–34.

Maass, John. "Foreign Travellers and American Hotels." In *Victorian Resorts and Hotels,* edited by Richard Guy Wilson. Published as *Nineteenth Century* 8, nos. 1–2 (1982).

Mahoney, Timothy R. *River Towns in the Great West: The Structure of Provincial Urbanization in the American Midwest, 1820–1870.* Cambridge: Cambridge University Press, 1990.

Mansberger, Floyd R., with Eva Dodge Mounce. *Historic Illinois Potteries* 2, no. 1 (1990).

Martin, Ann Smart. "The Role of Pewter as Missing Artifact: Consumer Attitudes toward Tablewares in Late Eighteenth Century Virginia." *Historical Archaeology* 23, no. 2 (1989): 1–27.

Martin, Edgar. *The Standard of Living in 1860.* Chicago: University of Chicago Press, 1942.

Martin, Patrick E. *Archaeological Investigation at Fayette State Park.* Lansing: Michigan Historical Museum, 1986.

Mayer, Robert. *San Francisco: A Chronological and Documentary History, 1542–1970.* Dobbs Ferry, N.Y.: Oceana Publications, 1974.

Mayhew, Edgar deN., and Minor Myers, Jr. *A Documentary History of American Interiors: From the Colonial Era to 1915.* New York: Charles Scribner's Sons, 1980.

McClymer, John F. "Late Nineteenth-Century American Working Class Living Standards." *Journal of Interdisciplinary History* 17, no. 2 (autumn 1986): 379–98.

McCord, T. B., Jr. *Across the Fence, but a World Apart: The Coleman Site, 1796–1907.* Alexandria, Va.: Alexandria Urban Archaeology Program, 1985.

McCracken, Grant. *Culture and Consumption: New Approaches to the Symbolic Character of Consumer Goods and Activities.* Bloomington: Indiana University Press, 1988.

McDannell, Colleen. *The Christian Home in Victorian America, 1840–1900.* Bloomington: Indiana University Press, 1986.

McEwan, Bonnie G. "The Archaeology of Women in the Spanish New World." *Historical Archaeology* 25, no. 4 (1991): 33–41.

McLane, Charles B., and Carol Evarts McLane. *Islands of the Mid-Maine Coast: Penobscot Bay.* Vol. I. Gardiner, Maine: Tilbury House, 1997.

McMurry, Sally. "City Parlor, Country Sitting Room: Rural Vernacular Design and the American Parlor, 1840–1900." *Winterthur Portfolio* 20, no. 4 (winter 1985): 261–80.

———. "Progressive Farm Families and Their Houses, 1830–1855: A Study in Independent Design." *Agricultural History* 58, no. 1 (January 1984): 330–46.

Meisel, Martin. *Realizations: Narrative, Pictorial, and Theatrical Arts in Nineteenth-Century England.* Princeton, N.J.: Princeton University Press, 1983.

Miller, Danny. "Structures and Strategies: An Aspect of the Relationship between Social Hierarchy and Cultural Change." In *Symbolic and Structural Archaeology,* edited by Ian Hodder. Cambridge: Cambridge University Press, 1982.

Miller, George L. "Classification and Economic Scaling of Nineteenth Century Ceramics." *Historical Archaeology* 14 (1980): 1–41.

———. "The 'Market Basket' of Ceramics Available in Country Stores from 1780 to 1880." Paper presented at the Society for Historical Archaeology meeting, Tucson, Ariz., January 1990.

———. "Marketing Ceramics in North America: An Introduction." *Winterthur Portfolio* 19, no. 1 (spring 1984): 1–5.

———. "A Revised Set of CC Index Values for Classification and Economic Scaling of English Ceramics from 1787 to 1880." *Historical Archaeology* 25, no. 1 (1991): 1–25.

Miller, Philip. "What's in a Name?" *Newsletter* of the Northern Ceramic Society, no. 72 (December 1988).

Miyoshi, Masao. *The Divided Self: a Perspective on the Literature of the Victorians.* New York: New York University Press, 1969.

Moore, George M. "Bennington Ware." *Old China* 2, no. 2 (November 1902).

Morris, Wright. *The Home Place.* 1948. Reprint, Lincoln, Nebr.: Bison Books, 1968.

Mrozowski, Stephen A. "Nature, Society, and Culture: Theoretical Considerations in Historical Archaeology." In *Historical Archaeology and the Study of*

American Culture, edited by Lu Ann De Cunzo and Bernard L. Herman, 447–72. Winterthur, Del.: The Winterthur Museum, 1996.

Mullins, Paul R. "Negotiating Industrial Capitalism: Mechanisms of Change among Agrarian Potters." In *Historical Archaeology and the Study of American Culture,* edited by Lu Ann De Cunzo and Bernard L. Herman, 151–91. Winterthur, Del.: Winterthur Museum, 1996.

Mumford, Lewis. *The Brown Decades: A Study of the Arts in America, 1865–1895.* 1931. Reprint, New York: Dover Publications, 1971.

Myers, Susan H. "Edwin Bennett: An English Potter in Baltimore." *Ars Ceramica,* no. 4 (1987): 31–35.

———. *Handcraft to Industry: Philadelphia Ceramics in the First Half of the Nineteenth Century.* Washington, D.C.: Smithsonian Institution Press, 1980.

Newark Museum. *The Pottery and Porcelain of New Jersey, 1688–1900.* Newark, N.J.: Newark Museum, 1947.

Phillippe, Joseph S. "Archaeological and Historical Investigations at the Drake Site: a Nineteenth Century Farmstead in Northern Illinois." Normal, Ill.: Midwest Archaeological Research Center, Illinois State University, 1988.

Prown, Jules David. "The Truth of Material Culture: History or Fiction?" In *American Artifacts: Essays in Material Culture,* edited by Jules David Prown and Kenneth Haltman. East Lansing: Michigan State University Press, 2000.

Ramsay, John. *American Potters and Pottery.* New York: Tudor Publishing, 1947.

Reckner, Paul A., and Stephen A. Brighton. "'Free from All Vicious Habits': Archaeological Perspectives on Class Conflict and the Rhetoric of Temperance." *Historical Archaeology* 33, no.1 (1999): 63–86.

Remensnyder, John F. "The Potters of Poughkeepsie." In *The Art of the Potter,* edited by Diana Stradling and J. Garrison Stradling, 123–28. New York: Main Street / Universe Books, 1977.

Rice, D. G. *The Illustrated Guide to Rockingham Pottery and Porcelain.* London: Barrie & Jenkins, 1971.

Riles, Loretta M. "James Bennett." Untitled manuscript. Manuscript collection, Ohio Historical Society at the East Liverpool Museum of Ceramics. East Liverpool, Ohio, 1980.

Roberts, Daniel G., and Betty J. Cosans. *The Archeology of the Nineteenth Century in the Ninth Ward, Philadelphia, Pennsylvania.* West Chester, Pa.: John Milner Associates, 1980.

Rogers, George E. *The Crockery Companion.* Boston: n.p., 1881.

Rorabaugh, William J. *The Alcoholic Republic.* New York: Oxford University Press, 1979.

———. "Beer, Lemonade, and Propriety in the Gilded Age." In *Dining in America,* edited by Kathryn Grove, 24–46. Amherst: University of Massachusetts Press, 1987.

Roth, Rodris. "Tea Drinking in Eighteenth Century America: Its Etiquette and Equipage." *Bulletin* 225 (1961), United States National Museum. Paper 14, Contributions from the Museum of History and Technology. Smithsonian Institution, Washington, D.C.

Ryan, Mary P. *Cradle of the Middle Class: The Family in Oneida County, New York, 1790–1865.* Cambridge: Cambridge University Press, 1981.

Savage, George, and Harold Newman. *An Illustrated Dictionary of Ceramics.* London: Thames and Hudson, 1985.

Schlereth, Thomas J. *Material Culture: A Research Guide.* Lawrence: University Press of Kansas, 1985.

Schmitt, Dave N., and Charles D. Zeier. "Not by Bones Alone: Exploring Household Composition and Socioeconomic Status in an Isolated Historic Mining Community." *Historical Archaeology* 27, no. 4 (1993): 20–38.

Schrier, Arnold, and Joyce Story, editors and translators. *A Russian Looks at America: The Journey of Aleksandr Borisovich Lakier in 1857.* Chicago: University of Chicago Press, 1979.

Schwartz, Marvin D. *Collectors' Guide to Antique American Ceramics.* Garden City, N.Y.: Doubleday, 1969.

Sears Roebuck Catalogue. Edited by Fred L. Israel. 1897. Reprint, New York: Chelsea House, 1968.

Shogren, Samuel W. "Lifeways of the Industrial Worker: The Archaeological Record (A Summary of Three Field Seasons at Blacksmith Hill)." Wilmington, Del.: Hagley Museum and Library research files. 1986.

Shortridge, James R. *The Middle West: Its Meaning in American Culture.* Lawrence: University Press of Kansas, 1989.

Skinner, D. S. *Hops and Venom; or, Looking into Frog Mugs.* Stoke-on-Trent, England: Stoke-on-Trent City Museum & Art Gallery, 1988.

Slosson, Annie Trumbull. *China Hunters Club.* New York: Harper & Brothers, 1878.

Sotheby Park Bernet. *The Jacqueline D. Hodgson Collection of Important American Ceramics.* New York: Sotheby Parke Bernet, 1974.

Smith, Charles R., and Shawn K. Bonath, comps., "A Report on Phase I and Phase II Historic [sic] Archaeological Investigations on Three Segments of the F.A.P. 408 Highway Corridor, Adams, Pike, and Scott Counties, Illinois." Normal, Ill. Midwest Archaeological Research Center, Illinois State University, 1981.

Smith, Samuel D. *An Archaeological and Historical Assessment of the First Hermitage.* Nashville: Division of Archaeology, Tennessee Department of Conservation, 1976.

Smith-Rosenberg, Carroll. *Disorderly Conduct: Visions of Gender in Victorian America.* New York: Oxford University Press, 1985.

Spargo, John. *Early American Pottery and China.* 1926. Reprint, Rutland, Vt.: Charles E. Tuttle, 1974.

Spencer-Wood, Suzanne M. "Feminist Historical Archaeology and the Transformation of American Culture by Domestic Reform Movements, 1840–1925." In *Historical Archaeology and the Study of American Culture,* edited by Lu Ann De Cunzo and Bernard L. Herman, 397–445. Winterthur, Del.: Winterthur Museum, 1996.

———. "Miller's Indices and Consumer-Choice Profiles: Status-Related Behaviors and White Ceramics." In *Consumer Choice in Historical Archaeology,* edited by Suzanne M. Spencer-Wood. New York: Plenum Press, 1987.

Spencer-Wood, Suzanne M., ed. *Consumer Choice in Historical Archaeology.* New York: Plenum Press, 1987.

Spencer-Wood, Suzanne M., and Scott D. Heberling. "Consumer Choices in White Ceramics: A Comparison of Eleven Early Nineteenth-Century Sites." In *Consumer Choice in Historical Archaeology,* edited by Suzanne M. Spencer-Wood. New York: Plenum Press, 1987.

Springsted, Brenda Lockhart. "A Delftware Center in Seventeenth-Century New Jersey." *American Ceramic Circle Bulletin,* no. 4 (1985): 9–46.

Stillinger, Elizabeth. *The Antiquers.* New York: Alfred A. Knopf, 1980.

Stone, Gary Wheeler. "Artifacts Are Not Enough." In *Documentary Archaeology in the New World,* edited by Mary C. Beaudry. 1988. Reprint, Cambridge: Cambridge University Press, 1993.

Stradling, Diana, and Ellen Paul Denker. *Jersey City: Shaping America's Pottery Industry, 1825–1892.* Jersey City, N.J.: Jersey City Museum, 1997.

Stradling, J. Garrison. "A Dream of 'Porcellain' in Cincinnati: William S. Merrell's Personal Account of Experiments and Travels, 1824–1828." *American Ceramic Circle Journal* 10 (1997): 74–90.

———. "Puzzling Aspects of the Most Popular Piece of American Pottery Ever Made." *Antiques* 51, no. 2 (February 1997): 332–37.

———. "The Southern Porcelain Company of Kaolin, South Carolina: A Reassessment." *Journal of the Museum of Early Southern Decorative Arts* 22, no. 2 (winter 1996): 1–39.

Stratton, Herman John. "Factors in the Development of the American Pottery Industry 1860–1920." Ph.D. diss., University of Chicago, 1929.

Sutherland, Daniel E. *The Expansion of Everyday Life, 1860–1876.* New York: Harper & Row, 1989.

Swank, Scott T., with Benno M. Forman, Frank H. Sommer, Arlene Palmer Schwind, Frederick S. Weiser, Donald Fennimore, and Susan Burrows Swan. *Arts of the Pennsylvania Germans.* Winterthur, Del.: Winterthur Museum, 1983.

Taussig, Frank William. *The Tariff History of the United States.* New York: G. P. Putnam's Sons, 1914.

Thistlethwaite, Frank. "The Atlantic Migration of the Pottery Industry." *The Economic History Review* 11, 2d ser. (1958): 264–78.

Towner, Donald C. *English Cream-Coloured Earthenware.* London: Faber and Faber, 1957.

Tower, Lillian Leslie. "The Quaint Old Ware of Bennington." *Country Life in America* 19, no. 5 (January 1911).

Transactions of the American Institute of the City of New York for the Year 1851. Albany, N.Y.: Charles Van Benthuysen, 1852.

Twain, Mark. *Life on the Mississippi.* 1883. Reprint, New York: Harper and Brothers, 1929.

Upton, Dell. *Holy Things and Profane: Anglican Parish Churches in Colonial Virginia.* New York: Architectural History Foundation, 1986.

Wakefield, Hugh. *Victorian Pottery.* 1962. Reprint, New York: Universe Books, 1970.

Wall, Diana DiZerega. "Examining Gender, Class, and Ethnicity in Nineteenth-Century New York City." *Historical Archaeology* 33, no. 1 (1999): 102–17.

————. "Sacred Dinners and Secular Teas: Constructing Domesticity in Mid-Nineteenth-Century New York." *Historical Archaeology* 25, no. 4 (1991): 69–81.

Waselkov, Gregory, Robert T. Bray, and Linda Waselkov, *Archaeological Investigations of the Hyrum Smith Site*. Columbia: University of Missouri, 1974.

Watkins, Lura Woodside. *Early New England Potters and Their Wares*. 1950. Reprint, n.p.: Archon Press, 1968.

————. "Henderson of Jersey City and His Pitchers." *Antiques* 50, no. 6 (December 1946): 388–92.

Webster, Thomas. *An Encyclopaedia of Domestic Economy*. New York: Harper and Brothers, 1845.

Weidner, Ruth. "Gifts of Wild Game." In *The Material Culture of Gender/ The Gender of Material Culture,* edited by Katharine Martinez and Kenneth L. Ames, 337–64. Winterthur, Del.: Winterthur Museum, 1997.

Welter, Barbara. "The Cult of True Womanhood: 1820–1860." *American Quarterly* 18, no. 2, pt. 1 (summer 1966): 151–74.

Wetherbee, Jean. *White Ironstone: A Collector's Guide*. Antique Trader Books, Dubuque, Iowa, 1996.

Williams, Susan R. Introduction to *Dining in America, 1850–1900,* edited by Kathryn Grover, 3–14. Amherst: University of Massachusetts Press, 1987.

————. *Savory Suppers and Fashionable Feasts: Dining in Victorian America*. New York: Pantheon Books, 1985.

Williamson, Harold, P. *The Growth of the American Economy*. New York: Prentice-Hall, 1955.

Winter, Susan E. "Social Dynamics and Structure in Lower Town Harpers Ferry." In *An Archaeology of Harpers Ferry's Commercial and Residential District,* edited by Paul A. Shackel and Susan E. Winter. Published as *Historical Archaeology* 28, no. 4 (1994): 16–26.

Wiseman, Frederick Matthew. "Folk Art and Antiques: A Different View." Pt 2. *Maine Antique Digest* (May 1987).

Wood, Ruth Howe. "Memories of the Fentons." *Antiques* 8, no. 3 (September 1925): 150–54.

Worrell, John, Myron O. Stachiw, and David M. Simmons. "Archaeology from the Ground Up." In *Historical Archaeology and the Study of American Culture,* edited by Lu Ann De Cunzo and Bernard L. Herman, 35–69. Winterthur, Del.: Winterthur Museum, 1996.

Worthy, Linda H. "Classification and Interpretation of Late-Nineteenth- and Early-Twentieth-Century Ceramics." In *Archaeology of Urban America: the Search for Pattern and Process,* edited by Roy S. Dickens, Jr., 329–60. New York: Academic Press, 1982.

Yentsch, Anne. "Minimum Vessel Lists as Evidence of Change in Folk and Courtly Traditions of Food Use." *Historical Archaeology* 24, no. 3 (1990): 24–53.

Young, Jennie J. *The Ceramic Art*. New York: Harper, 1878.

Zierden, Martha. "A Trans-Atlantic Merchant's House in Charleston: Archaeological Exploration of Refinement and Subsistence in an Urban Setting." *Historical Archaeology* 33, no. 3 (1999): 73–87.

Zusy, Catherine. *Norton Stoneware and American Redware: The Bennington Museum Collection*. Bennington, Vt.: Bennington Museum, 1991.

Baltimore, Maryland

Fagan, William H. *Baltimore Wholesale Business Directory and Business Circular, for 1852.* 2d ed. Philadelphia: J. Craig, 1852.

Jersey City, New Jersey

Directory of Jersey City, Harsimus and Pavonia, for 1849–50. Jersey City, N.J.: John H. Voorhees, 1849.

Philadelphia, Pennsylvania

Philadelphia City Register. Philadelphia: C. E. Howe Company, 1910. The same listing for the years 1911, 1912, and 1913.

Pittsburgh, Pennsylvania

Harris, Isaac. *General Business Directory of the Cities of Pittsburgh and Allegheny.* Pittsburgh: A. A. Anderson, 1841.

Troy, New York

The Troy Directory for the Year 1833–4. Troy, N.Y.: N. Tuttle, 1833. The same listing for the years 1834–1835, 1835–1836, 1836–1837, 1837–1838, 1838–1839.

Index

Entries for "Rockingham ware" and "Rockingham-ware" refer to Rockingham ware made and used in the United States unless otherwise identified.